Ghosts of the New City

Southeast Asia

POLITICS, MEANING, AND MEMORY

David Chandler and Rita Smith Kipp

SERIES EDITORS

Ghosts of the New City

*Spirits, Urbanity, and the Ruins
of Progress in Chiang Mai*

ANDREW ALAN JOHNSON

University of Hawai'i Press
Honolulu

Library of Congress Cataloging-in-Publication Data

Johnson, Andrew Alan, author.
Ghosts of the new city : spirits, urbanity, and the ruins
of progress in Chiang Mai / Andrew Alan Johnson.
    p.   cm.—(Southeast Asia—politics, meaning, memory)
Includes bibliographical references and index.
ISBN: 978-0-8248-3939-0 (cloth : alk. paper)
ISBN: 978-0-8248-3971-0 (pbk. : alk. paper)
1. Urban renewal—Thailand—Chiang Mai—Public opinion.
2. Haunted places—Thailand—Chiang Mai. 3. Chiang Mai
(Thailand)—Public opinion. I. Title. II. Series.
HT178.T52 C535 2014
                                            2013049884

Designed by Janette Thompson (Jansom)

Printed by Sheridan Books, Inc.

For Daena

CONTENTS

ACKNOWLEDGMENTS

This book was written in parts while I was based in the anthropology depart-ment at Cornell University, the Sogang Institute for East Asian Studies, the Asia Research Institute of the National University of Singapore, and the Weatherhead East Asian Institute at Columbia University.

First, my thanks go to those people in Chiang Mai who tolerated my questions and presence during my fieldwork. In particular, I would like to thank Chayan Vaddhanaphuti, Duangchan Charoenmuang, Jamaree Chiengthong, Jiraporn Witayasakpan, and Sureerat Sombatkiri, as well as the excellent teaching staff at the Advanced Study of Thai (AST) program at Chiang Mai University. Elsewhere in Chiang Mai, I am indebted to Chokanan Waanichloetthanasaan, *phi* Tui, *phi* Sir, *phi* Nok, and *nong* Aong for their friendship during my research. In Bangkok, I received support from the Princess Maha Chakri Sirindhorn Anthropology Centre in Bangkok.

The ethnographic research for this book in 2006–2008 was supported by a Fulbright-Hays fellowship from the United States Department of Education. I also acknowledge the support of travel grants to Thailand in the summers of 2005 and 2009 from the Einaudi Center for International Studies at Cornell University, and I am continually grateful to the staff at the Southeast Asian Summer Study Institute (SEASSI) at the University of Wisconsin-Madison for their unparalleled commitment to Southeast Asian languages. I wish to acknowledge that parts of Chapter 1 have been published as "Progress and its ruins: Ghosts, migrants and the uncanny in Thailand" in *Cultural Anthropology* (May 2013).

I am indebted to the Cornell Southeast Asia Program (SEAP), directed by Thak Chaloemtirana, a close and supportive academic environment and a wonderful place in which to write. In particular, James Siegel was (and is) an endless source of inspiration. Also, Anne Blackburn, Magnus Fiskesjö, and Eric Tagliacozzo provided me with valuable feedback and support. Ngampit Jagacinski deserves particular mention for her devotion to Thai-language instruction at Cornell and her dedication to her students. Gregory Green, the curator of Cornell's Southeast Asian collection, deserves mention as an individual genuinely interested in promoting scholarship. I must also thank Claudine Ang, Lawrence Chua, Pamela Corey, Alexandra Denes, Jane Ferguson, Tyrell Haberkorn, Erik Harms, Nina Hien, Samson Lim, Quentin "Trais" Pearson, Pittayawat "Joe" Pittayaporn, Christophe Robert, Ivan Small, and Chika Watanabe. Michael Bobick, Tarandeep Kang, Townsend Middleton, and Saiba Varma merit my particular gratitude, as does David Rojas, who has commented on a previous draft of this manuscript and given me valuable direction and advice. Elsewhere, I am grateful for the advice and friendship of Claudio Sopranzetti.

Four people who deserve particular mention are Dominic Boyer, Tamara Loos, and Andrew Willford, who were extremely helpful in formulating the ideas that eventually led to this book; Michael Herzfeld offered continual advice and guidance on the craft of ethnography. I am also grateful for Michael's ability to find the best possible restaurant in any city.

In Singapore, I wish to thank Tim Bunnell and Michelle Miller for welcoming me to the Asia Research Institute, and Prasenjit Duara for his leadership there. Maurizio Peleggi was generous with his time and his conversation, and Jane M. Jacobs was always supportive. In addition, Charnvit Kasetsiri, Pavin Chachavalpongpun, and Thongchai Winichakul provided guidance and advice on my work. Finally, I wish to recognize Pattana Kitiarsa, whose pursuit of ethnography was an inspiration to me. He is sorely missed.

At Columbia, I am indebted to the Weatherhead East Asian Institute under Myron Cohen, where I put the finishing touches on this book. Jayne Werner and Duncan McCargo in particular were helpful as I put it together. Elsewhere, I wish to thank Hoon Song and Joel Kuipers for their inspiration in the formative years of this project. Finally, Justin McDaniel remains a tireless force for Thai and Lao studies and provided helpful feedback on ideas presented here.

At the University of Hawai'i Press, I wish to thank Pamela Kelley, David Chandler, and Rita Smith Kipp for their careful reading, suggestions, and help during the review and production of this manuscript. Also, Charles Keyes offered a wealth of suggestions and advice in the later stages of writing. All photographs are my own.

Finally, my parents, Jean and Robert Johnson, were supportive during the long period of research and writing and forgave many missed holidays. Most of all, I wish to thank my wife, Daena Funahashi, for her endless advice, suggestions, and inspiration in the research and writing that went into this book, as well as the devotion and passion that she gives to anthropological work as well as to life. I owe her much more than I can possibly repay.

NOTE ON TRANSCRIPTION

This book follows the Royal Thai General System of transcription for all Thai terms, except in the case of proper names of individuals, where I have followed their own preferred Romanization (e.g., Shalardchai, Sarasawadee).

Introduction

The Broken Building

Upon travelling to the northern city of Chiang Mai, Reginald Le May, a British adviser to Siam in the early twentieth century, observed of its residents: "In spite of the vast number of temples built, the innumerable images of the Lord Buddha fashioned and venerated, the endless pilgrimages to the more famous shrines, the countless store of money spent on gold leaf and incense, and the armies of priests that have been ordained during all these past centuries, the [Chiang Mai] Lao people remain at heart what they have been from time immemorial . . . animists" (1986, 125). Le May was referring to the persistence of spirit veneration alongside the very public display of Buddhist piety, and how references to ghosts or spirits (*phi*) crept into unexpected corners of everyday life.

This book is about the idea of the city as a space similarly "haunted" by magico-religious notions of charismatic power—power that retains its significance even in the face of Thailand's transformation into a nation-state and current entrance into the neoliberal economic moment. This charisma (*barami*) comes to frame how residents of Chiang Mai perceive "culture" (*watthanatham*) and "progress" (*khwam charoen*).[1] In this ethnography, I show how urban planners and spirit mediums cast themselves as professionals uniquely suited to resurrect the *barami* of the ancient kingdom of Lanna, the polity that once ruled what is now Northern Thailand. Yet in the wake of a series of economic and political crises, as the possibility of a Lanna renaissance grows more and more dubious (and, at the same time, is perceived to be more and more necessary), stories of ghosts inhabiting the shells of new high-rise construction have increased, attesting to the doubt implicit in planners' and mediums' calls for a restoration of charismatic potential.

This book is also an anthropologist's response to Tony Day's (2002) call for historical studies that take culture into account and draw connections between premodern ways of interpreting new forms of power and modern ones (see also Kapferer 1988). Day and Kapferer see new regimes of truth as entering into a relationship with other ways of looking at knowledge. In this way, discourses such as development, nationalism, neoliberalism, or a reified "culture" merge with ideas such as *thamma* (dharma), *charoen,* and *barami.*

Both Day and Kapferer are primarily concerned with the state. Yet these states, in their origins and at their cores, are cities. The mandalic state, *mueang* in Thai,[2] radiated out from an urban center, a place whose layout, design, and beauty mobilized and enabled the power and charisma of the ruler to realize prosperity for his (or her) domain. The city is the foundation upon which fantasies of the Buddhist heavens were built; they were sites of national development and control; and they are at present places where consumption and prosperity are most manifest. In short, the city in Northern Thailand is still a "stage"—to play upon Clifford Geertz's metaphor of the "theatre state" (1980). It is a site where rituals of cosmological power are performed, even if that power is defined in such diverse ways as "cultural heritage" (*watthanatham*) or sacrality (*sak*) or simply as the monumentality of glossy new shopping malls. These new cities, like the Northern Thai urban "sacred center" (Swearer 1987), are places where demonstrations of progress and prosperity are enacted, performances intended to ensure that, owing to the potential of the past, the future will be equally prosperous.

CITIES

Looking at the city as an idea is not in itself a new concept. At the beginning of the twentieth century, in the face of rising urbanization and the prospect of the new century, many European writers explored the possibilities of the urban as such. What would the city's effect upon its inhabitants be? How best could the city be designed in order to realize its potential?

In early twentieth-century Europe, the division between rural and urban has been characterized as one of collectivity versus atomization, emotion versus intellect, and sentimentality versus rationality. Georg Simmel emphasizes the effects the city has had upon the individual: the sheer amount of stimuli it generates requires a new psychosocial mechanism, he writes, one that creates new possibilities along with new problems. Ultimately, the city is alienating: "one never feels as lonely and deserted as in this metropolitan crush of persons" (Simmel 1950, 334), culminating in an urban character of "reserve with its overtones of concealed aversion" (ibid., 332). The individual in defense of his individuality intellectualizes and rationalizes interactions to the detriment of emotional relationships, yielding to a worldview where all things are objectively evaluated.[3]

Raymond Williams (1975) argues that in English literature the country has been consistently represented as the site of intimately connected community in opposition to the city. As with Simmel's hyperrational but unfeeling urbanity, the city becomes the realm of the mind, the country the realm of the heart. The urbanite becomes more intellectual but less feeling, less deeply committed to others. In Simmel's "blasé outlook," the urban experience is one fraught with anxiety, disgust, and alienation. Here is the quintessential Freudian subject—on the surface rational and in control, but troubled within by deeper affective forces. The Freudian uncanny is something that haunts notions of urban rationality (Vidler 1994).

However, it would be a mistake to jump from this idea of the urban, formed in early twentieth-century Paris, Vienna, Berlin, or Chicago, to present-day Asia. But might we see at least shades of Simmel's blasé affect in Chiang Mai? Certainly the "floating world" (*ukiyo-e*) of Edo-era Japan seems similar to Baudelaire's Paris as an environment of sensuality-seeking, detached observers. In doing so, we cannot assume that simply because two places are urban, "the urban" carries the same meaning in both.

Studies of urban centers in Southeast Asian history emphasize their intimate connection with religious concepts of prosperity and order. Chief among the characterizations of Southeast Asian urbanity has been the notion of the "mandala," a polity revolving around the charisma and prestige of a particular ruler (Tambiah 1976; Geertz 1980; Wolters 1999). The power of a mandala would depend on the ability of the urban center to attract vassal lords and residents more than on its ability to police or administer a large region. But how is the legacy of such urban models reflected in modern-day Thai cities? In short, to reverse Day's proposition of seeing culture in history, how can we take seriously the issue of history in culture? How does the idea of the mandala become reinterpreted through and reconciled with contemporary narratives of culture, nation, and mass media?

Recent scholars have looked at the vast changes undergone by cities such as Bangkok and Jakarta, the sociological impacts of urbanization (Rimmer and Dick 2009), the web of international commerce stretching across regional and national borders (Bunnell 2013), and the various "texts" to be read in order to foster or challenge nationalism (King 2010). In his excellent book *Saigon's Edge*, Erik Harms (2010) addresses Raymond Williams' binary between city and country on the outskirts of Vietnam, where people skillfully and selectively deploy urban and rural categories in order to negotiate their own position vis-à-vis a rapidly expanding Saigon.

But in these new studies of nation-states and communities, of traffic circulation and the flows of international finance, where is the legacy of the great Southeast Asian mandala states of the premodern period? What makes urbanity in Southeast Asia distinct from how it has been conceived in the West? How might the legacy of the city as a vehicle for articulating religious notions of power come to articulate "secular" notions of power and progress? Answering these questions involves an engagement with the intense forms of presence that cannot fit into—or be accounted for within—mainstream narratives of urbanization. In short, a new study of urbanity involves engaging with ghosts.

CRACKS

"This city doesn't have a future," Bon told me. He was a man in his late forties, whose family had run the largest Hainanese-style coffee shop in town, and with whom I regularly discussed urban change in the city. Traffic noise from nearby Chang Phueak road routinely drowned out our conversation, and we had to choose the few quiet moments in between in which to talk. We had been discussing the weather—blazingly hot for December—and how it had wreaked havoc on the Thai government's new floral festival near Doi Kham, killing whole fields of flowers and frustrating Thai tourists and planners alike. Now, in the pause of traffic noise, Bon had switched the topic to the future of the city as a whole.

He had good reason to know. His family's coffee shop had been running just to the north of the city walls for three generations. They used long, Hainanese-style coffee filters and condensed milk, what is labeled in nationalist terms all across Southeast Asia as the particular drink of some specific country—for example, "Vietnamese coffee," "Thai-style coffee," "Malay *kopi*," and the like. Over time, Bon's shop had continually watched its business shrink, especially as younger people developed a taste for the increasingly available "good-smelling coffee" (*kafae hom*) produced by espresso machines. New stores had proliferated in recent years, marketing espresso as particularly "Northern Thai" in such outlets as the hill-tribe-themed Waawee Coffee or Doi Chaang Coffee, or the royal project–based Doi Tung. What had originally been Chinese coffee and had become Thai coffee was being replaced by Italian coffee marketed as Lanna coffee.

Bon showed me pictures of his business when it was in its prime: two shops, side-by-side, with long benches and stools were packed with customers, generally older men. "Chinese men," Bon clarified, "early in the morning. Too early for you! They talk about politics, their lives, these kinds of things. But this was when I was younger." Now, according to Bon, he makes ends meet by serving iced coffee in plastic bags to people commuting to work in the morning and by renting out the neighboring shop. Bon doubted that his computer enthusiast son would carry on with the shop. "Perhaps he will become an engineer," he mused.

Shortly after his dire pronouncement on the future of the city, Bon grabbed his car keys. "Today we're going to Lamphun [a city about twenty minutes to Chiang Mai's south] for *khao soi* [Northern-style egg noodles in curry]." Bon had been eager to show me Wat Haripunchai, one of the oldest Buddhist temples in the North and located at the center of the first Buddhist city in the North. However, instead of going straight to Lamphun, Bon pulled his pickup truck off the busy Canal Road at the western edge of Chiang Mai and pointed to a tall apartment building on the edge of the road. It was made of concrete, and, as on many of the other buildings along the road, car exhaust and rain had drawn sooty black streaks down its formerly whitewashed sides. What drew Bon's attention, though, was a jagged crack running from the building's base up to its top. "Do you see that?" he asked me. "The concrete there is no good. One day, it's going to snap in two." He paused, keeping his eyes on the building. "Also, it's haunted," he added. Continuing, Bon said:

A girl was crossing the road late one night. Then, she was struck by a car and killed. If you go to sleep in one room in that building at the same hour that she died, the bed will shake. It's the ghost of that girl [that is causing this]. You have to be careful when staying in tall buildings in Chiang Mai. Many of them have ghosts. I was staying in one, years ago, for just one night when I visited my sister studying at the college [Chiang Mai University]. I woke up three or four times in the middle of the night to hear the sound of arguing just outside my door. Like there were people right outside the door. The third time, I got up from the bed and opened the door. I opened it very quickly. I didn't want the people to run away, so that I could yell [at them]. Tell them to be quiet. There was no one in the hall. It was absolutely silent.

My sister later told me that a teacher used to live in that room. He[4] was heartbroken [about something]. Late one night, at three a.m., he took a gun and put it in his mouth [and killed himself]. It was exactly at three a.m. when I heard those voices for the third time. When I knew that story, I never went back [to that building].

Bon continued to tell me other stories of haunting incidents in Chiang Mai, including some that he had experienced personally and others that he had only heard of. Each one occurred in the same kind of space: tall, one-room hotels and apartment buildings.

In Bon's stories, buildings, death, and haunting are all somehow connected—the ruin of a young life, the ruin of a broken building, and the ruinously bad traffic. He also links each with the future of the city—specifically, with the impossibility of "progress" and forward motion within its confines. Spirits, unable to be reborn, cars stalled in traffic, and abandoned buildings crumbling in the heat are all linked to the inability of the city to progress. It is this connection between ghosts, progress, and the city that I shall follow throughout this book.

I situated this study in Chiang Mai rather than Bangkok because the Northern Thai capital has often been described by Thai authors as a place that preserves some kind of cultural essence (Seri 1966; Sit 1980; Charuphat and Thirapap 2007), either an essence of "Thainess" preserved from corrosive "Western" influences in Bangkok or a similarly pristine "Lanna." In these utopian readings, Northern Thailand is a place where material development (*kan phatthana*) exists alongside spiritual progress (*khwam charoen*). It is this harmonious progressiveness that is being challenged by the spirits inhabiting Chiang Mai's high-rise architecture. The ghosts haunting the abandoned buildings can be seen through Jacques Derrida's sense of "hauntology" (Derrida 1994, 161), by which he means seeing both the instability of what we assume to be taken for granted and the impossibility of ever having such certainty (and the subsequent haunting of that which we thought we knew). In this case, the haunting of Chiang Mai's abandoned architecture points to a failure in the system of charisma and power, a haunting of which the broken buildings are a sign. In Bon's characterization, there was even something flawed in the concrete used to build them. The foundations are bad. The buildings are cracking. Ghosts come in.

1 | Progress and Its Ruins

In the 2010 film *Laddaland* (Golden Land), one of the highest-grossing Thai horror films, a father, Thi, moves his family from Bangkok to a suburban gated community in the city of Chiang Mai, where he has accepted a new, high-ranking job. Their first drive through the community is a montage of Americana-inspired clichés: broad streets, freshly mown lawns, two-story homes, and even a pair of children playing with a golden retriever in the spray of a sprinkler. Nonetheless, Thi's family is reluctant to leave Bangkok, knowing they will miss their extended family and suspicious of the new life in the north.

The family's reluctance soon proves to have been well-founded: Laddaland is revealed as having a dark underbelly beneath the manicured lawns and well-kept streets. The neighbor's wife shows signs of being abused, and Thi's new boss turns out to be "lending" himself money from the company's coffers. But the event that begins the community's slide into ruin is the murder of a Burmese maid by a white male foreigner (*farang*) living in a nearby house.[1] As the maid's ghost returns to haunt the streets, this clean and modern veneer begins to peel off. "Selling Urgently" signs appear on the neighbors' houses, the streets become overgrown by grass and littered with palm fronds, and the gate guard disappears, leaving the gates wide open. Other aspects of Thi's life also crumble: his boss, having embezzled much of the company's fortunes, flees, leaving his business behind to collapse; he suspects his wife of infidelity; and his daughter begins coming home late or not at all. In the end of the film, as ghosts multiply throughout the community, Thi, no longer able to distinguish between his family and malevolent ghosts, accidentally shoots his own son.

Laddaland, with its themes of chaos, poverty, and violence lying under-lying a seemingly modern, clean, and rational suburban life, resonated with many of the horror stories told to me during my field research. In the film as well as in these stories, things that appear to be modern and signs of a pros-perous life are in fact tainted by foreign presences—indeed, the communities themselves come to epitomize an unhomely way of life. As they did in Bon's story of the cracked building, financial crisis, moral crisis, and supernatu-ral crisis intertwine. In short, *Laddaland* and the tales of haunted communi-ties show the idea of (and desire for) progress made uncanny. In other words, entering an orderly, prosperous, and exclusive community does not protect one from ruin. Despite the gates and security guards, ghosts and criminals are able to infiltrate it, and the dream of living in such a place has in itself become something foreign.

For many, the film neatly captured a sense of crisis at large in Chiang Mai, especially since the Asian economic crisis of 1997. Many of my interlocutors saw high-rise buildings and suburban gated communities—both of which I will henceforth term "communities of exclusion"—as symbols of Chiang Mai's progress and development; but the images of ghosts and foreigners that appear repeatedly in these sites in everyday popular stories are manifestations of this anxiety over something fundamental felt to be lacking in this "prog-ress." Here, the ideas of the urbane dwelling within the city, that quality of urban life which civilizes and renders things prosperous, is seen to have failed, opening the gateway to admit forces thought to have been overcome.

Indeed, the present moment becomes a ruinous one. As tropes of cul-ture (*watthanatham*) promise to mobilize the charismatic power of the past for future benefit, they do so in a present full of doubt. In this chapter, I analyze stories of ghosts and hauntings as expressing anxiety about the possibility of knowing for sure whether one has actually attained progress, a quality that, in the Thai sense of *khwam charoen,* points to the inner essence of a place and of a person. In this way, I complicate Avery Gordon's (2008) idea of haunt-ing as an unexpected reminder of "historical alternatives" or past injustice in present-day social relations by bringing such "haunting" into dialogue with Buddhist conceptions of progress and development as well as a deep engage-ment with haunting as a Thai concept.

In each of the stories that follows, those living in these communities of exclusion express their desire for a particular form of existence—one that is progressive (*charoen*), orderly, and prosperous. But also in each story, the com-munity is not what it had seemed to be. Instead, it is invaded by forces that this discourse of *charoen* purports to have overcome—namely, "undeveloped" ethnic others or "superstitious" ghosts.

THE UNCANNY, *CHAROEN,* AND ESSENCES

As I argue that Thai residents interpreted abandoned buildings as being haunted by supernatural forces, I do not mean to suppose a direct binary between "Thai" and "Western" thought, or of Thai thought "old" and "new." Such a construction would present a Victorian-era anthropological character- ization of culture as consisting of exotic "survivals" from a prior time, or at best create an image of a "Northern Thailand" that, as Pemberton cautions for Java, would "be so recognizably different that it would have to be acknowl- edged as a self-contained totality: another time, another epistemological space, another culture" (1994, 17). Indeed, as Day suggests, just as the past was not a totality, neither is "modernity." Rather, as the literature on the re- enchantment of modernity suggests (Dube 2010), neoliberal ideas of space as standing reserve become loaded with other meanings, ones that fall outside of the realm of the "rational" and thence become categorized as "superstitious." In other words, the supposition of the "modern" as such has the side effect of categorizing all of that which becomes considered not a part of it as some- thing else—something "superstitious," "traditional," or "Northern Thai." Such reifications do not do justice to the nuances of modern Chiang Mai or to anthropological data in general.

Magic within this category of the modern can be teased out through examining Thai terms about prosperity, specifically *khwam charoen.* When I described the abandoned buildings dotting the Chiang Mai skyline to Choke, an architect friend of mine, he smiled and shook his head, repeating a com- mon saying: *"phatthana, tae yang mai charoen"* (developed, but not yet pro- gressed). In other words, while the bricks and mortar appear "developed" (*phatthana laeo*), something insubstantial is lacking, something that causes all that wasted capital and space.

The Thai word *charoen* derives from the Khmer (Cambodian) word *chamraon,* meaning "to advance, progress" (Headley et al. 1977, 196–197), or "to expand until complete in a positive sense" (Thongchai 2000a, 531), a forward motion that allows a thing to reach its fullest potential. The use of the term *charoen* links ideas about tangible progress (e.g., development) to an essence of progressiveness, the quality that is promised by sources of char- ismatic power (*barami*). There is, in this idiom, an animating force behind the city: that charismatic property—articulated by the word *watthanatham* for some and embodied by the guardian spirits of the city for others—that allows for *charoen* and the drawing-in of prestige, new immigrants, power, and wealth. Lucien Hanks, in his classic study "Merit and Power in the Thai Social Order" (1962), terms this power "merit" (*bun*), although I prefer to focus on the more specific *barami*. *Barami* contrasts with *atthan*—cursedness, misfortune, the result of bad ghosts and spirits. Each is selectively deployed in the new supernatural imaginary of Chiang Mai, as plagues of bad ghosts rise at the same time as upsurges in charismatic spirit mediumship.

When I began to ask about concepts of space in the city, the subject of the supernatural repeatedly arose, ranging from the influence of the city's guardian spirits to the supernatural power (*sak*) of sacred space and from there to sacred space's inverse: places like the cracked and haunted building to which Bon pointed, places of misfortune and malevolent ghosts (*phi*). Thai academics (cf. Mala 2008) often frame such beliefs in benevolent or malevolent spirits as "cultural" remnants of a prior worldview attributed to Chiang Mai's "Lanna" past in ways that mirror the construction of "Java" (Pemberton 1994); although in the case of Northern Thailand, academic writing on "Lanna" is juxtaposed not only with "the West" but also with Bangkok. In Thai academic writing, Northern beliefs are often mined for gems of "local wisdom" (*phumpanya*) deemed to have practical value (see Johnson 2011; also cf. Charupat 2007) or, when this attempt fails, dismissed as "not deeply meaningful" (Sit 1980, 22). Authors such as Sit, Mala, or Charupat present this quantity of "Lanna wisdom" or "culture" as being under threat by a homogenizing force stemming from the West, an anxiety that is also reflected in other representations of Thai nationalism (Amporn 2003). In this way, Lanna beliefs are framed as a homogeneous, unchanging set, charming and occasionally wise, but in decline under the onslaught of rationalization (Kraisri 1967). This stands in stark contrast with other anthropological work in Thailand (Irvine 1984; Mills 1999; Pattana 2003) that documents the increase in fears and hopes projected upon the supernatural in the present.

THE EDUCATED CLASS

In Freud's notion of the uncanny, it is precisely those who believe themselves to know better—"supposedly educated people" he writes (2003, 242)—who are susceptible. Feeling haunted reminds the educated that he or she has not yet overcome superstitious beliefs. One's unconscious fears betray a secret savagery within.

It is perhaps for this reason that Chiang Mai's "educated people" figure prominently in this story of the uncanny haunting of progress. Many of my interlocutors took pains to draw a distinction between "those who are educated" and those who are not. In many discussions with me, middle-class shop owners pointed to their formal schooling in drawing a clear distinction in Chiang Mai's society in the same way that my less well-off interlocutors self-deprecatingly pointed to their lack of it.

Benedict Anderson describes such a split in his influential essay "Withdrawal Symptoms" (1977). He characterizes a divide between traditional middle-class sources of prestige (e.g., the military or the civil service) and the new middle class, schooled at Thailand's then new universities. While Anderson frames the conflict in 1970s Thailand as one between recently educated middle-class students and their older, less iconoclastically oriented parents, in the case of mid-2000s Chiang Mai, his distinctions between "old/Right" and "new/Left" forms of middle-class prestige no longer carry the same ideological weight. This marks a profound shift from the political landscape of the late twentieth century, when liberal students formed an influential and active political unit, and Left/progressive/democratic versus Right/capitalist/military/traditional units made coherent sense (Klima 2002; Saitip 1995). As faculty have grown more conservative and students become less likely to join in mass movements—as the lack of student leadership in recent political protest movements in comparison with the 1970s attests—the previously ideological split between generations has instead become something akin to a class divide between the middle and lower classes, and traditional poles of Left and Right have lost their explanatory power. The new, 2000s-era ideological divide separates the largely rural and largely lower- and middle-class "Red Shirt" supporters of former prime minister Thaksin Shinawatra from largely Bangkok-based, middle- and upper-class "Yellow Shirts." But these groups blur former ideological boundaries: Red Shirts incorporate former Communists and former killers of Communists, while the Yellow Shirts include army generals and former student leaders.

Yet the distinction between "educated" and not educated that Anderson draws remains, especially when the issue of culture, spirit beliefs, and urban anxiety is concerned. Those residents of Chiang Mai who style themselves the "educated class," a term by which I attempt to evoke such Thai categories as "people with education" (*khon mi kan sueksa*) or "people who have learning" (*khon mi khwam rian ru*), point to a sharp division between the rationality of national narratives of culture and Buddhism on one hand, and local spirit beliefs and Buddhist magic on the other (Pattana 2005, 174). I argue that such a rejection of the localized spirits of place in favor of a reified "culture" does not necessarily disenchant, but rather, that this culture becomes the new source of enchantment, operating with a similar logic to that of sacred magical power (*sak*). Each serves to address the problem of anxiety and misfortune in the same way that mediumship does, by mobilizing an edited, reconfigured authority rooted in past ideas of the city for future benefit.

Such a "re-enchantment of modernity" has been observed elsewhere in the world, and I analyze the Thai case in light of this. Saurabh Dube argues that modernity in itself requires other forms of magical thinking—for instance, the abstractions and mythical thought involved in imagining such things as capital and nations (2010, 729). Such "new" forms of magic often blend with and complement ways of thinking that are normally termed "magical" or "religious." As Phillip Taylor suggests for Vietnam, folk religions are often the first points at which the enchantments of modernity become expressed in the trappings of "traditional" culture—in Taylor's case, a Vietnamese goddess experiences a dramatic surge in popularity as the Vietnamese economy liberalizes (2004, 5).

In Thailand, the positive and negative associations between wealth and magic are present: the hopes and the fears inherent in economic change are manifest in supernatural form. Pattana Kitiarsa (2005) describes how the booming business of spirit mediumship serves to address the anxieties of Thailand's modern-day lower class, and Mary Beth Mills (1995) similarly shows how the figure of the young woman as the malevolent "widow ghost" represents for poor northeastern farmers an uncanny return of modernity (*khwam thansamai*) when a wave of panic over "widow ghost" deaths swept the region. For Mills, the widow ghosts are the uncanny return of the failures of the market to deliver on promises of nationwide prosperity.

Previous studies of modernity's enchantments concern images and the fickle spectrality of the economy, an invisibility that renders economic concerns ghostly, much like the specters that emerge from them. Yet Chiang Mai's haunted buildings are concrete, in both the physical and figurative sense. Unlike in the previous studies, these ghosts are anchored in space. Indeed, fears of chaos in Chiang Mai often revolved around fears of space and concern over what dwelled in urban spaces. In the case of Chiang Mai, I argue that the "ghosts of bad death" (*phi tai hong*) inhabiting abandoned construction represent for those who fear them the unknowability of a place's inner essence and the (potential for) progress's fragility. Such anxieties and fears appeared as the precise inverse of the models of urbanity detailed elsewhere in this book.

Max Weber (2003) famously predicted that modernity would disenchant, a prediction that is contradicted by much recent anthropological work on the uncanny reemergence of the magical and ghostly. Mladen Dolar argues that this should be no surprise: modernity and the uncanny in fact became connected when the decline of the formal religious sphere as the sole location of the unearthly led to the release of the uncanny into the realm of the everyday (Dolar 1991, 7). In citing the uncanny, Dolar draws, as I do, upon the Freudian idea of *unheimlich*, the species of horror that emerges when that which had previously been thought to be surpassed (not merely repressed) reemerges (Freud 2003). As such, the uncanny is therefore especially relevant when looking at concepts of progress.

In Diane Nelson's view, fears of occult forces have to do with the breakdown of national (middle-class) conceptions of the home. For her, when indigenous groups began to assert their differences from the body politic, for many the end result was a horrific doubling of the national "family," that is, "modes of ladino identification—being that which everyone else aspired to because of its attachments to whiteness, the modern, and the future—are suddenly under question and rendered uncanny" (Nelson 1999, 26). Such a breakdown of familial ideas—in the Thai case, the obligations between of the living and the dead—is what distinguishes my work from that of others working in Thailand and Laos (cf. Klima 2002, 2006; Langford 2009). In these studies, the living have active relationships of exchange and obligation with the returned dead. In my work, such familiar ties no longer exist: as notions of progress break down, the ghosts that emerge are as alienated from the living as the living are from them.

Tracing the internal logic of haunting in Chiang Mai, the kinds of ghosts that emerge and how they emerge provide clues to the nature of Chiang Mai's crisis: ghosts emerge owing to the failure of *older* magic, *charoen*. *Charoen*, "progress," encloses prosperity, enlightenment, wisdom, and wealth all in one term. It is a word that points to the inner progressive state of a thing rather than its outward appearance.

Imagine a ladder. Every being in the cosmos is somewhere on that ladder and in motion. Some are climbing slowly, some quickly, others are staying still, and still others are slowly descending. Beings on higher rungs sometimes aid those on lower rungs to climb higher, just as beings on low rungs occasionally pull others down. At each new rung, there is a new level of prosperity, but also of understanding.

This act of climbing is the act of *charoen*. The beings nearby one on the ladder are fellow humans. Wealthy and kind patrons or wise teachers might be a few rungs up, while wise kings might be just beyond them. Men who ordain as monks may not start on a high rung but are actively climbing quickly, while wealthy but selfish individuals are descending from a higher place.

But humans are not the only beings on the ladder. At rungs farther up are benevolent spirits, including the *chao mueang* (described later). Beyond them might be the Hindu deities: Brahma, Vishnu, and Shiva (among others), lending support to their followers in their climb. By mirroring the technique of higher climbers, those below seek to improve their speed. That which seeks to become enlightened or wise first imagines the desired state of being. Below, the misfortunate, poor, or ill also struggle. Farther below them on the ladder lie ghosts and demons, still in motion but with great distances to climb. Worse, owing to their ignorance and wickedness, they pull others down with them or hold them back.

During the twentieth century, this religiously informed notion of *charoen* became associated with idioms of national development, the figure of the Thai monarchy, and reform Buddhism to assure Thais of the inevitable, supernaturally powered, and moral nature of increasing wealth and prosperity (see Jackson 2010, especially in regard to the monarchy, and Morris 2000 for modernity). In this line of thought, the twentieth-century project of national development thus occurred under the auspices of supernatural forces that secured the motion of *charoen* and the forward march of progress. Such a sense of spiritual, moral, and rational progress ensured that there would be no uncanny visitors from lower down the ladder, in other words that ghosts would not emerge—an assurance not built into other idioms of progress (e.g., *thansamai, kan phatthana*). It is now, however, as crisis after crisis challenges these assumptions about progress, that uncanny specters gain ever greater power.

This concern with the inner essences of things might at first seem to run counter to some earlier ethnography on Thailand. Penny Van Esterik (2000) and Peter Jackson (2004), for example, characterize Thai society as concerned with surfaces over essences, a reversal of Western privileging of essences over surfaces. For Jackson, in Thailand, "[i]t is the surface image that has the power to mould the inner being" (Jackson 2004, 211). But these studies focus on the point of friction between the public sphere and the private sphere, where state power acts swiftly to correct any disruptions in the public order and remains unconcerned with private practices. In contrast, Chiang Mai's disruptions occur in intimate spaces: homes, hotel rooms, and so on. Haunting, in this sense, is not the private invading the public, but the destabilization of the homely. It is a reflux on the ladder of *charoen* and a destabilization of the assumed-to-be-inevitable motion of progress.

Following Jackson's idea of the "regime of images," the *charoen* home is one that is assumed to inform, direct, and reflect the *charoen* status of its inhabitant. But, as I argue, moving into these new spaces was, for many of my interlocutors, traumatic. The strangeness of these spaces is productive of doubt—my interlocutors doubted their (or the homes') inner quality of *charoen,* and by extension their own. In other words, it was the failure of Jackson's regime of images. While every effort to ensure that the home's image would remain *charoen,* as cracks began to appear (sometimes literally, as Bon showed me) in infrastructure, society, and economy, those thought-to-be overcome elements reemerged in the form of ghosts and migrants. These stories, then, are the discursive cracks in Thai middle-class desires for *charoen.* As in the film *Laddaland,* ghosts become the uncanny reminders that the regime of images does not always act as it should, that poverty and death can and do exist beneath manicured lawns and behind white concrete.

CRISIS

Thailand's recent political history has been dominated by the figure of Thaksin Shinawatra (prime minister 2001–2006). The Chiang Mai–born police official turned businessman turned prime minister embraced a technocratic idea of the Thai future, one that rejected the status-obsessed monarchical and military-oriented Central Thai elite in favor of neoliberal rationality. His slogan "Think New" (*Khit mai*) and his numerous North-based construction projects promised a fundamental change in Chiang Mai's fortunes and the potential for Thailand's second-largest city to emerge from Bangkok's shadow. Academics and activists (Thai and foreign alike) were often critical of Thaksin's plans, but for many others he embodied a real, physical connection with an intangible well of modernity; like other Southeast Asian "men of prowess," he channeled outside forces and turned them into tangible profit for his supporters (Sidel 2004). Thaksin's policies also funneled wealth into the provinces, and his business partners in Chiang Mai were awash in contracts. After his ouster in 2006, his supporters blamed even unrelated problems on his absence. For example, when Chiang Mai experienced a citywide Internet slowdown, one older supporter[2] confidently told me that such a thing would never have happened under Thaksin; according to this man, Thaksin had had a plan to give every Northern Thai his/her own personal Internet link—"by stars, by satellite."

These promises were especially appealing to a Chiang Mai still reeling from the 1997 economic crisis. During that year, the Thai baht lost nearly half of its value and Thailand became technically bankrupt. Especially hard-hit were real-estate speculators who, as much of their wealth was based on debt, found themselves defaulting on their loans and losing their property. Chiang Mai became a clear demonstration of the Thai real-estate market's overreach—the crisis left behind a ring of abandoned structures around the city and empty high-rises dotting the skyline—there was even a stock exchange, complete with banks of monitors and a trading floor, that fell into ruin, never used.

Chiang Mai's recovery largely coincided with Thaksin's rise to power, and, for many in the city, he represented a new face to the Thai government, someone they saw as clued in to the actions of the international market instead of inwardly patronage-oriented, and therefore capable of preventing a recurrence of 1997. In the eyes of his supporters, the face of the Thai political scene had changed from one favoring the well-connected to one that favored the common man. To his detractors, in contrast, Thaksin represented amoral, avaricious power—progress without *charoen,* rule without morality, power without merit.

Responding to the latter view, the Thai military ousted Thaksin in a royally backed coup d'état in September 2006 and replaced him with military-
appointed rulers. As a result, many among his supporters feared that the
Asian financial crisis of 1997 would occur all over again, while among his
detractors, many assumed that Chiang Mai's development under Thaksin had
been carried out purely for profit, without regard to quality. For both groups,
the remains of post-1997 construction after ten years of being exposed to the
tropical elements and the shells of new construction halted during the uncertainty of 2006 looked identical—only the darker gray hue of the old concrete
and the vines growing over the structures indicated which one had no future
and which one's future was merely unlikely (figures 1–4).

These fears were somewhat warranted. The Thai economy did suffer
(although not to the extent it did in 1997), and the coup's destabilizing
influence echoed throughout Thai politics for years. My study came at the
moment before the anti-coup sentiment coalesced into political action. In
2006 and 2007, during my field research, anxiety about the country's future
was more diffuse than it would become in 2008–2010, when protest and
political violence rocked Bangkok's streets. Elsewhere, other authors (Keyes
2006; Wassana 2010) have explored the magico-religious interpretations of
such political and social anxiety.

FIGURE 1 | Abandoned building, Hai Ya district

FIGURE 2 | Abandoned gated community

FIGURE 3 | New construction

FIGURE 4 | Cars in the abandoned Boi Luang Hotel

HAUNTINGS

"It's Not the Real World"

Chim owned a jewelry shop on fashionable Nimmanhaenmin Road and lived for a time in the same high-rise as I did. Her store specialized in Lanna designs and she styled herself as a "Lanna woman."[3] Chim purchased a house in a gated community in the suburb of San Sai, a district immediately to the northeast of the city center. When I interviewed her in her store during a slow period of the afternoon, she told me how at first she had been excited by the prospect of living in an exclusive community. "They talk about the places like there will be a nice community [of neighbors]. [As if] there's only doctors [in the community]. But I never saw my neighbors. Many of the houses were empty." She paused, trying to summarize what she meant: "It's not the real world [*man b'maen lok ching*]. I got so scared that I moved out, back to the city."[4] When I asked her why she was so frightened, she described to me how she was terrified to live in the house—she would wake up many times during the night, listening for strange noises from downstairs. Already alert to the link between empty spaces and ghosts, I asked Chim whether she was afraid of ghosts. She laughed. "Maybe there are ghosts," she mused, "but I fear criminals [*chon*] more. My neighbors wouldn't say anything if there were criminals [coming into my house], they wouldn't be interested [in looking outside], they would just stay inside."

Chim, already styling herself along neotraditionalist lines,[5] took up the fantasy of the gated community in which "there's only doctors." This was a common slogan for the new communities—as one advertisement read, "Come and live with people of your status [radap khun]." Chim's desire is to be part of this exclusive club of interesting people, a desire that was never realized. Instead, as in *Laddaland,* the moment Chim achieved her desired state of *charoen,* she became disturbed by it. In her new, *charoen* village, the neighbors were either not present or were entirely uncaring. Crime in these communities is in fact no greater than crime elsewhere in Chiang Mai, but Chim feared it to the point where, in a reversal of the American phenomenon of "white flight" (cf. Low 2003), she fled the gated community for the city center. What I am seeking to understand here is how the mismatch between Chim's desire for this progressive, intellectual community and the reality of the empty streets is productive of fear. I argue that Chim's questioning of the security of the gated community is an effect of this fantasy—and her very desire for it—being made uncanny.

While in her story Chim did not refer to ghosts, others—indeed, most of my interviewees—did. Som, another gated-community resident in her early thirties, told me about how she remained in the community only because her husband liked it. On the very day he left for his overseas work trips, she would rent a room in the city rather than stay in an empty house, surrounded by other empty houses. "Ghosts," she said to me in a low voice as we sat on the porch of her suburban house, "there are so many [here]!"

"Another Kind of Noise"

Chiang Mai has a lively and varied assembly of ghosts, much recent discussion of which in Southeast Asia points toward the dead as partners in connections of exchange or kinship (cf. Klima 2002; Langford 2009). But the dead in Klima's and Langford's ethnographies are identifiable; they are family, either actual relatives or the fictive kin of political comrades. Chiang Mai's high-rise ghosts, in contrast, are strangers. In almost no case was a ghost identified with a name or a family, and the one ghost who was in fact identified appeared to his former friends as a strange, inhuman thing to which nothing was owed. In short, these ghosts are something different, removed from the bonds of familial obligation.

The ghosts were all referred to as *phi tai hong,*[6] "ghosts of bad death," and most of them were associated with murders, suicides, or (most commonly) traffic accidents. *Phi tai hong* are intimately bound to ideas of motion and stasis, and many sites for their propitiation lie alongside highways. Stopping at or otherwise acknowledging the site (except for perhaps a quick beep of the horn) was considered dangerous, however, and would open one up to an unwelcome visitation. As we passed one such site along the road, Noi, the daughter of a spirit medium from San Sai, warned me of what would occur should we stop there (as I wanted to do): "You would fall ill. You would have bad luck. You would not *charoen.*"

This ghost at the roadside had been the victim of a traffic accident. It was both the cause and the result of bad luck. Should I be haunted by the ghost and therefore die violently, I too would be unable to move beyond the trauma of my death to be reborn and instead become a ghost. In short, ghosts of violent death, caught in and unable to progress beyond their traumatized state to be reborn, threaten to cause others to remain in stasis as well. They prevent the movement of individuals up the ladder of progress and spread this same hindrance to others in the manner of an epidemic—hence their uniquely antagonistic relationship to *charoen.* The (perceived) violence, disorder, and urban chaos in the city, reflected and amplified by newspaper reports that splash ghost stories and bloody deaths across the front pages (cf. *Chiang Mai News* 2007a, 2007b, 2007c, 2007d), support the sense of impending crisis: the explosion in violence and the economic decline of the city are both causes and results of the rise in bad ghosts. In short, ghosts represent a lack of mobility: they block "correct" motion.

Many ghost stories were concentrated around Chiang Mai's most rapidly growing part of town, Nimmanhaemin Road. This was also a place most identified with wealthy visitors from Bangkok, fashionable boutiques, and expensive cafés. The area was lauded as the center of Chiang Mai's revitalization (expressed as *khwam charoen*) by many architects, artists, and writers, and had become a hotspot for new construction projects. But even though (or, rather, because) Nimmanhaemin was cited as the center of Chiang Mai's boom by much of the popular press, it was also the location for many of its ghost stories.

"One day at work, a man died," said a middle-aged laborer, referring to the construction of a high-rise building along this road. "A beam fell through his head and he died *bup!* Just like that. Now these days at night you can hear him sometimes. I went over there with the guard from up the road and we heard it. It wasn't a noise like any animal would make, or any person—it was *another* kind of noise." His friend, the night watchman, nodded understandingly and pointed out toward the busy street. "That's why this place will never *charoen!* There are too many ghosts around here!" He waved his hand at

Nimmanhaemin. His statement that the avenue would never *charoen* was a jab at the expensive restaurants, luxury condominiums, and rocketing real-estate values—in other words, this road seems to be prospering, but the prosperity is hollow.

In addition to this hollowness, the laborer's story introduces an element of foreignness into the construction site: he recognizes his coworker's ghost as a ghost by *not* recognizing his voice as that of his friend. The ghost could have called out to the laborer by name, and the laborer could have recognized his friend's voice, but he does not. He could have identified a debt to his friend's ghost and talked about how one should erect a shrine for the spirit (as do the relatives of the war dead in Langford's 2007 study), but he does not—he simply avoids the place at night. The spirit that lives in the construction site, for the worker, is a *thing* with which communication and exchange are impossible.

The Bird-Shit *Farang*

The building next to this construction site was also haunted. It was a high-rise condominium building popular among foreign expatriates. Maew, a Thai resident of this building, related to me a story popular among her friends about the ghost that haunts one of these. According to Maew, he was a "*farang khi-nok*" [bird-shit *farang*]—a rude term indicating a foreigner who is poor or stingy. While most *farang,* such as those seen on billboards or television, were thought of by Maew as sources of wealth, others were poor and simply pretending to be someone important. This particular pretender to riches plunged from the top floor to his death on the road ten stories below in what Maew assumed to be a suicide.[7] Now, he stands in front of the window out of which he jumped and urges Thais to do the same. His appearance is a curious mixture of a Hollywood and traditional Thai ghost: "You will think that he is just some *farang,*" Maew continued, "but then you will see that he has no feet!"—footlessness being a common attribute of Thai ghosts.

Why did this story strike Maew and others as particularly frightening? Why is it significant that the ghost is *farang,* and why does he appear in a new building? Both the man and his building are things that seem progressive from the outside. Indeed, the person and the building are linked through the continual use of *farang* in advertisements for new housing projects. I argue that what makes this ghost story particularly frightening is that in it the veneer of progressiveness covers a cursed place. As the ghost's lack of feet suggests, what lies beneath the veneer is all too familiar—he seems to be a wealthy and urbane figure from abroad, but upon closer inspection he is in fact ghostly in the same way as any local village ghost. Progress, cosmopolitanism, and wealth have proved to be illusions.

Too Cheap to Get a Monk

Aong worked as a night watchman at a high-rise building in one of Chiang Mai's quickly growing suburbs. A Shan,[8] he had fled from Burma[9] as a child and was raised in Mae Ai, a town on the Thai-Burmese border. In his early twenties in 2006, he had just come to to Chiang Mai. Without formal refugee status or a listing as a registered hill-tribe member,[10] Aong faced a host of difficulties involved with life in the city: he was subject to a forced bribe or deportation to a hostile Burma should the police discover him; he lived in a squatter's community on the outskirts of the city without running water; and he was working outside the bounds of any sort of labor law. Each of these factors contributed to the instability of his life in the city, and each weighed on his mind. One of these probably led to his disappearance, as after three months of working every night, seven days a week, he suddenly vanished without a word to me, his Shan friends who worked on the same street, or his employer. But, before his disappearance, when I sat alongside Aong as he worked, eating noodle soup and drinking instant coffee with him, his chief concern about the city was its ghosts.

After telling me how a girl who lived in his Shan squatter compound was possessed by a wandering spirit, a possession that manifested in shouting fits and violent spasms until an exorcist could be located, Aong pointed across a parking lot to a nearby nightclub that catered to wealthy local youth. "You heard about the shooting, right?" Aong asked me, referring to a fight that had broken out in the nightclub the week before. A police officer, the son of a sergeant, had flown into a drunken rage at a table of youths who had bumped into his table while dancing. The officer pulled out his gun and pointed it at one youth, and when the officer's friend intervened, the friend was shot and killed. The officer fled, escaping prosecution, it was assumed, through his family ties within the police force. "[The friend's] blood sat in the corner of the club," Aong continued, "and they [the club owners] were too cheap to hire a monk [to exorcise the place]. When the club reopened, a girl was dancing [there]. Her foot kept stepping on the place where the blood had stained the floor. Then, when she left, she was struck by a car and killed."[11] When I pressed Aong to make the connection between the blood and the traffic accident more explicit, he grew frustrated with me: "It was the ghost of the officer! They were too cheap to hire a monk!"

Aong contrasts his own compound's commonsense approach to ghosts to the nightclub's. Whereas his community would have pooled money to hire an exorcist[12] in order to solve such a supernatural crisis, the nightclub owners simply cleaned up the visible stain of violence and chose to ignore its invisible trace. This lack of attention or care was something which, to Aong, made the city so dangerous: it was quite possible, and even likely, that similar inattentions had occurred throughout Chiang Mai, leading to the proliferation of hidden dangers lurking beneath the city's veneer. As for the northeastern Thai farmers about whom Mills writes, for Aong promises of urban prosperity imperfectly conceal a hidden violence.

Just as the ghosts of formerly mobile people—youths on motorcycles, migrant workers, foreigners—are thought to move into newly built communities and bring their progressiveness to a halt, so the parallel figure of the criminal "Burmese" (*chon* Phama) migrant also appears. In a similar manner to ghosts of bad death (*phi tai hong*), the figure of the haunting criminal also arises from motion only to settle into construction and impede progress. Here, I turn to that other figure of motion and stasis.

The Lurking Population

When touring one abandoned high-rise with the guard, I had taken photos of graffiti written on the walls, but I was unable to read the writing. Some of it was in Shan, which I do not read, but even the Thai writing had words that I did not recognize. Thinking it might be Northern dialect, in which I had had less training than the Central one, I brought back photos to discuss with Chai, a Northern Thai engineer and friend of mine. Chai read the script and then shuddered. "What is it?" I asked him, hoping for a good story. "It's not what he's saying," said Chai. "It's everything. Half the words are misspelled; you can tell he's not Thai. . . . Looking at this, I feel like I have no idea of the person that wrote it."

I went through the text with Chai, and he pointed out to me the numerous errors in aspiration and tone. For instance, in places that required the Thai equivalent of a *d,* the author instead had used a *t* (e.g., the word *dai*, "to be able to," was written *tai,* "south"), and the tone markers were incorrect throughout the script. Naturally, it could be that this was simply the result of someone with atrocious spelling, and not at all the sort of person Chai imagined (or, rather, found himself unable to imagine). But here, it is not the *writer* of the text with whom I am concerned. Rather, it is Chai's reaction, his recoiling from the camera image. Chai imagined the author of the text as a dangerous, unknowable person rather than a foolish or confused but ultimately understandable person with awful grammar. Chai did not say, "What an idiot!" He said, "I do not know what that person might be thinking." The horror that Chai felt came from the idea that someone with whom he found himself unable to identify was secretly dwelling in the abandoned spaces in the city. His horror, like the fear of the ghost, was related to the disturbance of finding what was familiar made uncanny.

Most urban residents with whom I spoke were aware of the presence of foreign laborers in their midst and described to me their own technique for identifying them. Many confessed that they could not distinguish a Shan person from a Northern Thai person physically, but spoke (as Chai did) of seeing foreignness in unexpected places—for instance, a Burmese-language magazine near a market vendor, yellow chalk used as a traditional sunscreen, or a strange accent emerging from a Thai-looking face.

I explained Chai's reaction to Choke, the architect. He identified Chai's fear as one of the "lurking population" (*pratchakon faeng*)—those people who live among the "regular" population but remain unseen. They are feared, he said, because they are believed to lack any sense of moral or social duty—indeed, their very existence depends on their being able to blend into the general Thai populace without being seen but not sharing that "Thainess" (*khwam pen Thai*) which ordinary citizens possess. Katherine Bowie (1997), Thongchai Winichakul (1994), and Pavin Chachavalpongpun (2005) have all written extensively about Thainess and the construction of dangerous others in Thai nationalist writing. Others are assumed to be capable of criminal and immoral acts, and, as my interlocutors expressed, when their existence is revealed, neighbors can suddenly become foreign. While in a previous generation this fear of the lurking alien would have been fear of the Communist infiltrator, in the present time the locus of fear is more disparate: the imagined criminal, like the ghost, has no goal or purpose, but simply exists to sow chaos and destruction.

However, these stories of migrants-as-criminals often fail to mention that it is the same migrants who provide the foundation of Chiang Mai's new middle-class lifestyle. The guards (as well as the imagined criminals guarded against) are also often Shan (as was Aong), and so are the maids and caretakers (as in *Laddaland*). In short, Shan migrants, in the minds of the residents of these communities, contribute to at the same time as they detract from the potential for *charoen*. This intimacy—the *homeliness* of the "invisible" Shan laborer—renders his figure all the more unhomely when he "emerges" as a criminal: one is suddenly, forcefully reminded that one has been living among such intrinsically alien people all along.

When my interlocutors referred to Shan (rather than simply "illegal alien" or "foreigner"), they did not use the word "Shan." Nor did they use the word that Shan use for themselves, Tai, or even the Northern dialect *ngiao* (currently used to refer to those Shan who were in Chiang Mai before the recent wave of migration, and a term often used in Northern historical records). Instead, they simply referred to migrant Shan as Burmese nationals, *khon* Phama.[13] The association of Shan migrants as "Burmese" highlights their foreign-ness. While communities and people referred to as Ngiao and Thai-Yai have histories that predate the Thai nation in Thailand's north, "Burmese" people labeled as such are obvious foreigners.

This identification is telling. While Chiang Mai has a long and intimate history with Burma, having been its vassal for two hundred years and sharing many religious and cultural traditions with it, Burma in modern Thai nationalist historiography plays the role of the principal villain (Pavin 2005). Recent royally funded historical epics such as *Suriyothai* or *Naresuan,* as well as other historical films such as *Bang Rajan,* depict royal Thais as protonationalists, defending the (ethno-)nation (*chat*) from the violent Burmese, who are portrayed as gleefully engaging in the slaughter of children and monks (Amporn 2003). Even films set in the modern day often depict Burmese as dangerous others, as in the recent "Backpackers" segment of the horror film *Phobia 2,* where (assumed-to-be) Burmese migrants, stuffed with amphetamines and suffocated in the back of a truck (recalling the 2004 killing of eighty-five Thai Muslim protesters, who also suffocated when crowded into the back of a police truck in the southern town of Tak Bai), reemerge as zombie-like killers. These associations—Burma (Myanmar), violence, and drugs—bleed into everyday stories about migrants in the gated communities.

The Village of Sparkling Gold

Somboon ran a noodle stall in front of a nearly abandoned gated community, Ban Thong Prakai (The Village of Sparkling Gold), and was full of stories about the dangerous house next door. It was abandoned during the day, Somboon told me, but at night it would become filled with Burmese drug addicts. "They had their motorbikes filling the yard; they were out drinking and taking *ya ba* [methamphetamine]. They were not good people." Somboon recalled hiding in the closet of his stall as the sound of "shouting in a foreign language"[14] echoed from the abandoned building. Eventually, his fears got the best of him, and he phoned the local army barracks. Soldiers descended on the house and cleared out "over fifty criminals," according to Somboon.[15] Before the army captain left, he lent Somboon a gun so that he could shoot any outsiders who returned. Somboon's story echoes those of the abandoned construction site—hostile foreign sounds echo out of a space that should be empty and spread a sense of menace around the neighborhood, rendering the entire place, so auspiciously named, a place of danger.

Migrants parallel ghosts in other ways. Bon, the shopkeeper who showed me the cracked building, described "Burmese" thieves as supernaturally gifted at sneaking into houses. "[The communities] are full of criminals [*chon*]. [Illegal] aliens. . . . They even figure out ways to steal things inside of [your] apartment. They take a long piece of bamboo and fashion a hook on the end of it. Then, they reach it through the balcony window into the apartment. Very, very long, *na?* They will take everything!" Bon stretched his arm out, imitating the long bamboo "arm" reaching into the supposedly secure apartment.

The image of a long arm reaching into one's domestic space has clear parallels in ghost stories. Arguably (Central) Thailand's most famous ghost, Nang Nak, is identified as a ghost when her arm grows impossibly long and reaches down through the floorboards of her riverside hut. In the case of the migrants, the impossibly long arm stems, not from any supernatural powers, but from their criminal ingenuity, born out of knowledge of the wilderness. They have fashioned the "long piece of bamboo" out of jungle materials, and the extension of the (backward, violent) jungle into the (clean, rational) home is the element that Bon stresses in his story.

I thought about Bon several days later when I opened the *Chiang Mai News* to read that "Shan bandits" had been caught stealing motorcycles in the city (*Chiang Mai News* 2007a). This story was one of many specifically describing the foreign origins of common theft or violence in the city, although more often referring to "Burmese." The feature linking the migrants to the uncanny is that they appear to be Thai (and therefore familiar) until they reveal themselves to be *other*, an unveiling that casts suspicion upon neighbors and recalls, in the film *Laddaland*, Thi's wild confusion of ghosts with the living. Thai and Burmese are hopelessly mistaken for one another, and one cannot easily tell the difference.

An example of such a confusion of dangerous others with "safe" Thais is an incident that took place in 2004 when unidentified men opened fire on a school bus near Ratchaburi. Lertrat Ratanavanit, the army's assistant chief-of-staff, commented that the perpetrators were likely to be Burmese or from hill tribes, as "Thai people are not that evil" (*Bangkok Post,* June 5, 2002). He added: "We wonder why incidents like this usually happen in Ratchaburi. There must be some alien movements in the province. A number of Burmese people work there. The [guilty] men might have fled to the forest, changed their clothes and then come out looking like ordinary people" (ibid.).

Presences

In all of these stories, clean, ordered, and modern Thai communities are suddenly imagined to be invaded by reminders of disorder, violence, and backwardness. Spaces that were meant to be symbols of progressiveness and exclusivity bring with them the specter of decline and invasion in the form of the foreign presences that haunt them.

The English word "haunt" implies a reminder of a past moment, and it is in fact this idea of a sudden, unexpected connection between two points in time that dominates scholarship about haunting (Gordon 2008; Cheung 2010, 176). In many ways, Thai ghosts and criminals also "haunt"—they forcefully draw connections between a place and a past (thought to be overcome) time. But a more productive analysis may be gained by looking closely at the words used in Thai to describe ghosts.

Ghosts can *sing:* "possess" a person or place (e.g., a "haunted house"). They can do so in an angry fashion (*hian*), lashing out violently around them. The word *lon,* often used in the combination *lok-lon,* implies something more similar to the English "haunt": it means a frightening recollection of a past event, although without the tinge of melancholy implicit in "haunt" (e.g., "a haunting tune"). But the most common term used to describe the actions of ghosts in my interlocutors' stories was *lok:* to trick, fool, cheat, cruelly deceive.

Criminals can also *lok,* especially when they appear to do something innocuous but end up doing something harmful. In this way, criminals who appear "normal" but then turn out to spread violence, ghosts who emerge suddenly in an empty street, and communities that seem modern but are not, all have inner essences that differ from the way they look. In a sense, they are deceits.[16] This deceit, combining surface progressiveness with inner ruin, becomes important when analyzing Thai ideas of progress in the idiom of *khwam charoen.*

PROGRESS, DEVELOPMENT, AND GHOSTS

The association between gated communities, social isolation, and fear is not unique to Thailand. Indeed, it seems at first glance to be a peculiarly American phenomenon. Setha Low (2003) points to the connection between inhabitants of gated communities and fear in the American context, arguing that, contrary to a statistical decrease in crime, stories of criminals and fear of crime actually increased among those living in such places. In American narratives, the gated community is considered a refuge from a sea of danger, a culturally and ethnically homogeneous island in a country perceived to be overrun by danger and diversity. But in Thailand, rather than as a retreat where the homogeneous few can take refuge from a worsening city, gated communities are thought of in aspirational terms as places where the wealthy congregate (as Chim says, "there's only doctors"), and where one can live like and among wealthy foreigners. The fears, when they appear, are not of the urban hordes howling at the gates, but rather are fears that these aspirations have in fact become hollow, that the foreigners and "doctors" (as in Maew's story and the film *Laddaland*) are in reality petty and violent, that the utopian community will turn out not to be a community at all (as in Chim's story)—in short, that the empty spaces next door will be filled with danger and contagion (as in Bon or Maew's story). Chiang Mai's ghosts emerge at a particular point in time, when hopes about increasing prosperity and future progress fall into doubt. For those who fear them, when one finally achieves the desired state of modernity (i.e., perhaps when one moves into a gated community), suddenly one becomes afflicted by ghosts.

How are we to interpret these fears? How might Chiang Mai's ghosts help us better understand the notion of the uncanny and questions of progress? How do such ghosts play into and question the idea of the city as a font of prosperity and merit, and as a place that actualizes and mobilizes *khwam charoen*?

In the context of northeastern Thailand, Mary Beth Mills (1995) suggests that fears of "modern" ghosts are a critique of modernity. In her account, cases of "Sudden Unexplained Nocturnal Death Syndrome" (SUNDS), a condition wherein a seemingly healthy young man died in his sleep among Thai factory workers in Singapore, was interpreted in rural northeastern Thailand as a problem of "widow ghosts"—sexually attractive and stylishly dressed spirits assaulting young men. These ghosts, Mills argues, reflected an ambiguity surrounding figures of modern femininity in Thailand, where the increasing presence of migrant female workers and the decreasing importance of male labor led to an unspoken concern about the effects of such an economy.

For Mills, haunting has an oddly carnival air. The village gathers in the evening to dole out protective measures. Old women dress young men up as women in order to mislead the spirits, and every household hangs up a large wooden penis to "distract" the ghost—all amid an atmosphere of "much joking and laughter" (1995, 254). Those who fear widow ghosts turn to traditional spirit beliefs for defense against a modern plague and do so in the confidence that they have found the solution to the epidemic. But, although the subjects of these two studies might seem similar (modernity, ghosts, Thailand), from my study I learned that haunting was seen as a profoundly isolated and isolating experience. *Phi tai hong* haunted isolated individuals, and there was no community response to the problem of ghosts: the only precaution taken against them was avoidance.[17] While Mills' interlocutors in northeastern Thailand were still aspiring to the lifestyle promised by gated communities, mine were people who imagined themselves as having already successfully achieved this quality of "modernity." In short, whereas Mills' villagers placed the threat of ghosts as coming from outside and thus able to be resisted through community solidarity, my interlocutors felt that their own communities were the sites and source of haunting. It is for this reason that I have invoked Freud's concept of the uncanny (*unheimlich*) in order to understand the haunting of gated communities: there, the home has become an unfamiliar place, and one's idea of oneself as modern and advanced (as well as one's desire to be so) is likewise estranged. Unlike a public menace, which can be combatted by collective action, Chiang Mai's fears encroached upon the most intimate and individual spaces of the home.

I now return to Choke's statement, "[Chiang Mai has] *phatthana, tae yang mai charoen*"—"it has developed, but not yet progressed." The humor in this expression hinges upon the similarity between the terms *phatthana* and *charoen*. These words are occasionally used interchangeably to refer to things that are modern, high-tech, or advanced.[18] They place the referent in a hierarchy of development, as when my interlocutors would refer to a country such as Japan or the United States as *charoen laeo* or *phatthana laeo*,[19] meaning that it was already a "developed" place. At first glance, the idea that something could be *phatthana* but not *charoen* seemed paradoxical, but the example of Chiang Mai's new construction is one that nonetheless is one and not the other—hence the joke. The chief distinction between these two terms is that *charoen* refers to the hidden, unseen qualities of an object, while *phatthana* refers to its more superficial qualities. It is this reference to the unseen qualities of development that forms connections between a lack of *charoen* and the figure of the ghost.

Recall that, in its original Khmer meaning, *charoen* pointed toward Buddhist enlightenment, although in present-day Thai it is also used to refer to advancement in the secular world, but advancement of a more substantial and meaningful sort. *Khwam charoen* is that quality which inheres in something and renders it wise, advanced, or progressive in actuality rather than simply in appearance. For Choke, while the communities appear "developed," they lack something insubstantial, something that causes the structure's potential to fail and the buildings to fall into ruin. *Khwam charoen*, in this idiom, is what renders potentially prosperous things actually prosperous. This power contrasts with the idea that something is haunted (e.g., innocuous on the surface but actually dangerous). Thus, to say that the city has "*phatthana* but not yet *charoen*" is to describe a place where the surface only appears to be developed, whereas beneath the surface still lies that which was thought to have been overcome and left behind.

Charoen/phatthana shares with the idea of haunting a concern with invisible essences, essences that are unknowable but nonetheless powerful. One does not know if a place has *charoen* (and will therefore give prosperity and become prosperous) or just has *phatthana.* Thus, the seemingly progressive and prosperous veneer never lies comfortably, as doubts always arise with regard to these essences. Hanks, too, notes how prosperity is always laced with uncertainty, as one does not know whether one's wealth has come to one based on the results of past karma or if it is the action of amoral "power" (*amnat*), and therefore fleeting (1962, 1254).

When these doubts emerge, they emerge as stories of hiding migrants and haunting ghosts. Migrants and ghosts have their roots in mobility: one group flees a drug-fueled civil war and the other emerges from bloody deaths on the sides of highways. But when they emerge they are signs of stasis. They all show failed moments of potential and introduce foreign elements into the everyday. Like the fictional ghost in *Laddaland,* they question the inevitability of progress and its ability to change lives for the better.

But more than this, it is my argument here that Northern Thai urbanites find Chiang Mai's high-rise structures and gated communities particularly haunting because they introduce unwelcome associations that question the assumed-to-be inevitable and morally informed notion of progress expressed by the term *charoen.* Even at the moment when modernity is seemingly under way, possessing (*sing*) ghosts or concealed (*faeng*) migrants are believed to have the power and the will to render such spaces hollow, infertile, and meaningless. This was doubly the case during the political turmoil and subsequent economic crisis of 2006 when, for many, promises of change and Chiang Mai's reinvention were rendered hollow. *Charoen* promises forward motion; but for my interlocutors, the fantasy of incipient prosperity is haunted by the specter of decline, the idea that such progressiveness has not been truly achieved, a fear that manifests itself in the images of dangerous, lurking others.

To return to the image of *khwam charoen* as a ladder, Chim, Maew, and Som believe that they have reached a new rung upon it. They have a certain fantasy about what life on that next rung will look like, a fantasy the gated community feeds into, often quite explicitly (recall the ad that everyone is "on your level," or Chim's idea that "there are only doctors"). But when they arrive, they discover beings from the bottom of the ladder (ghosts or criminals) already there. This discovery throws their conception of the forward march of *khwam charoen* into doubt. What they assumed to be progressive is tainted by something ruinous—it becomes unhomely. This is why exclusion here is so much more than the excluding of others (e.g., "A community where everyone is on your level") or exclusion from one's own domestic space; here it is an exclusion from the very idea of progress.

Yet this fear of the failure of progress to materialize, and the emergence of ghosts/migrants as emblematic of this fear, is not new to the post-2006 crisis period. Indeed, it has occurred repeatedly at various points of political and social crisis in Northern Thai history. Just as the successful city is one that enables *khwam charoen,* the failed city is one where *khwam charoen* has ceased to happen.

2

Foundations

In Chiang Mai during a time of crisis, anxieties about ghosts trouble the city. This situation is not new, rather, it resembles other crisis points in Northern Thai history. David Wyatt describes one such incident reported in the *Nan Chronicle* of 1795 wherein *pret* and *yak* ghosts were said to have emerged to attack the populace of the Northern Thai city of Nan:[1] "Ghosts [went] around the city assaulting monks and people. After these beatings they dropped off written messages saying that they had come from the *deva* [angelic beings] guardians of the *cetiya* [stupa] . . . now in a very bad state of disrepair" (Wyatt 1994, 173). When the city's monarch lacks charismatic power (*barami*), the city falls into ghostly inspired violence and chaos. Ghosts emerge, like the ghosts of bad death already mentioned, as the city's infrastructure crumbles.

Wyatt assumes, based on the corporeality of their assaults, that the reference to "ghosts" was not to be understood in a religious or supernatural light, but instead referred to dissatisfied subjects who were protesting against a lack of political authority in the Nan royalty (1994, 176). Yet this trope of ghostly invasion and supernatural crisis reappears at other points in other chronicles, such as the *Chiang Mai Chronicle* (Wyatt 1989, 175n2). Indeed, fears about ghosts or witches proliferate during times of crisis elsewhere in Southeast Asia—plagues experienced by those involved as the very real emergence of the supernatural, not as political metaphors (Sidel 1995, 166; Siegel 2006). How, then, to contextualize the assaults of these *phi tai hong, pret,* and *yak*? What is the role of "centered-ness," space, and construction?

For Chiang Mai, another "assault by ghosts" is recounted in the *Suwan Kham Daeng* chronicle. In this story, the city was suffering from an invasion of ghosts.[2] Indra, feeling sorry for the inhabitants, gave them seven magical fountains of gold, silver, and crystal along with, most importantly, a pillar with an attendant guardian giant (*yak;* Aroonrat 1982, 3). The pillar provided them with prosperity and the giant chased away the malevolent ghosts, but the city dwellers later lost the pillar. However, Indra forgave them and gave them a copy of the original to venerate instead—a copy that is now Chiang Mai's city pillar, the *sao inthakin.*

These chronicles, compiled in Northern Thailand during the eighteenth and nineteenth centuries, emphasize the importance of urban centrality in protecting the city from dangerous external forces. It is through the intervention of charismatic royal power,[3] *barami,* that the city can actively incorporate "wild" power and potential, subsuming it and rendering it a resource (see Johnson 2012). In this chapter, I juxtapose this productive power of the center (and the dangerous power of the margins), drawing from chronicles, historical sources, and present-day ethnography. I maintain that this idea of a centered well of magico-religious power in the city capable of opposing a chaotic and destructive wildness shares a link with current notions of urban charisma in Northern Thailand, albeit one altered and informed by nationalism and neoliberalism.

LANNA

"Lanna" (lit.: one million rice fields) refers to the Tai[4] kingdom that existed in Northern Thailand from the thirteenth until the nineteenth centuries, with Chiang Mai largely serving as the polity's capital. In modern usage, "Lanna" also denotes Thailand's northern provinces,[5] especially with reference to culture or cultural tourism. As I shall argue in subsequent chapters, Lanna, in both Central and Northern Thailand, invokes ideas of origins, authenticity, and both national and regional belonging.

Founding

The physical geography of Lanna consists of river valleys separated by mountain peaks. These rivers, the Ping, Wang, Nan, Kok, and others, flow into three larger river systems: the Chao Phraya, which runs southward into central Thailand and empties into the sea near Bangkok; the Mekong, which forms much of the border between present-day Thailand and Laos before becoming a major waterway in Cambodia and Vietnam; and the Salween, which runs through Burma. While these rivers toward the sea form wide alluvial valleys, inland they provide narrow strips of wet-rice–producing land separated by high mountains. This division between forested highlands and river valleys is a key feature of cultural and political life in the region. Scholars beginning with Edmund Leach (1973) and continuing to recent work on "Zomia" (Scott 2010) have emphasized the tension between lowland, wet-rice, Buddhist state and highland, swidden, animist populations, while recognizing the continual flow of people across this divide. In this book, I speak to this literature in showing how Lanna incorporates "animist" ideas of power into a notion of urbanity. But I think it useful first to address the standard narrative of Lanna history.

Chiang Mai was not the first city in the region. Previously, a Buddhist, likely Mon-speaking polity was located near the present-day city of Lamphun on the Ping River. Like most lowland states in Southeast Asia, the Mon coexisted with a non-Buddhist population living in small settlements in the countryside and over which they occasionally claimed hegemony (Srisak 1994).[6] During the first millennium CE, Tai or Tai-Lawa warrior chieftains built a series of fortified cities along the tributaries of the Mekong to the north and began to move southward. Eventually the two urban powers in the region— the Tai and the Mon—clashed, and the Mon were defeated. Mangrai, the Tai king, established a new capital in 1296, Chiang Mai (lit.: New City),[7] roughly twenty miles upstream on the Ping to the north (Sarasawadee 2005, 57).

Chiang Mai soon became a powerful city-state in the region and a key player in the regional politics. Lanna coexisted and competed with Sukhothai, the city-state now touted by Thai nationalists as the ancestor to the current Thai state, as well as with Luang Prabang, in present-day Laos, and Kengtung, in present-day Burma. In 1558, forces from the city-state of Ava, also in present-day Burma, captured the city, and Chiang Mai became a vassal of Ava for over two hundred years.

These two centuries are of special importance in Chiang Mai's history owing to their startling absence from Chiang Mai's historical narrative (Sarasawadee 2005, 109), an omission that reflects nationalist Thai antipathy to the prospect of a non-Thai Lanna, especially one controlled by the Burmese, who have functioned in Thai nationalism as a dark, violent "other" (see Pavin 2005; Sunait 2000). In mainstream Thai historiography (cf. Sit 1980), these two hundred years of Lanna history are mentioned only in describing the revolts against Burma, revolts that Thai nationalist writer Seri Aajasaalii describes as the "blood of freedom" demanding that Lanna subjects never be slaves (*khi kha;* Seri 1966, 94).[8] However, Sarasawadee notes that the later founder of the future Chiang Mai royal family, Thipchang, received numerous accolades and titles from the Burmese and regularly sent war tribute back to Ava—in other words, historical reality, especially spanning two hundred years—is too complex for a simplistic reading of Lanna independence and Burmese despotism (Sarasawadee 2005, 129).

The year 1767 marked the apex of Burmese control over the region, as it was then that Burmese forces (including those from Lanna) sacked Ayutthaya and scattered the Siamese; but the Siamese regrouped at Thonburi under King Taksin, who led a steady campaign that reclaimed Burmese advances and directly targeted Chiang Mai. In 1776, Siamese forces occupied Lanna and scattered Chiang Mai's population. The city was abandoned for nearly twenty years.

As Siam consolidated its control over the region, the Siamese began to appoint local warlords to serve as vassals. One of these, Kawila, was charged with re-creating Chiang Mai after its abandonment. He did so by making excursions into nearby war-torn areas, areas that today are part of Burma, Laos, or Sipsongpanna in China's Yunnan region (Sarasawadee 2005, 133). This process of rebuilding the city by the reclamation of war captives was referred to as "collecting vegetables to put in the basket, collecting serfs to put in the *mueang* [*kep phak sai sa, kep kha sai mueang*]" (Kraisri 1965), the remnants of which are still evident in the various ethnic communities in and around Chiang Mai's suburbs—communities that are "tied" to a particular temple (see Vatikiotis 1984), what in earlier times was a form of temple-bound serfdom (*kha wat*).

Cities, then, were created by accumulating people (Wolters 1999, 16–17). Projects like Kawila's focus on the coercive aspects of this urbanization, a focus that corresponds with James Scott's (2010) model of a coercive state attempting to round up a population in the lowlands and refugees fleeing its project in the hills. But this process was not solely carried out by force. Charles Keyes notes how Thai and Lao leaders highlighted their store of merit and, in that light, their access to otherworldly sources of power and prestige (Keyes 1973, 98).

In addition to Chiang Mai and Ayutthaya, Chiang Saen and Vientiane likewise were to be destroyed, depopulated, and then restored. But histories like Sarasawadee's Lanna triumphalist narrative or Seri's Thai nationalist one ignore the dislocation and trauma associated with the destruction of a city and with its repopulation. Kawila's raids into nearby city-states parallel similar raids that Siamese (and Burmese) forces conducted in neighboring regions. Anne Hansen cites the journal of John Crawfurd, an English diplomat who visited the region in 1821 and 1822:

> [T]heir wars are conducted with odious ferocity. Prisoners of rank are decapitated, and those of the lower orders condemned to perpetual slavery, and labour in chains. The peasantry of an invaded country, armed or unarmed, men, women,

and children, are indiscriminately carried off into captivity, and the seizure of these unfortunate persons appears to be the principal object of the periodical incursions which are made into an enemy's territory. (Crawfurd 347, cited in Hansen 2008, 51)

Kawila's *kep kha sai mueang* specifies the sort of slave the war captive will become: a *kha,* or "servant." *Kha* were people tied to a particular place and a particular trade, and a community of *kha* bound to a certain district (centered on a temple, hence "temple-slaves" [*kha wat*]) was a common feature of city-states. Many of the communities formed by the captives of Kawila's raids were resettled in communities from a certain origin (e.g., Lue or Yong) and tied to a certain trade (e.g., silverwork or lacquerware), and often this trade then served as part of Chiang Mai's tribute paid to its overlord(s)—in Kawila's time, in Siam. The diversity of the assembled collection of war captives and their handiwork would weigh toward proving the wide-ranging power of the monarch: the immediate suburbs of the city became a trophy case to display the king's power. In other words, the more ethnically diverse the city, and the more various the nations that paid tribute to the monarch, the greater his status.

Kawila's rule began Lanna's long phase as a Siamese vassal state, and his dynasty (the "Seven Kings") saw Lanna undergo radical changes. Beginning in the nineteenth century, British and other European merchants began to aggressively exploit the teak forests of the North. In the latter part of that century, owing to this new influx of capital (in British colonial rupees) and to an increasingly expansionist Siam, the status of local royalty began to decline. As European merchants sought teak contracts, kings (*chao*), through greed or inattention, often granted multiple contracts to different companies on the same plot of forest (Pasuk and Baker 1995, 104; Sarasawadee 2005, 169–171). Responding to European complaints about the local lords' mismanagement of teak, Bangkok appropriated the forests, redirecting what had become a significant source of income for *chao* and beginning what would become a long process of redefinition of Siam's and Lanna's relationship.

With increasing integration with Bangkok and the influx of (British) Burmese and Chinese traders, another ethnic community was built up, albeit one over which Chiang Mai's lords had little control. Foreign merchants (whether Muslim, Chinese, or British Shan), missionaries, and diplomats were directed to settle toward the banks of the Ping, to the east of the old city, and this is where Chiang Mai's central market grew. Chiang Mai's Chinatown and its Muslim quarter are still located in this area, as are the old structures of the American mission and the French and British consulates. In addition, the foreign settlements along Tha Phae Road were started by a large number of ethnically Shan communities, remnants of merchant communities linked to British Burma (Vatikiotis 1984, 83).

The growth of foreign trading communities marked the last attempts to preserve the ethnically segregated city planning of Chiang Mai by its lords. By the late 1800s and with the rise in the teak industry, Chiang Mai had become a place where people intermingled: "Lao, Chinamen, Indians of many castes and races, and women of all descriptions, passed in a seemingly endless stream before us, some with the day's work manfully done, some perhaps with it never begun" (Le May 1986, 81; Vatikiotis 1984, 67). But, in contrast to the resettled war captives, the Chiang Mai monarchy had little power over the city's new residents, most of whom were under the protection of either British law or Bangkok. Despite local anger over the behavior of Europeans and Americans within the city limits, little could be done to censure those who offended the local powers (Le May 1986, 56). Tensions reached a crisis point in 1866 when American missionaries converted two Lanna men. Enraged, the then king Kawilarot ordered the execution of the converts, claiming that, though he could do nothing to the foreigners, he still had power over his own subjects (Le May 1986, 126)—in his words, he was the Taker of Life (*chao chiwit ao*), who could order someone's beheading by saying "take" or "want"(*ao*; Sarasawadee 2005, 140). But this act was to prove the breaking point of the local monarchy's power. Kawilarot was soon called to prove his allegiance in Bangkok, where he died of unknown causes. The kings who followed him ceased using the term "Lord of Life" (*chao chiwit*), instead referring to themselves as "Great Lord" (*chao luang*), and whereas Chiang Mai's kings who followed Kawila (and, indeed, since the Burmese conquest) had always been vassals, after Kawilarot's death they became powerless.

As Siam's government began to adapt to fit European ideas of absolute monarchy, Bangkok exerted more and more control over the internal politics of Lanna (see Loos 2006 and Thongchai 1994 for other examples in Thailand). In 1884, Lanna became an administrative district (*monthon*) rather than a vassal kingdom, although more worrying to the local population were internal economic and religious reforms (Keyes 1975). For instance, Siam began to interfere directly with Lanna royal monopolies—a key source of income for *chao*—by collecting taxes on goods such as betel, which had previously been the purview of local lords. This was done via third-party tax farmers, a process that alienated both the local nobility and farmers, as tax farmers would often ask for advances on crops not yet extant. Local anger, directed against the Siamese and their Chinese representatives, erupted into revolt on several occasions around the turn of the twentieth century (Nopakhun 2003, 13). Although the uprising of 1902, where bands of Northern Thais and Shan attacked the bastions of Central Thai power in the province of Phrae, is perhaps the most famous, a similar event happened in 1889 in the Chiang Mai suburb of San Sai, where a local leader, Lord (*phaya*) Phab, led an uprising of Shan and Northern Thais to Chiang Mai in order to rid the north of *chao* Chek Tai—"Chinese people and 'southern' [Bangkok] Thais" (Nopakhun 2003, 15).[9]

Other destabilizing effects of national integration were more subtle and speak to the Northern Thai king's role as a keeper of spiritual peace and prosperity as well as worldly peace. As Bangkok took on a greater role in controlling other sources of income, *chao* began to appropriate tracts of farmland and extract higher rents from their tenants (Pasuk and Baker 1995, 315). This was framed as a reaction to an outbreak of witch-spirits (*phi ka*) in the countryside. *Ka* are lineage spirits (*phi pu ya*) that have become malevolent owing to neglect and inattention (see Anan 1984). In order to restore harmony, *chao* expelled from the polity families believed to be harboring *ka*, driving them into marginal areas (where some converted to Christianity). Such accusations of a lack of respect for proper religious authority reflect other anxieties abroad at the time—just as *chao* faced subordination and perceived disrespect at home from foreign lords, so *chao* accused local citizens of neglecting to respect their own home spirits.

During the early twentieth century, Siamese dominance over Lanna became absolute. Siamese policy attempted to bring Chiang Mai into closer accord with Bangkok through the implementation of Central Thai script as the only language to be used in education (passed in 1903); the revision of Northern Thai Buddhism to bring it more in line with Central Thai practices and the Bangkok-based sangha administration (Keyes 1975); and the discrediting and imprisonment of a charismatic Northern monk, Khuba Siwichai, in 1935 (Sarasawadee 2005, 212–213). Siwichai remains extremely popular in the North, adorning many if not most Northern-owned establishments alongside images of the Thai king.[10] A list of "charges" supposedly leveled at him by the Bangkok religious authorities remains popular as a demonstration of the superior magical power of Lanna monks; it includes such feats as allowing the rain to fall upon the monk from Bangkok while Siwichai remained dry, or walking several meters above the ground while the monk had to tread on the earth (in the latter case, Siwichai's position in the air above the Siamese monk is a symbol of magico-religious superiority). The image of a spiritually pure, if less cunning and savvy North juxtaposed with a worldly but impure Bangkok remains a common trope both in Northern self-stereotyping and in Central Thai depictions of Lanna.

Lanna history ends—in those terms, at least—abruptly in the 1930s. When Bangkok appointed a governor to administer Lanna directly, Northern royalty were divested of any administrative power they had retained. This process, for Northern Thai authors such as Sarasawadee, marked the end of Lanna. During the twentieth century, Chiang Mai grew at a stunted pace in comparison with Bangkok, despite the construction of rail lines in the 1920s and the establishment of Chiang Mai University in 1964.

Yet, spurred by nationalist reinterpretations of Chiang Mai, another idea about Northern identity began to grow during the 1990s. Prior to this time, regional identity was discouraged because of the fear that it would lead to support for the Communist Party of Thailand (CPT); after the decline of the CPT, regional identities were allowed, and even encouraged. Nidthi Eoseewong details the creation in Thai national discourse of a new "image" (*phap*) of the North, one with beautiful women, cool weather, and flowers (Nidthi 1991)—one, like Goldilocks' bed, that is not *too* foreign or *too* familiar but just foreign enough (Nidthi, in Charuphat 2006).

Such an image went hand in hand with the promotion of national and international tourism to Chiang Mai as a "city of culture." Roughly one and a half million visitors per year were listed as tourists by the Tourist Authority of Thailand's Chiang Mai office in 2006 and 2007, over half of them domestic tourists,[11] large figures when one takes into consideration the fact that Chiang Mai's metropolitan area only holds about one million residents. Recently, during the tenure of Chiang Mai native Thaksin Shinawatra as prime minister, new tourist projects such as the Chiang Mai Night Safari were proposed and some of them built. As I shall describe later, these sites were controversial in the eyes of many activists and academics, but to many others they were a symbol of "development" finally arriving in Thailand's North.

As shown in the film *Laddaland*, another trend in the city's transformation is a glut of luxury-housing projects and home-furnishing stores supplying the emigrant (national or international) population that lives in its condominiums or gated communities; or, to put it more accurately, these stores and spaces were built in anticipation of a hoped-for influx of emigrants. Such a discourse of waiting for the boom is widespread. As a real-estate agent who became my friend and interlocutor in Chiang Mai said, ever since the 1990s she has been flooded with poor landowners trying to invest in a second home (on credit) "for the *farang* to rent" in the hope that this will make them wealthy.

Construction, domination, destruction, abduction, reconstruction, and reconfiguration all have transformed Chiang Mai from Mangrai's "new city" to its present-day state of middle-class life and Thai tourist nostalgia. But in each case, there remains a concern with maintaining the intangible quality of urbanity in the face of wild dissolution. It is this urban charisma to which I now turn.

THE *MUEANG*

Lanna as a city-state with fluctuating allegiances and degrees of independence was not unusual in mainland Southeast Asia in its time. As Thonghchai (1994) details in his excellent account of the influence of the European concept of borders and maps upon Siamese ideas of space, the precolonial[12] *mueang* was something relatively unbounded, where the charisma of the center was more important than the line demarcating the ending of one polity and the beginning of another. Tambiah (1976) describes the *mueang* as what he terms a "galactic polity," an urban center that in turn both orbits other centers and has minor satellites orbiting it.

Within the *mueang,* there is also a discrete center: a guardian spirit, a king, or another repository of *barami.* This system of center and orbit is replicated down to the level of the neighborhood (*mu ban*), which has its own guardian spirits (*phi a-hak*), and from there to the individual family household complex (*ban*), where familial spirits (*phi pu ya*) provide a small radius of protective charisma. Thus, the mandala can be thought of as a fractal: the same centered-circle pattern is replicated from home to kingdom to inter-kingdom relations to the cosmos. Georges Condominas describes this replicative hierarchy as *systèmes à emboîtement* ("emboxed systems"; Condominas and Wijeyewardene 1990, 35–36). As each segment of the *mueang* is potentially independent (able to orbit the *barami* of its own center) and also potentially absorbable by other, larger segments (e.g., Chiang Mai could just as probably fall under a Burmese or Laotian sphere as a Siamese sphere), and as the power of central *mueang* waxes and wanes, their spheres of influence likewise wax and wane; and thus the careful maintenance of the charisma and image of the center lies at the heart of statecraft (for an excellent treatment of Lao *mueang* as relates to *phi* and Buddhism, see Holt 2009).

Clifford Geertz (1980) describes the nineteenth-century Balinese mandala state—what he terms a "theatre state"—in an attempt to shed more light on precolonial Southeast Asian polities. In Bali, as in Condominas' notion of *emboîtement,* smaller centers replicate larger ones, which in turn are replications of the cosmos. Geertz proposes that dramatic displays of power by the Balinese state were attempts to create order and prosperity in the kingdom by imaging the ideal. With regard to the creation of spectacle to bring about order, Geertz writes:

> [The Balinese state] was always pointed not toward tyranny . . . but rather toward spectacle, toward ceremony, toward the public dramatization of the ruling obsessions of Balinese culture: social inequality and status pride. . . . [These

dramatizations] were not means to political ends: they were the ends themselves, they were what the state was for. . . .

Behind this . . . lies a general conception of the nature and basis of sovereignty that . . . we may call the doctrine of the exemplary center. This is the theory that the court-and-capital is at once a microcosm of the supernatural order—"an image of . . . the universe on a smaller scale"—and the material embodiment of political order. It is not just the nucleus, the engine, or the pivot of the state, it *is* the state. (Geertz 1980, 13)

Geertz is writing about the precolonial Balinese state, a polity that, though technically practicing its own brand of Hinduism, shared the concept of the mandala or exemplary center with much of the Theravada Buddhist world (see Keyes 1975; Duncan 1990; Swearer et al. 2004). While Geertz focuses on the spectacle involved in the Balinese state, he pays less attention to the stage on which the spectacle is set—namely, the city.

The Thai word *mueang* points to the importance of the walled city as the exemplary center. *Mueang* means both city (as in *mueang* Chiang Mai) and polity (as in *mueang* Thai).[13] Its distinction from other terms for urban areas lies in the idea of an inhabiting sacred force (e.g., *barami*). *Mueang* are animated sites: centers of civilization, refinement (to varying degrees), and spiritual antennae that radiate prosperity and wealth to the countryside. They are the home of politics, religion, and rulers. They claim to have within them a spiritual and civilizational force that the countryside and wilderness lack. Northern Thais use *mueang* to distinguish themselves from others. The term also means Northern Thai language (*kam mueang*) or Northern Thai people (*khon mueang*), including all the various Buddhist, Tai-speaking ethnic groups that have been subjects of Northern kings (Yuan, Lue, Tai Yai,[14] Khoen). This term also excludes those who are non-Buddhist, upland dwellers, or speakers of non-Tai languages. *Mueang,* then, when applied to people, becomes a term used to separate city dwellers (or those lowland rural subjects of a city)—those with refinement—from forest dwellers.

As the importance of cultivated space demarcated from wild space might suggest, historical and mythic Northern representations of the origins of urbanity stress the city's magico-religious separation from the jungle. As in Bali, the Northern Thai king performed a religious role in rites "whereby the realm was oriented to a sacred cosmos" (Keyes 1975, 62). With the king and temple at the center of the world and the cultivated farmland (*na*) at its edges, this replication of the cosmos and the fount of *khwam charoen* it supplied ended where the jungle began. Yet in Northern Thai ritual, as the Buddhist city conquers the non-Buddhist jungle, the city incorporates those elements of the non-Buddhist world. The conflict does not simply make believers out of heathens but narrates a drama wherein the conquerors adapt and appropriate the power of the conquered for the city's benefit: the urban Buddhist ruler conquers not only with forceful, worldly power (*phra-det*) but also with assimilatory, charismatic *phra-khun*. Indeed, such a process can be seen in Central Thai discourse on Chiang Mai, casting the North as a place of unrealized cultural and spiritual potential waiting to be used for the good of the greater Thai nation.

Lanna as a vassal state and now as a cultural capital can be seen as "emboxed," to use Condominas' helpful term. As it expends both *phra-khun* and *phra-det* into the countryside, Bangkok exerts its own hegemonic force upon Chiang Mai. To expand upon Condominas' meaning, just as remote villages replicated larger urban centers' systems of spirits on a smaller scale, we can see how ideas about progress and urban refinement persist across tropes of the city. This is no surprise, given Day's emphasis on the repetition of certain features across levels of scale and location in Southeast Asia. Animist tropes find themselves in Buddhist clothing, and, as I shall argue later, each of these becomes bound into the modern-day "boxes" of culture, heritage, and progress.

THE CITY AS A BUDDHIST CENTER

Temples and monasteries in Lanna produced a number of religious and secular manuscripts in palm-leaf books (*tamnan;* cf. Thon 1974; Thong 1974; Thawii 1976). Of these, the narratives that have received the most attention are those dealing with local matters. In these (cf. Swearer 1998; Wyatt and Aroonrat 1998), history begins with the act of creating a Buddhist city out of a non-Buddhist jungle, cultivating wildness into something civilized.

This is the theme of the conflict between Wilangkha, king of the forest-dwelling animists, and Chamadewi, queen of the city-dwelling Buddhists, retold orally as well as in palm-leaf texts such as the *Camadevivamsa* (Swearer 1998) and the *Jinakalamali* (Buddhadatta 1962). The *Camadevivamsa* was composed in Pali by Mahathera Bodhiransi in the 1400s out of preexisting materials written in a language that the monk considers "inferior and unsuitable for Buddhist city dwellers" (Swearer 1998, xxi), presumably Northern Thai, thus reflecting the ongoing tension between popular vernacular religious practice and orthodoxy. While the *Camadevivamsa* makes no mention of the ethnicity of its protagonists (indeed, as many studies—not least Hirschman 1987, Leach 1973, and Scott 2010—have shown, ethnicity as a concept was a late nineteenth-century arrival to Southeast Asia), many Thai and foreign authors

(Swearer 1998; Condominas 1990, 11; Kraisri 1967) attribute Chamadewi's people to the Mon and Wilangkha's to the Lawa.[15]

Chamadewi's story begins atop Doi Kham, a mountain just to the south of where Chiang Mai is today. On its densely forested slopes lived a family of giants (*yak*): a father and mother and their son. The parents were named Pu Sae (Grandfather Sae) and Ya Sae (Grandmother Sae). They terrorized the local humans, killing and eating them. One day, the giants came upon the Buddha, who was wandering in Northern Thailand.[16] They fell upon him preparatory to eating him, but the Buddha stopped them, warning them of the sin they would commit by killing such an enlightened being. They were chastised and expressed the wish to become Buddhists. While the son became a holy hermit, the parents still felt hungry. They wanted to be allowed to continue to prey upon the local human population and were angry that the Buddha would not let them do so. They then begged the Buddha to allow them to kill and eat a human once a year (Swearer et al. 2004, 84). The Buddha stood firm, but granted them the freedom to kill and eat a buffalo instead so long as its ears were just as long as its horns.

Grandfather and Grandmother Sae remained on the mountain, but the son, Wasuthep the hermit, did not. The Buddha gave him a relic before moving on, and Wasuthep came down to the banks of the Ping River. There, he and another hermit, Sajjanaleyya, invoked a magical bird to fetch a conch shell from the sea (Swearer 1998, 53).[17] Pressing the shell into the ground, the sages caused the conch-shaped city of Haripunchai (Lamphun) to rise, complete with walls and palaces but lacking a ruler.[18] Wasuthep mystically gave birth to an infant daughter, Chamadewi.[19] Afterwards, she was sent to the Mon kingdom of Lavapura (Lopburi) to be educated in the ways of queenship, but returned to rule Haripunchai.

Years passed. Trouble with the local forest dwellers began to brew. Their king would not stop courting Chamadewi. But his advances were crude, and crudely coupled with displays of violence: though he sent gifts, he also threw spears toward the walls of Lamphun from the peak of Doi Kham. Two of these nearly reached the walls, and Chamadewi became frightened of his strength. However, instead of giving in to his advances, she played coy and outwitted him. In the oral legend that I recorded at Doi Kham, she makes Wilangkha a gift of a turban; but what the jungle king does not know is that the turban is made out of her bloodstained menstrual undergarments (as noted in Swearer's introduction to Swearer 1998, 24). Menstrual blood is one of the most dangerous and polluting of substances in Thai magic, and the human head is the point from which power flows (Terwiel 2012, 90). The two in combination are disastrous.

The contact of menstrual blood with Wilangkha's head destroys the magical source of his kingly strength. Yet he does not know that his power has been secretly disabled. Confident as ever, Wilangkha agrees to a demonstration of power. But when Chamadewi challenges him to throw another spear, the spear reverses in mid-flight, doubling back to impale him. Wilangkha's power that enabled him to throw spears from one city to the next had been invisibly sapped owing to its contagion. This contagion also takes a spatial turn, as what should be low (undergarments) becomes high (the kingly brow). While he still appears to be potent, this potency is a sham. The image of the hollow king, full of his own pride and prowess but destined for ruin, recalls the new developments rising in Chiang Mai's periphery that I have discussed in Chapter 1. In both cases, contagion, corruption, and ruin are undetectable but unavoidable.

The *Camadevivamsa* and *Jinakalamali* tell the story of the struggle to create an urban center in the midst of wildness. It is the foundation myth of the North's urbanity. Lamphun, in Bodhiransi's mythico-history, was created before it was inhabited—the *urbs* arose by itself via magic, not from a slow and natural concretion of formerly rural people, or through the genius of a conqueror-king, or as the result of mythical settlers from afar. For local historians and nationalists alike, Chamadewi and her Mon Buddhist city are now seen as being the predecessors of Thai and Northern Thai civilization—including a film in the works starring Thai princess Ubolratana. On the other hand, in the nationalist narrative, Wilangkha's Lawa, as Kraisri Nimmanhaeminda writes, "possessing a culture obviously inferior to that of the Mon" (Kraisri 1967, 100), become the "forest people" of nineteenth- and twentieth-century Siamese ethnography (Thongchai 2000b).

The tropes in these stories are repeated. The peak of Doi Kham, on the edge of both Chiang Mai and Lamphun, is the home of something fearful: Wasuthep's demon parents, Wilangkha's forest horde. In each case, clever bargaining averts the forest-based evil and nullifies it. It is this power of pacification and assimilation—the *phra-khun* of the Buddha and Chamadewi both—that comes to the fore in present-day dramatizations of these events.

Grandfather and Grandmother Sae

Doi Kham remains the center for the propitiation of Wasuthep and his parents, the cannibal demons Grandfather and Grandmother Sae (Swearer et al. 2004, 84). These monsters of the wilderness, oddly enough, are claimed as ancestors by the mediums of Chiang Mai's possessing urban spirits (Shalardchai 1984, 67). In a reversal of the stories of haunting in Chiang Mai's abandoned buildings, the violent power of Grandfather and Grandmother Sae, assimilated and tamed, reemerges to become prosperity.

Despite Kraisri's prediction that the rite of propitiating the spirits "will soon pass as the [Chiang Mai] University brings modern learning to the coming generations" (Kraisri 1967, 99), the ritual in June of 2007 was flooded with devotees of Chiang Mai's urban spirit cults; indeed, as Walter Irvine (1984) shows, urbanization has brought a boom in spirit rituals, not a decline. The road to the festival was hard to find, and I arrived on my motorcycle several hours late, but the ceremony to feed Grandfather and Grandmother Sae had not yet begun. The rite was to take place in a clearing in the woods of Mae Hia subdistrict. A fenced-off area contained several spirit shrines—the homes of the spectral attendants to Grandfather and Grandmother Sae, but what garnered the most attention from onlookers was a small, dark hut in the back of the field.

In this hut was one of the two principal spirit mediums of the rite. They were both young men—unusual for Northern Thai spirit mediums, who are usually older women, although there is an increasing trend of having gay or transgendered mediums.[20] One was heavy and had the dyed-blond hair of a fashionable young urbanite; the other was slim and wore a serious expression. Both were dressed in an "ancient" style: white shirts and checked cloths wrapped around their waists and red turbans. Their attendants wore the indigo-dyed *mo hom* shirts that marked neotraditional costume. In the already hot early morning of late May, the first medium lurched back and forth inside the hut, while visitors asked her[21] questions in low voices. Suddenly, letting loose a cry, she rushed out of the hut and people backed away from her. Coming out into the sunlight, she danced her way to the rows of spirit shrines, following a group of older men. A camera crew leaned in front of her as she visited each shrine.

As she went on her rounds, an announcer described the event over a loudspeaker, alternating between Pali chanting by the attendant monks and speculation over the scientific origins of Grandfather and Grandmother Sae's power. "Science will discover," said the announcer, "that these mediums have nanotechnology. Nanotechnology! [This is] something very small, so small that you can't see, but [something that] will allow you to communicate with other worlds."

Here we see the connections drawn across all corners of Thai belief but intersecting only at *khwam charoen*. On the one hand, Buddhist monks call out, pacifying and blessing animist spirits. On the other, spirit belief is equated with technology. These links should not be surprising: the functioning ideology is one of *charoen*—its trappings as technological or spiritual are less relevant than demonstrations of its effectiveness. In this way of seeing, the technological, the magical, and the religious fuse.

The main course of the day's rite for the audience was the eating of raw buffalo meat. The buffalo—already slaughtered and its meat laid out on skewers—was lying on a tarp on the ground along with its head and empty (but still bloody) skin. Grandmother Sae, now joined by Grandfather Sae, grabbed a hunk of bloody meat and ate it messily, slinging it around her neck as she did so. Grandfather Sae, after devouring a good share of the raw flesh, sat astride the buffalo with a giant-sized toothpick, fixing the audience with a baleful stare. Men with cameras—one of them a European with an enormous moustache—crowded in close to each action of the mediums, who seemed unfazed by the attention.

The rite continued to rise to a climax wherein Grandmother Sae buried herself under the skin of the buffalo, grubbing for more meat, and Grandfather Sae lifted a bucket of blood, drinking some but spilling most of it down the front of his white shirt. Many in the crowd held cameras aloft to get a good shot of the spectacle. The buffalo having been devoured (at least the skewers of meat—several pounds of raw flesh at least), Grandfather Sae was escorted out of the cordoned-off area toward where a giant tapestry of the Buddha had been raised. He stood in front of the image, fixing it with his unnerving stare, then fell to his knees with his bloody hands pressed together in a respectful *wai* (figure 5). Kraisri (1967) suggests that, according to the ritual, the demon is tricked into believing that the banner *is* the Buddha, mistaking

FIGURE 5 | Grandfather Sae submits to the Buddha

its fluttering in the wind for signs of life, and as such keeps his promise not to kill and eat humans. (One wonders what would happen if the rite were performed on a calm day.) Grandmother Sae, after paying her respects to the Buddha, then passes around strips of string that have been blessed: the dangerous demons have been reinvented as good Buddhists and can now share some of their fearful power with the visitors.

These spirits, so long as they are safely propitiated, guard the city from misfortune and ensure its prosperity. It is the slopes of Doi Kham (home of Grandmother Sae and Grandfather Sae) and Doi Suthep (home of Wasuthep) that still provide clear water and cool breezes to the city, presumably sent by the goodwill of these once dangerous spirits. By appropriating the spiritual power of the jungle-dwellers, the Buddhist city is able to mobilize the natural world for its own good. Though the clear water promised by the spirits has since disappeared, turning my motorcycle onto Suthep Road outside of Suan Dok gate was always refreshing in the hot season. Suthep Road led straight to the mountain, and in the later afternoon and evening cool air descended from the heights, rushing down the street and, on particularly hot days, making one secretly give thanks to the demonic family (or perhaps simply the cool, damp forest in which they were said to dwell).

Chamadewi

Just as Grandfather and Grandmother Sae have their own ritual of propitiation in which the wilderness is subjugated for the good of the city, so Chamadewi has hers. Chamadewi's medium was once a minor soap-opera star, but she now commands a large spirit cult in Lamphun and Chiang Mai. In one of her shrines, nestled in a shop-house half-buried in Chiang Mai's outer wall, she holds a yearly festival (*yok khru*) for Chiang Mai's urban mediums.

Perhaps because of its lack of grotesque displays of raw flesh and blood, Chamadewi's rite is devoid of the local and national tourist attention the Grandfather and Grandmother Sae ritual attracts, although, as at many mediumship rites, there was a camera crew present.[22] A crowd of devotees stood around outside the shop-house, listening to a live band and eating free food provided by the spirit cult. Mediums, at rest, sat in the entranceway, talking and joking with one another. Inside, the throng of mediums was so closely packed that my attempts to pass through to greet Kham, a medium friend and key interlocutor, were impossible without shouldering my way past whirling and gyrating older women.

The act of dancing oneself into a trance—"ghost dancing" (*fon phi*) in local parlance—characterizes spirit mediumship in the Chiang Mai region. As amplified brass-band music plays, the mediums, under the influences of their possessing spirits, whirl in an often frantic version of folk dance. In the shop-house, this chaotic foreground provided such a contrast to the figure of utter stillness and composure seated at the back of the room that I at first took her for one of the department-store mannequins that was often converted to a spirit image in folk ritual (Johnson 2012). Chamadewi's medium sat, covered in Indic-inspired costume regalia and surrounded by brightly painted concrete stone snakes. She held one hand up in the manner of a Hindu god and wore a serene smile that recalled the Buddha. On occasion, a dancer would stop, come to the forefront, sit, and bow to her, hands pressed against the floor. Toward the afternoon, she abruptly stood up, and, as the music rose to a crescendo, the dancing mediums stopped and turned toward her, hands clasped in a *wai*. She tottered off of her throne, burdened by the weight of regalia on her head, its precariousness, or simply by pains in her legs from having sat so still for so long, and moved slowly toward a waiting car. As she left, the mediums parted to make way for her, and an aide made sure she could lower her crown into the back of the tiny sedan that waited at the curb.

Such a marked contrast between composure and chaos vividly portrays Chamadewi's role—and by extension, the role of urban power—in Northern cosmology. She remains so still as to resemble a divine image, all the while receiving obeisance from the hodgepodge of local spirits and causing them to cease their motion one by one and pay her homage. The frenzy of motion that characterizes animist spirits, from the dancing of Chamadewi's devotees to Grandfather and Grandmother Sae's gluttony, is sharply contrasted with the stillness that both Chamadewi's medium and Grandfather Sae, after the unveiling of the Buddha tapestry, convey.

In this way, we can think of the conceptualization of the city in both the Chamadewi tale and that of Grandfather and Grandmother Sae as one where the city contains within itself the charismatic power (*phra-khun*) to calm and assimilate the wild. The Buddhist city—magically created by holy hermits—stills and defeats the destructive power of the wilderness, much as Chamadewi's power caused Wilangkha's spear to rebound against its thrower.

What we can see from those aspects emphasized in the Chamadewi narrative that are incorporated into modern-day Northern Thai ritual are the wilderness/urban distinction as one of violence versus civility, chaos versus order, heat versus coolness, and ignorance versus learning. In each, the story hinges on the cleverness of city dwellers in deceiving violent rural antagonists (e.g., Grandfather Sae obeys the Buddha only so long as he imagines him as alive, confusing the waving painted banner of the Buddha with the Buddha's living body). Also evident is the choice of making the "Lawa" Sae ritual a spectacle, coupled with the relative obscurity of Chamadewi's *yok khru*. Indeed, the former is precisely the ritual that Kraisri predicted would be eliminated by the spread of "knowledge," yet it is the former that the municipality has transformed into "cultural heritage."

Why is the spectacular display of the conquest of bloody animism achieved by a cheap trick (the substitution of a picture of the Buddha for the real thing, with the implication that the demons are too stupid to figure it out and too morally suspect to honor an agreement made with a dead person) preferred by state authorities and audience alike over the spectacular display of the obeisance of lesser lords to their mistress? The answer is threefold: first, the Grandfather and Grandmother Sae narrative does not challenge a nationalist narrative of Thai hegemony and dominance over the area. In the Sae rite, demons are subjugated by the Buddha. Recognizing a rite that had Tai spirits bowing to a Mon queen might have offended Tai-centrist viewpoints, especially given the modern-day association between Mon and Burmese. Second, mediumship has always had an uneasy relationship with middle-class Thai sensibilities (see Morris 2000; Pattana 2005; White 2004). Often considered a sign of lower-class or provincial naïveté by Chiang Mai's "educated classes," mediumship becomes a part of Northern Thai religious practice that, because of its very ability to change and adapt, is often denied and excluded from the archive of "Lanna" culture. While the Sae mediums can be considered by a skeptical audience to be performers showing mediumship's surrender to an image of the Buddha, the Chamadewi ritual has mediums bowing to yet another medium. Finally, in a related point, the Buddha image in the Grandfather and Grandmother Sae ritual is just that—an image. Unlike a medium, it cannot speak, does not offer advice, and cannot comment on the current state of affairs. In short, it is a symbol without the power to enter into dialogue with its supplicants.

This removal of the active component from Chiang Mai urban religious practice (and its return in popular practice) mirrors the removal of the active component from Chiang Mai's political practice as well (e.g., the replacement of the cult of local monarchs with that of the Thai monarch). It recall's Bon's city with its empty center. Yet in each, the idea of the city as a vehicle for *charoen* remains. The Buddhist center reaches out to the animist hinterland and incorporates it, converting potential danger into benefit. As many studies of modern Thai Buddhism point out (Tambiah 1975; McDaniel 2011; Terwiel 2012), this relationship of continual incorporation and appropriation is characteristic. "Buddhism," Hinduism/Brahminism," and "animism" in Thailand are not independent units but continually reinforce and influence each other. Common themes of progress and ruin, city and wilderness, and order and chaos run through them all.

THE CITY AS FOUNTAIN OF CHARISMA

James Duncan, in *The City as Text* (1990), shows how the Sri Lankan city of Kandy was designed and redesigned in order to access magico-religious sources of power for Sri Lankan kings. These designs shifted between Hindu-influenced models of the city, which placed the ruler in the position of Indra thus rendering him a god on earth, and Buddhist-influenced models, which placed the religion at the center and the ruler as its guardian. Here, "center" is to be taken literally. In the former model, the central position of the city was given to the king's palace; in the latter, to the principal Buddhist relic. As Duncan notes, such models of urban planning spread beyond South Asia to become the basis of such cities as Angkor, Sukhothai, the Shan *möng* in modern-day Burma, and the Northern Thai *mueang*. But in these latter far-flung places, the tension between Hindu and Buddhist that characterized Sri Lankan society was muted. As the story of Chamadewi's subjugation and assimilation of the forest dwellers might indicate, Buddhism (adopting liberally from Hindu ideas of kingship) blended with local animism to create a hybrid. All three ideas are reflected in the urban planning. At the center of the city are an animist pillar, the royal palace, and a Buddhist temple.

The blending of animist and Buddhist beliefs at first evokes the idea of syncretism, and indeed this has been the prevailing model behind characterizations of Thai religious practice (e.g., Kirsch 1977; Terwiel 2012). Pattana Kitiarsa, however, criticizes the characterization of these practices as "syncretic," arguing that "syncretism" implies the fusing of two separate belief systems, resulting in something "contentious, unauthenticated, and impure" (Pattana 2005, 484). Instead, Pattana highlights the fact that much of the development of beliefs surrounding tutelary spirits, for instance, occurs away from the purview of the state and its homogenizing force and actively incorporates—and has been actively incorporating—elements from a variety of sources (ibid.). Mediumship, like Buddhism, is not a unitary or timeless thing. Pattana favors the term "hybridity" to indicate that neither Buddhism nor animist spirit ritual is in any way a pure or unchanged or even a unified entity. And his term is supported by the fluidity among animist, Hindu, and Buddhist ideas of sacred urban space that I found through my own research, as well as how understandings from these bleed into popular, "rational" imaginings of space in the city.

So it is with the central point in Chiang Mai's magico-religious city plan. The city pillar, which echoes both the *shiva-linga* of Hindu cities and the animist spirit pole (*sao ban*) of Tai villages, is housed in a Buddhist temple. In Chiang Mai, this central pillar is "Indra's Pillar" (Inthakin), highlighting the close relationship between the Hindu deity and the king. It is the central pillar that houses the spirits responsible for urban "order and prosperity" (Wijeyewardene 1990, 135) in contrast to nature spirits such as Grandfather and Grandmother Sae, who are tamed *by* the urban spirits of order (such as Chamadewi). This central pillar was originally housed at Wat Sadue Mueang, in the direct center of the city—indeed, the temple's name literally means "the city navel." Yet now it is modestly enshrined at one of the most important temples in Chiang Mai city, Wat Chedi Luang. This temple is the center of Chiang Mai's Thammayut sect—the branch of reform Buddhism that was created by the Central Thai monarch Mongkut (Rama IV, r. 1851–1868) in order to purge supernatural elements from mainstream Buddhism. Accordingly, the coexistence of the monks and the pillar is an uneasy one, as the city pillar represents the most obvious example of magical belief that the Thammayut was intended to eliminate. As such, for the Thammayut monks at Chedi Luang, the city pillar is a symbol of all that is unrefined and unreformed about the North. Yet for the shrine's believers, it is a place where another primordial spirit of the city is worshipped: another demon (*yak*) that has been recruited to ensure the city's prosperity and persistence.

In ancient times, according to the Suwan Kham Daeng chronicle, the people of "Lord Lua" (i.e., Lawa) living near what would become the city of Chiang Mai were suffering (Sarasawadee 2005, 30). Ghosts had invaded the town (Aroonrat 1982, 3), an invasion that recalls Wyatt's description of the invasion of Nan by *phret* and *yak* ghosts as well as my own description of present-day hauntings in Chiang Mai. As we recall, taking pity upon the people, Indra gave the Lawa the Inthakin pillar, along with mystical fountains of gold, silver, and crystal and a guardian spirit. But the people grew lax and impious, and lost all of these gifts. Indra forgave them and made a copy of the city pillar, the current Inthakin.

The invocation of the Lawa as the source of the Hindu/Buddhist-derived spirit pillar *lingam* reinforces the fact that one must examine these legends not as ethnohistory but as origin myths that organize the spatial world of Northern Thailand. Indeed, it may be better to see the invocation of "Lawa," not as representing the Lawa people, but as a stand-in for spirits of place— Lawa were often invoked by Northern Thai chronicle writers as a surrogate for locality (Wijeyewardene 1986, 84–85), much as Kraisri (1967) and Cholthira (1991) see them as autochthonous inhabitants who inform present-day practice. By invoking Lawa spirits in the city pillar as well as in the Grandfather and Grandmother Sae rites, one is invoking an autochthonous presence at the site (and therefore origins and legitimacy). The city, then, is always present, only improved upon by the actions of later kings. Indeed, in later Lanna practice, the figure of the Lawa inviting the Tai to settle was repeated—when Lanna kings on official processions were to enter the city, they had to be preceded by a Lawa leading a dog, thereby recapitulating the creation of the city out of base nature (i.e., the Lawa and the dog). While, according to contemporary spirit mediums, Tai spirits are generally considered to have come from elsewhere, Lawa spirits represent the soil of Chiang Mai. By tracing the pillar back to the Lawa, the cult of the Inthakin defines Chiang Mai as an indigenous part of the landscape, naturalizing a Northern Thai Buddhist hold over the area, which, while foreign, has appropriated the indigenous and animist powers of the Lawa for the city. The pillar, in turn, becomes an antenna by which the merit of the Lanna king radiates out to the countryside, bringing rain and causing the crops to grow.

Inthakin

In mid-June 2007, the rite for the propitiation of the Inthakin was held for several days at Wat Chedi Luang. Vendors lined the street leading up to the site of the ritual, selling food, joss sticks, and flowers. I had arranged to meet at the festival with Kham, a spirit medium in her fifties who worked in a tobacco field during the day, and her daughter Noi, a Nivea sales representative at the Tesco-Lotus megastore, and as usual I arrived early. Dusk was descending on the temple, but it was a riot of noise and activity. As the rainy season had almost begun and the sky had been lowering and threatening rain all day, local people thronged the place, trying to accumulate as much merit as they could before they were washed out. In this sense, their worship may have been counterproductive, as the Buddha image at the entrance to Wat Chedi Luang was the Buddha of the Hundred Thousand Rains.

Despite the non-Buddhist origins of the Inthakin, and despite the antipathy with which the Thammayut monks at the temple viewed such "magical" practices, from the perspective of Kham and Noi, non-Buddhist and Buddhist aspects of the rite wove into each other seamlessly.[23] They visited the shrine of the guardian *yak*, the Inthakin, the temple's main Buddha image, monks' cremation relics, and received blessings from the abbot all within the context of "making merit" (*tham bun*), which in their conception was this-worldly wish granting. For instance, Noi asked the Inthakin and Buddha images to grant her a husband in return for merit made, a request clashing with orthodox Buddhist theory, which holds that merit made in this lifetime is realized in the next. Even Indra and the guardian spirit of the pillar, as I argue later, were variations upon (or adapted into, or both) the principal guardian spirit of cities in the region, namely Chao Luang Kham Daeng.

We met outside the gates, and Noi presented me with some bundles of homegrown flowers and incense sticks she had bought at the market near her mother's house in Mae Taeng. These were cheaper than flowers purchased from the vendors, and bringing their own flowers made economic sense. We began our merit making by laying these flower bundles at each corner of the hall housing the Inthakin at the shrines of its guardian spirits, and then Kham and Noi gave me their bundles to lay at the foot of the pillar itself.

They had given me these bundles because they were not allowed inside. Instead, they were waiting on the edges of the Inthakin shrine, looking in at me with their offerings, along with other women also waiting. Many sites in Northern Thailand that have to do with Hindu angelic spirits (*deva*) or autochthonous spirits (*phi*) bar women from entry, just as the area directly adjacent to a temple stupa is often off-limits to women in the North. In a similar manner to how the deity behind the city pillar varies from Hindu-Buddhist to animist, the arguments as to why women cannot approach it vary (if only slightly), the Buddhist answer being that, since the Buddha did not touch women, and since the stupa houses a Buddha relic, then a woman touching the stupa would be just as defiling as a woman touching the Buddha. Such an explanation sufficed for the middle-class Thais, monks, or academics with whom I talked, and was intended to be a polite rebuttal to accusations of misogyny, of which Northern temples had recently been accused by a feminist member of parliament. In contrast to these explanations, Noi echoed what I had heard before in less formal settings as the reason she was not allowed to go in to offer flowers to the Inthakin: "Women are dirty," she said, "not clean." When I asked her to clarify what she meant, she laughed: "Menstruation!" she answered, using the English-derived *men*. "You aren't allowed to be near sacred objects if you are menstruating, and they keep all women away all the time just to be safe." This begs for a sexual interpretation: the fertility symbolism of the pillar, derived from the phallic Khmer *lingam,* being offered flowers at the beginning of the rainy season seems obvious, as would the prohibition of women who are menstruating (and thence at that moment infertile).

I walked into the brightly lit shelter of the Inthakin and tried to find a spot to drop my flower bundle, feeling rather uncomfortable and conspicuous. Complicating the matter were the multiple pairs of eyes focused on me: the caretaker drowsily looking up from where he had been asleep in the corner of the shrine to watch the foreigner; Noi and Kham, nearly invisible in the evening gloom outside, hoping that I would put their offerings higher up on the pillar (so as to absorb more merit); and the other young men waiting to pay their respects. I placed the offering on a middle tier, not wanting to risk accidentally falling on the pillar in my attempt to get to the top and in the process possibly thwarting Noi and Kham's wishes for the year.

After the three of us had made our principal offerings and visited the abbot for a blessing, the rain began to fall in earnest. Noi, Kham, and other refugees from the downpour waited on a porch in front of the hall where the abbot was blessing supplicants. An older woman who had recently moved to Chiang Mai from Bangkok waited with us. She became interested in the three of us and started to question Kham about spirits. What sort of spirit did she channel? Was it true the Northern Thai spirits were particularly effective? What kinds of advice did the spirit provide? Could she come and see Kham for advice? Kham demurred, suggesting that there were other, more skilled mediums who took paying clients.

The woman from Bangkok's treatment of Kham as a counselor was part of a long tradition in spirit mediumship throughout Thailand, but Kham's reluctance to accept her as a client bears some analysis. Kham was not a high-profile medium and channeled the spirit of a small community in Chiang Mai's suburbs. She had many supplicants (lit.: "children of the spirit") in her home community, but she was less comfortable taking supplicants from elsewhere. Although spirit mediumship in Chiang Mai is rapidly changing, mediums generally give counsel to residents in the village as opposed to spirit mediums from other parts of Thailand, where supplicants came from various locations, attracted by the fame of the medium. The woman from Bangkok was thus asking Kham to have her spirits step out of their place as local guardians and apply their powers and advice elsewhere; but this might be the domain of other territorial spirits, hence Kham's discomfort. In short, the woman was asking Kham to violate rules surrounding proper space—Kham's spirits are tied to particular places and sites. They are feudal lords in search of serfs, not businesses in search of customers.

The woman from Bangkok exhibited an interest in Northern spirits. She believed them to be more powerful,[24] a belief based on the conceptualization of Northern Thailand as existing in an allochronous time. As a site where, as the woman assumed, essences are purer and *watthanatham* has more power, Chiang Mai exists as the reverse of Bangkok. While Mary Beth Mills (1999) detailed the flow of women from the hinterlands (in her study, the northeast) southward in search of modernity, the Bangkok woman had travelled to the North to find the premodern.

The woman from Bangkok associated the festival with Kham's mediumship through a common link with magic (*sayasat*)—an association the Thammayut abbot sitting behind her would have preferred she not make. As Rosalind Morris writes: "spirit mediumship is among the most reviled of ritualisms among conservatives of the *thammayut* patriarchy. In essence, it threatens the rationalist regime's claims to have achieved modernity through

the sublimation of such beliefs, and the magicality associated with them"
(Morris 2002, 79).

Yet, despite the Thammayut's best efforts, spirit possession and the
Inthakin rite do share a link in the minds of many. Morris describes a spon-
taneous possession at the Inthakin festival in which the possessing spirit used
the opportunity to lash out at high-rise construction in the area near the river
(Morris 2000). Wijeyewardene (1986) notes that spirit possession used to be
a feature of the Inthakin ritual, and the principal possessing spirit was that of
the ghostly founder of the North, Chao Luang Kham Daeng.

Chao Luang Kham Daeng

Another story of the origins of the city pillar replaces the figure of Indra
with a spirit called Chao Luang Kham Daeng (Great Copper Lord, hereaf-
ter "Kham Daeng"), an autochthonous spirit associated with Ang Salung
Mountain (Doi Chiang Dao). In venerating an "animist" spirit of a nearby
peak, Chiang Mai is far from unique in Thailand's North. The (historically problematic) "Ramkhamhaeng" inscription from Sukhothai (inscription no. 1, face 3) also mentions such a spirit: "The divine spirit of [Phra
Khaphung mountain] is more powerful than any other spirit in the kingdom.
Whatever lord may rule this kingdom of Sukhothai, if he makes obeisance to
him properly, with the right offerings, this kingdom will endure, this kingdom will thrive; but if obeisance is not made properly or the offerings are not
right, the spirit of the hill will no longer protect it and the kingdom will be
lost" (Wyatt 1994, 56–57).

The presence of Kham Daeng's mediums at early city pillar veneration
rites would indicate that, while for the Buddhist clergy the pillar was a site
to venerate Indra, for many, the figures of Indra and Kham Daeng overlapped
(Sommai and Doré 1991, 147). As the story goes, when Mangrai, the Tai
founder of Lanna, was planning Chiang Mai, he noticed an albino rat and its
followers living in a tree. More albino creatures emerged, servants of the local
guardian spirit—Kham Daeng. Mangrai, on seeing these animals emerge,
considered the site perfect for founding his city. By doing so, Mangrai, a foreign invader to the lands around the Ping, incorporated the sacred system of
the indigenous population into his Tai polity and used both to create the city
of Chiang Mai.

This time of the pre-Tai "indigenous" forms the basis for many popular stories and oral legends about the North. In these stories, there exists a
shadowy time outside of the historians' linear progression of dates and dynas-
ties whose narrative mirrors and mimics Thai historians' linear progression

of kings and armies. This alternate timeline includes a cast of characters that remain important to Chiang Mai's spirit mediums and popular local legend but have no place in chronological time, while their presence is inscribed on various sacred places around Chiang Mai.

Near Kham's home in Mae Taeng is a spring between two mountain peaks. The water is dazzlingly clear, but inaccessible except by way of a wooden cup on a long bamboo pole. Pong, a laborer in his forties and resident in Mae Taeng, explained to me why:

> There was a kingdom around here that was destroyed by its enemies. ["Who?" I asked.] Probably the Burmese.[25] There were two princesses, Buatong and Buakaeo, who escaped this destruction. They went a long way, over this peak, over that peak. [They were] searching for some place to hide. Then they found that cave up there. Have you been to the cave? ["Not yet," I responded.] You need to be careful when you go in. . . . But they hid here for a while. The Buddha felt sorry for them and made this spring. He also put a terrible spirit [*phi du*] here to guard it. The princesses were all right for a while. But later they were taken and killed. ["When was this?" I asked.] A long time ago. In a past age, in an ancient time [*samai kon, samai boran*]. Probably during the time of Chao Luang Kham Daeng.

What is interesting about this story is its temporal setting: while it deals with the fall of kingdoms and calamity, it does not fit into the sequence of events narrated by textual history, for example, the chronicles or any kind of official history— a narrative beginning with the arrival of Tai-speaking peoples in the region, the introduction of Buddhism, and the beginning of the reign of righteous kings (e.g., Mangrai, Ramkhamhaeng). Nonetheless, via this story, a kind of history is "written" in the geographical features of the landscape—a poetic one that is tied firmly to place.

Dipesh Chakrabarty (2000) describes a distinction between hegemonic, "official" history, "History 1," and subaltern history, "History 2." At first glance, the coexistence of a time of spirits, kings, and kingdoms outside of official Lanna-era history but superimposed upon the Northern landscape would seem to fit such a distinction perfectly. Kham Daeng and his lineage provide a mythical time period that is unconcerned with linear time. The blasé attitude toward fitting Kham Daeng into the temporal history of Lanna that Pong provides was echoed by Noi and others involved in spirit medium-ship. While Kham Daeng is, for them, a figure that existed and ruled in the past, his principal role belongs to the present. He is significant because he provides the supernatural power that sustains the city of Chiang Mai *now*, not because he played a pivotal role in historical events.

Such a clear split into a "dominant" and a "subaltern" history is probably too simplistic. Were we to imagine the division as an absolute one, we would be drawn into the sorts of essentializations and reifications that plague much other writing about Northern Thailand (e.g., Cholthira 1991). We would identify an "authentic local Lanna" knowledge that operates on a different—present-oriented—logic to be pitted against imperialist Central Thai versions of history. We would pit Pong against Sarasawadee. But the two ways of seeing history blend into each other. As I show here and later, characters (e.g., Kawila, Mangrai) and places (Chiang Saen) from History 1 become drawn into History 2 as sources of present and future potential, just as some of the present-oriented logic of History 2 bleeds into interpretations of History 1. To take an example from outside of Northern Thailand, Charles Keyes (2002) describes how Ya Mo, the local spirit of Khorat (Nakhorn Ratchasima) in Thailand's northeast, becomes laden with meaning in no less than three versions of history: she is an opportunist caught between two warring powers in academic texts (History 1); a national heroine fighting to free the Siamese nation from Laotian warlords in the nationalist narrative (History 1.2); and a local spirit who grants wealth and advice via her mediums to members of her spirit cult (History 2). The publication of a Thammasat University master's thesis by Saipin Kaewngarmprasert (1996) challenging the nationalist narrative sparked an unlikely alliance between nationalist historians and spirit cult leaders, culminating in mass protest and Saipin's effective exile from the province (Thak 2007, 249). History 1 and History 2 had united against a narrative that would deny Ya Mo power in either (Keyes 2002). The various interpretations of history not only coexist but reinforce each other in surprising and unlikely ways.

How, then, can we think of Kham Daeng and his relationship to the urban power of Chiang Mai? In some stories, he is the lord of Lanna during the nebulous period of history before the establishment of a Tai kingdom in the region. He is identified variously as Lawa or Shan, or more often he is not identified as belonging to any particular ethnic subset (and assumed to be Northern Thai). In local religious practice, he resides in Ang Salung mountain (better known as Doi Chiang Dao), several miles to the north of Chiang Mai, and is the lord of the tutelary spirits (indeed, all the good spirits) of the city. Rhum notes that "territorial spirits [like Kham Daeng] can be ranked according to the territory they protect in a hierarchy that closely parallels the traditional political hierarchy. At the top are spirits that protect whole principalities [Rhum specifically mentions Grandmother and Grandfather Sae; see Rhum 1987]. Below them are the spirits that protect capital towns, such as those associated with city pillars" (Rhum 1994, 43). Turton, translating the name differently, describes Kham Daeng and his cult as "the possibly historical culture hero *chao luang khamdeeng* (the Golden King)[26] who is regarded as having established or revived Theravada Buddhism in the North and having founded the first kingdom of Chiengmai. His cult is widespread throughout northern Thailand . . . the cult of the Golden King defines the nearest thing to a popularly generated supra-village political unit" (Turton 1972, 67). I doubt Turton's final point: spirits often claim allegiance to Kham Daeng, and despite the fact that Kham Daeng's yearly propitiation is a large event, mediums of vassal spirits do not all come together in an organized fashion. Mediums will claim a link to Kham Daeng as part of their claim to indigenous supernatural power (as do textual sources cited previously in this chapter) rather than as an articulation of regional political organization; and while there does exist a chain of medium teachers and students (Denes 2006; Shalardchai 1984), it does not automatically imply that the medium of a spirit (e.g., Lord Iron Wrist) who claims to be the vassal of a higher spirit (e.g., Kham Daeng) necessarily considers herself subordinate to the higher spirit's present medium. In other words, links claimed to exist *between spirits* may not exist *between people.* But this is not to deny all aspects of Turton's point. Kham Daeng was referred to by many of my spirit medium interlocutors as the ruler of the ghosts of Lanna, especially the tutelary spirits of neighborhoods and cities; even if the mediums themselves do not form a political unit, the spirits are conceived of as forming this unit during their annual retreats inside of Chiang Dao cave. In other words, while the political grouping of mediums may in fact not exist, it is imagined to exist in the spiritual plane. This "imaging," to use Geertz's term, of relations in miniature fits into Condominas' notion of *emboîtement.* Kham Daeng's mandala, like perhaps most, is how *ideal* and not actual relations are imagined.

How Kham Daeng acquired this post was not the greatest of beginnings. The eldest son of the kingdom of Phayao, he was advancing to attack an army coming from the west (see Swearer et al. 2004). Stopping near Doi Chiang Dao, he noticed a golden deer in the forest. Kham Daeng pursued the deer until it fell, exhausted, and assumed the form of a beautiful young woman. The places along Kham Daeng's path in pursuit are all named and specified: Advance Village, Intercept Village, (Deer) Corpse Village, Prostrate Creek (Swearer et al. 2004, 65). The pursuit, like the travels of the Buddha, assigns names and significance to specific places in the landscape, ties that bind the story of Kham Daeng to the landscape of the Chiang Dao region and give meaning to the mythico-history of Kham Daeng's domain in a way that is mapped upon physical space.

But the nude, beautiful woman that was Kham Daeng's prize was nothing of the sort. After an exchange of repartee in the style of young lovers courting (*so:* declarations of love from the man, doubts expressed by the woman), she invites him to visit her mother, who lives in the massive Chiang Dao cave. Kham Daeng instructs his troops to wait several days for him, but he never emerges. The army returns to Phayao in defeat, despite never having engaged the enemy, and a general recounts the story to Kham Daeng's father, suggesting that the woman may have been Chamadewi. The father, doubting that Chamadewi was so beautiful, decides that the woman must have been the cannibal demon (*yak*) In Lao, and his son her meal (Swearer et al. 2004, 67).

Despite Kham Daeng's ignominious end, he rose to a new dominion afterwards. His spirit, post mortem, still had the power to win over In Lao and the cannibal spirits of the mountain. In a parallel manner to the story of the Buddha conquering Grandmother and Grandfather Sae, the pious branches of lowland authority conquer the meat-eating mountains. His spectral empire then spread over the surrounding region and down into what was to become Chiang Mai, extending invisible lines of kingship and prosperity outward from an invisible (underground) city. It is to his cave that all the spirits retreat during the rainy season, the Buddhist Lent, when monks stay inside the temple. With Kham Daeng reigning over the good tutelary spirits of Chiang Mai, Chiang Dao peak now acts as a shadow *mueang,* the domain of the righteous lord to which lesser lords pay their obeisance. "History" here is less important as a recounting and more a statement of ideal relationships between lord and vassal.

This coexistence of History 1 and History 2 emerges clearly during the month of May, just before the monsoon begins. At this time, there are two rituals that occur at Chiang Mai's gates and corners. Mediums gather for festivals (*yok khru*) involving dancing and drinking whisky at each gate and corner, and monks along with city officials perform the Suep Chata Mueang (Enhancing the Fate of the City) ceremony (see Morris 2002). During the ceremony, monks and city officials gather at each gate, where a string connects the hands of chanting monks to the stone embedded in the gate, thus replenishing the fate (*chata*) of the city. It is a ceremony that explicitly bans mediumship, at least in its modern form. But for a ritual that otherwise expunges elements of animism, the city incorporates Kham Daeng and his kingdom beneath the mountain.

Before the ritual, city workers stretch a string from Doi Chiang Dao to Chiang Mai, circling around each gate and corner and also resting atop the Inthakin, thus recognizing the mountain's peak as the fount of sacred power that, once linked to Chiang Mai via the white thread, can be used to recharge the city's charisma. The battery analogy works well: the city pillar and the pillars embedded in each gate and corner of the city (as well as lesser pillars at the center of lesser neighborhoods and villages) are like antennae radiating power to the people living nearby. The Suep Chata has been performed every year in Chiang Mai since the 1990s. During the Lanna period, it was intended for use only in wartime (Sommai and Doré 1991, 158), and its recent resurrection can be seen as an attempt to revitalize Northern Thai ritual practice in a way that aligns it with official sources of power: monks and city officials appointed by the authorities in Bangkok. This new Lanna revival also removes mediums from ritual practice (note the absence of nearly all mediumship-centered rites from Sommai and Doré 1991 or Manee 1994).

These figures—Chamadewi, Indra, and Kham Daeng—are variations on a common theme of urban centrality, kingship, and the taming and incorporation of the wilderness. Much as the Buddha image calms the "cannibal" animist spirits of the mountain and Indra's pillar disperses the assault of bad ghosts, Kham Daeng likewise brings order to the cannibal spirits of Ang Salung Mountain and extends this power to calm the chaos of modern-day Chiang Mai. Although official historiography seeks to divide these practices, these spirits should not be seen as separate entities inhabiting discrete religious spheres of "Buddhism," "Hinduism," and "animism," respectively. Rather, they are variations on the common theme of urban order and rule. As I have argued elsewhere (Johnson 2012), in all of these cases spirit worship in Thailand serves to "name" a power that otherwise lies beyond communication, each acting as a source of transcendent authority. In this instance, that power is the orderly power of the city; and it is to this magico-religious power of the city to which I now turn.

THE CITY AS A ROYAL CAPITAL

Chiang Mai's premodern urban plan delimited a hierarchical series of spaces and ethnic enclaves ringing the city. The organizing principles were hierarchies of high to low, center to periphery, north to south, and east to west. Peter Stallybrass describes an implicit hierarchy of the body in relation to the nineteenth-century European city, wherein the head and spirit are associated with certain parts of the city, and "low" parts of the body with others (Stallybrass 1986, 145). In Chiang Mai's magico-religious plan (*thaksa*), the association was explicit. The north—explicitly referred to as "the head" (*hua wiang*) was the abode of the ruler. Conversely, the southwest was the direction of poverty, where sewage flowed, and it was also the direction in which corpses left the city, making it the direction of death and pollution— the southwest gate in the outer wall is called *hai ya* gate: *hai* with a rising tone from the *hai* with a falling tone (to throw away), and *ya*, which today has the primary meaning of "medicine" but is rooted in the term for "magic"

(Suthep 1986, 189). Magic entered the city from the north and flowed out through the southwest. Merit was allowed to enter the city from the northeast and pollution could be expelled to the southwest. The city was a body: clean food flowed in via the head, and feces flowed out from the bottom. This system remained a concern for city planners up until the early twentieth century, when city planning fell under the aegis of Bangkok-appointed commissioners (Vatikiotis 1984, 45; Surapol 1986, 176).

The symbolic meaning of various directions in Chiang Mai's *thaksa,* while it may seem an obscure point, is replicated in miniature form in everyday life. Suthep Sunthonphetsat describes not only how the east and northeast are identified with sacrality and positive qualities (masculinity, the right hand, humanity) and the south and west identified with negative qualities (femininity, corpses, lesser people) in religious texts, but how this system of spatial hierarchy also exists in the layout of temples, where lay people place their spirit shrine in their homes (at the northeastern side of the house), and even where one lays one's head when one sleeps (pointing east; Suthep 1986, 189).

James Duncan writes:

> Territorial space was structured in the image of celestial space. Many royal cities were explicitly built to represent the cosmos in miniaturized forms, with the central part of the city representing the celestial city of the gods, high upon the cosmic mountain. These cities were built as a square or rectangle and fixed at the cardinal directions. The square form of the city was actually conceptualized as lying within a *mandala,* a circular cosmic diagram fixed at the four cardinal directions and anchored by a fifth point in its center. [Here, Duncan is using "mandala" to refer to the model of a divine circle rather than in Wolters' sense of a center-oriented polity.]
>
> By paralleling the sacred shape of the *mandala,* these cities were transformed into microcosms of the cosmos. The king, by situating his palace at the center of this *mandala,* occupied the center of the universe, and the summit of Mount Meru [the mountain of the gods], and hence maintained the liminal status of a god on earth.[27] By occupying this position at the center of the cosmos, he became a *cakravarti* [Thai: *chakkawati*] who could control the world through the magical power of parallelism. (Duncan 1990, 49)

As such, the city's plan (figure 6) ensured the flow of power and prosperity. The walls began with Mangrai's square fortification, built in 1296 and consisting of a triple-layered square pierced with five gates (Penth 1986, 10). This earthen fortification was bolstered with brick during the reign of King Phayu in 1345 but retained the same square layout, keeping the city's reservoir at the northeast and two streams bringing fresh water around the city (ibid., 11). Tilokarat, one of Chiang Mai's most ambitious kings, demolished part of the walls to make a sixth gate (location unknown) and build a palace in the northeastern part of the town (ibid., 12–13). King Kaeo (around 1516) repaired the damage that Tilokarat did to the walls and may have constructed the earthen wall (*kamphaeng din*), which was not sufficient to defend the city from Ava (ibid., 14). During the period of Siamese suzerainty, Kawila installed towers and gatehouses at each corner and gate (respectively), and this is how the city remained until the walls were rebuilt in the mid-1980s (ibid., 15–16).

The supernatural quality of the walls that imbued the brick with extra force was and is preserved through a system of *sima* stones buried in each gate and at each corner in a manner similar to how temple grounds were consecrated. The resultant space—the entire city, in Chiang Mai's case—was consecrated and under the benevolent influence of a great power, whether the Buddha or the king (Thongchai 1994, 24). For this reason, ordinations could occur within the city walls outside of a temple before the Sangha Acts in the early twentieth century. In precolonial times, in order for these structures to remain pure, foreigners (those not under the rule of the king) were excluded

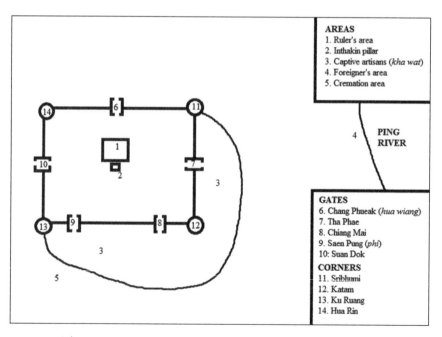

FIGURE 6 | City plan

from the city proper. For instance, Robert Schomburgk, the British consul-general in 1857, was denied entrance within the inner wall of the city and instead had to conduct his business near the river, well outside the sacred walls (Vatikiotis 1984, 45; Wijeyewardene 1986, 136).

The *Chiang Mai Chronicle* recounts how in 1465 an astrologer in the secret employ of Chiang Mai's enemies (the *Chronicle* claims Ava, while Hans Penth claims Ayutthaya) convinced the Lanna king Tilokarat to cut down a tree and build his palace at the auspicious northeastern corner of the city, with promises that this would lead him to acquiring supernatural power (Wyatt and Aroonrat 1998, 99; Penth 1989, 11). The *Chiang Mai Chronicle* tells:

> King Tilokarat sought out all the high dignitaries . . . and all the foremen to come with all their laborers to raze the city wall which King Mangrai had built, and to fill the moat and level it. Then he had them cut down the banyan tree which was the glory [*decha*, as in *phra-decha*] of the city of Chiang Mai, with its wide and beautiful shaded canopy, from its crown down to its roots, and clear the area to be completely flat. . . . Then he opened up the gate to the earthen city and named it the Si Phum gate. [Said the treacherous monk,] "the Si Phum [quarter] is filled with magical power; and sleeping quarters are auspicious. Whenever we hear that an enemy is attacking, from whatever direction, [you are to] arrange flowers and perfumed water and set them up above the royal throne in the sleeping hall, and knock on the [magical] pillar in that direction; and the enemy will flee from the majestic power of that magical pillar." (Wyatt and Aroonrat 1998, 98–99)

On the contrary, however, removing this tree and constructing the palace on its site caused Chiang Mai to become "a defiled place, as if the glory of the city had been sullied with urine and defecation. Harmful things befell the country, the ruling family, and all the high officials" (Wyatt and Aroonrat 1998, 99).

Another example of such treachery against Tilokarat had a similarly duplicitous monk in the employ of the Ayutthayan King Borommaracha hiding "wood remaining from a coffin, a piece of a water-buffalo bridle, joists from a verandah, pieces from a pig-sty, a bottom step from a staircase, and the lintel from a doorway" (Wyatt and Aroonrat 1998, 100) at the top of the gates to the city. Each of these objects is obviously a "low" thing, associated with pollution and death, and having them placed high on the gate, where all had to pass underneath, would have caused the city to become polluted as well. Such an inversion of high and low recalls the trick Chamadewi played on Wilangkha. Luckily for Tilokarat, he noticed that the monk himself would not pass under the arch and therefore became aware of his treachery.

This idea of the gates of the city as points of ingress for magico-religious pollution is not limited to the chronicles. Renovations in the 1980s stirred up resentment among the local community for this very reason. These renovations, made at the height of Chiang Mai's AIDS epidemic, were accused of allowing the disease to spread by an article in the national daily newspaper, *Matichon:* "AIDS-infected Gates in Chiang Mai" (Thammakian 1985). Of concern was the loss of something sacred in the brickwork. As a less fiery critic, Chaya, put it: "The new gate, even though it protects the old image [*rup lak*], it is still something new, and as for the gate which was thrown away, it was not just bricks and mortar that were thrown away, but it was history that was definite [*nae non*]" (quoted in Thiw 1989, 37). What is significant here is how closely the discourse of cultural heritage parallels that of supernatural power: a denial of heritage permits disease to spread in the city just as angered spirits do.

As the walled city was reserved for the *khon mueang* (meaning, it should be remembered, both "city people" and—at least from the nineteenth century to the present—"Northern Thais"), the outer regions were for outsiders, outsiders who, should they settle in Chiang Mai, would be placed in certain specific locations. The outer wall that stretches in an arc from the southwest corner of the city to the northeast is termed the *kamphaeng din*—the dirt wall of the city. It is this space, the "earthen wall," into which Tilokarat's new gate opened in the chronicle account I quoted above. The space inside this wall—like many other areas in Chiang Mai's close suburbs—was filled with the ethnic communities of "temple slave" artisans (Wijeyewardene 1986, 120).

With the fall of the Lanna monarch, this urban plan centered on the monarch also collapsed. As the Bangkok monarchy turned toward European models of nation-state and absolute monarchy (Thongchai 1994), the *systèmes à emboîtement* of replicating the cosmos in miniature was no longer considered seemly: a Northerner's only monarch was the one in Bangkok. As a result, the ethnic communities of artisans were no longer bound in place and, at any rate, no longer necessary, as Lanna was now paying taxes, not tribute, to Bangkok. In addition, the palace at the heart of the city was no longer necessary.

After the death of Kawilorot, the last of Lanna's absolute kings, the Bangkok government purchased his royal palace at the "head" of the city and converted it into a women's prison. The symbolic coup could not have been more noticeable: what had been the ritually highest point of the city—the residence of the king—was now where criminal women were incarcerated, recalling Wilangkha's defeat. Another part of the palace next to the "navel" of the city became the new city hall, and the remnants of the Chiang Mai royal family moved outside the walls to the eastern riverside. The Bangkok administration had moved into the literal heart of the city, and Chiang Mai's royalty had relocated to a stretch of riverbank next to Europeans, Muslims, and Chinese communities; spatio-symbolically speaking, the kings had become foreigners in their own town, and city layout began its modern phase.

Three Kings

These power relations are played out in the monument standing at the direct center of Chiang Mai, at the "city navel" (*sadue mueang*), where the Inthakin pillar had once been located, and also the site of a former royal palace. In 1924, as Chiang Mai was formally incorporated into the Siamese state, the palace was converted into the regional administration building (and later, in 1933, became the city hall of the year-old Thai state), designed in a British colonial architectural style. In 1997, the city hall moved to the north of the city, well outside the walls, and the building was converted into the Chiang Mai Art and Culture Centre. The local royalty—the living embodiment of Chiang Mai's *barami*—was removed and replaced by other signs of *barami*: first, Bangkok's political domination; and second, the reinvention and resurrection of "Lanna." Royal power became state power became cultural heritage.

The Three Kings monument decorates a rectangular plaza in front of this building. The monument was constructed by the Central Thai artist Khaimuk Chutoo, a relative of Queen Sirikit, and was commissioned by the Fine Arts Department in Bangkok to replace a smaller, earlier statue that had stood at the same site. The statue was transported over a ten-month period from Bangkok to Chiang Mai and was unveiled on September 23, 1983. The bronze monument depicts three muscled figures, each adorned with Central Thai–style royal regalia. Their faces are nearly identical, each with the chiseled good looks and Western-style features of modern-day Thai soap-opera stars. In all of these traits—the statue's appearance as a European-style bronze monument, the kings clothed in Central Thai regalia, and the fact of something Centrally-constructed and moved to Chiang Mai—the Three Kings Monument could be read as a symbolic form of the colonization of Lanna history, whereby the Central Thai (Chakri) monarchy comes to stand in for the Lanna monarchy. Indeed, the inscription under the statues describes the polity over which Chiang Mai ruled as "Lannathai" not simply "Lanna," a renaming that asserts that Chiang Mai was always "Thai."

The Three Kings are those kings who, according to the Yonok Chronicle, laid the plan for Chiang Mai over the site of a prior Lawa village. They are Mangrai, the founder of Chiang Mai; King Ngammueang of the neighboring city-state of Phayao;[28] and Phra Ruang of Sukhothai. This last figure is identified with King Ramkhamhaeng of Sukhothai, which, according to nationalist versions of Thai history, was the first truly Central Thai state.

Given the statue's origins in a workshop devoted to Bangkok's current monarchy, which traces its moral authority if not its actual lineage from Ramkhamhaeng, the statue at first glance presents a Bangkok-oriented reading. The lifelike metal statues stand with their heads close together, as if conferring over the future of Chiang Mai. Mangrai stands to the back, his arms spread and almost embracing his two friends and seeking their counsel—he is centrally located, but passive. Ngammueang stands faded into the background, much as Phayao as a city-state has become simply a lesser Northern province. Both Mangrai and Ngammueang look attentively at Ramkhamhaeng, who is pointing to the ground in an authoritative manner, as if saying *"Here* is where the city shall be!" Ramkhamhaeng's contribution to Chiang Mai's construction was, along with Ngammueang's, to keep Mangrai's ambitions in check.

Ramkhamhaeng's presence next to King Mangrai adds Thai nationalistic legitimacy to the founding of Chiang Mai. As the alleged architect of the Thai nation guides the architect of Lanna society, Lanna's fundamental relationship with Thai origins is assured. Indeed, the monument suggests that, although Chiang Mai was constructed by Mangrai, the basis of his knowledge stemmed from the Central Thai king.

Such a reading is the sort that a monumentalist view of the city would make. The imagined flaneur reads the statue in its space and imagines his or her relationship to Lanna and its founders. Yet the statue is not just a static text. In front of it is a small sandpit where offerings of incense and flowers can be made in order to pay respect to or ask for the intercession of the spirits of these kings. Passing by the monument in the morning (even those mornings when no ritual was held there) often brought one a whiff of incense or flowers from the offerings piled at the kings' feet. Indeed, the statue is the site of magico-religious power as much as it is a site for nationalist history. But the two discourses are not separate. Rather, idioms of progress, power, efficacy, and domination all have magico-religious ideas embedded in them.

These ideas came to the fore at the annual spirit possession rite honoring the Three Kings, when a white thread was extended down from the statues into of a series of tents that covered the entire central urban plaza, where it terminated at an altar complete with offerings of fruit, bowls filled with cash, bottles of orange and red Fanta, and whole pigs' heads. In front of the altar, as in the other tents in the plaza, mediums—mostly older women but including many younger, transgender women—danced to an amplified brass band. Each medium came in her/his possessing spirit's usual attire; this was a gathering of Chiang Mai's spirits wherein the supernatural lords of Chiang Mai's small neighborhoods could pay their respects to absent monarchs at the city's central point.[29] Some of them drank Thai rice whisky and exchanged raucous jokes; others were more reserved and solemn. All made a point of giving the monument and the altar numerous gestures of prayer and respect (*wai*), which they also liberally extended to each other. The noise and heat were overwhelming, and, above the din of the music and voices, a medium would occasionally emit loud retching noises as she expelled one spirit in order to welcome another. At the end of the rite at four o'clock, all of the mediums turned toward a portrait of the living (Central) Thai monarch as the royal anthem was played. Each bowed her head in a solemn *wai* as she acknowledged the country's highest source of *barami*.

What differentiated this rite from other mediumship rites (*yok khru*) held elsewhere in the city over the course of a year was its timing and size. The ritual was held just before the rainy season, at the culmination of the ceremonies surrounding Chiang Mai's gates and corners. As I have argued, while the city pillar and the figure of Kham Daeng would at one point be the site and possessing spirit for the final and central ritual, mediums' expulsion from many temple grounds meant that the final act of propitiation to the spirits had to take place in front of the Three Kings. The ceremony was held over the course of several days and at its height involved several hundred mediums in addition to a brass and electric band. Warrior spirits wore green (reflecting modern-day army uniforms), spirits of old ascetics wore white, those possessed by children wore purple, and those possessed by the spirits of Northern Thai warrior kings wore yellow (the color of the current Thai monarch).

The Three Kings Monument rite differs from a medium's everyday consultations in that it is performed, not for individual supplicants or for a particular place, but to draw forth the charismatic power of the Three Kings for the city as a whole: it is significant that during rites such as that of the Three Kings lay spectators are not the focus of mediums' attention, nor are they even afforded a privileged viewpoint. Rather, the rite is about the generation of the royal power of the city by showing the power of the monarchs to attract, even in death.

THE CHARISMATIC CITY

In this chapter I have outlined four different conceptions of the city: the city as Buddhist sacred center; the city as fount of prosperity to the countryside; the city as supernatural entity; and the city as the body of the ruler. Each of these conceptions draws upon popular history and mobilizes the prestige and power of the past to affirm the civilizing and assimilatory power of the city in the present. In all of these models, importance is given to the inchoate attractive power of the city, that quality which will invite *khwam charoen*. Religious ritual invokes moral power or charisma (*barami*), a quality that derives from kingship[30] and authority, with urbanity and centeredness and opposition to wildness. The hearts of urban centers are sources of royal authority, of power that civilizes and tames the wilderness. The city absorbs and appropriates Grandmother and Grandfather Sae, the city builds upon the "Lawa's" Inthakin pillar, Kham Daeng defeats death, and the Three Kings radiate charismatic power to the chaotic crowd in front of them. Even as the announcer at the Grandmother and Grandfather Sae rite equates medium-ship with nanotechnology, the discourse of urban *khwam charoen* defeating and assimilating rural, wild power continues.

In modern-day Chiang Mai, this royal power is conceived under the idiom of *watthanatham,* culture. *Watthanatham,* as I argue, is a quality that flows downhill: it stems from sources of this authority downwards toward supplicants. For instance, a royal museum in Chiang Mai describes in detail how the Thai queen "gave" silverwork designs to Karen artisans in an effort, as an official at the center said, "to make them *charoen.*" While outside observers might think it strange to understand how an aristocrat with no experience in silverwork can advise lifelong artisans, this makes perfect sense in the royalist Thai idiom: *watthanatham* radiates out from the spirits and kings toward the hinterland. Wherever it happens to land, it inspires *charoen.* As Surin Maisrikrod, a royalist academic, writes (1999): "the monarchy is a primary source of Thai culture and values"—a stark contrast with Herderian notions of culture organically brewed from a "folk."

This hierarchical idea of culture is reflected in early Thai projects of ethnographic description of the provinces. Central Thai scholars began to take an active interest in the provinces in the late nineteenth century when Bangkok was aggressively integrating its outlying territories (such as Lanna) into the forming Thai state. The Siamese elite began a campaign of ethnographically describing the provinces they were then incorporating into greater Siam. In this process, two (occasionally competing) concerns predominated: first of all, Siamese writers wanted to demonstrate their similarity to European colonial powers as chroniclers and documenters of savage others, but they also sought to incorporate these others into the Siamese realm. Historian Thongchai Winichakul writes:

> Alongside the colonial enterprise, the Siamese rulers had a parallel project of their own, concerning their own subjects, a project on the "Others Within." In the late nineteenth and early twentieth century (roughly speaking 1885–1910), travels had mediated the construction of an ethnographic classification in the eyes of the Siamese elite. Discursively formulated through travelogues and ethnographic notes, it was an abstract scheme which differentiated Siamese subjects spatially within the geo-body in relation to the superior space of Bangkok. The

two principal categories of people, of "Others Within," are the *chao pa,* the forest, wild people, and the *chao bannok,* the multi-ethnic villagers under the supremacy of Bangkok. . . . this Siamese ethnography of Siam was also a temporalizing practice, locating and juxtaposing people, including the elite themselves, in a new linear (progressive, temporal) cosmic order called civilization. (2000b, 41)

For Fifth Reign (1869–1910)[31] elites, this ethnographic construction reaffirmed their place at the fore of Siam's *siwilai* ("civilization," a loanword from English) and the provinces as the home of the backward past. Thongchai notes how during the late 1800s, peasants were described by royal observers such as Damrong in his collection of village tales as literally voices from the past. Damrong's work, titled *Nithan Borankhadi,* implies that stories (*nithan*) from contemporary villagers were actually archaeological (*borankhadi*) relics, preserved in the modern day—they were Fabian's other in time for the elite observers (Thongchai 2000b, 536). This idea persists. In fact, as I began my own research project, a senior Thai academic pulled me aside and confided to me that my project was flawed in my choice of Chiang Mai. "Pick a small town," he cautioned me. "Talk to some old people. Chiang Mai is just too much like Bangkok nowadays."

Khun Chang Khun Phaen, a Thai epic that originated in the oral tradition but was finally compiled and edited by Damrong in 1910, portrays Chiang Mai as a place that is undoubtedly both foreign and lower on a scale of civilization than Ayutthya. In *Khun Chang Khun Phaen,* Soi Fa, the daughter of the king of Chiang Mai, laments having to marry an Ayutthayan Thai because of the gap between Central Thai and Northern (called "Lao" in the epic) customs: "How can I manage a household in the Thai style when I don't know the customs? I'll be blamed, derided, and shamed. . ." (32:14).[32] Her mother comforts her: "Though your partner is foreign and speaks a different language, and you're not even familiar with each other's faces, the main thing is he's a good person. . ." (32:15). Yet it is Soi Fa's fears and not her mother's hopes that are confirmed. Once Soi Fa is at the court, she is regularly abused for being Northern. For instance, her grandmother-in-law scolds her: "You're making such a racket, you rude Lao, it fills the whole house, you busted beam. I'm fed up with you, you seven hundred dogs, you're past loving. Just a tricky, noisy, Lao hillbilly" (37:4).

King Chulalongkorn writes in 1893 of the need to end the division between "Lao" and "Thai" with regard to the North:

I hope that this [education] will instruct and give knowledge to the kingdom, and [give to the Chiang Mai "Lao"] the knowledge that unity with the Thai is a good thing. This will come with mutual knowledge and understanding, and having the same viewpoint. I mean that I hope for progress [*charoen*] in their city and [in their feelings of] unity. People that study have to be people that aren't so arrogant. The [Chiang Mai] Lao are slandered [by Central Thais] as all being more base and wicked than the Thai. We have to find the intelligence to teach them how to be servants of the Kingdom and of the same *mueang* as the Thais. If they do good [deeds] they will receive good things, the same as the Thais. The schools have to teach about the benefits of the [Bangkok] government at all levels, just like the [European and American] missionaries [teach about the benefit of Christianity in their schools]. They [the missionaries] use all levels [of society] to support religion. . . ." (Quoted by Sarasawadee 1982, 33; translation mine).

Chulalongkorn sees a fundamental cultural or racial difference between the Northern "Lao" and the Central "Thai," but a difference that can and should be overcome by emulating the Western missionaries' success. He references the prior negative image of the "Lao," and does not in fact directly contradict it, but points to its potential resolution in the "conversion" of the Lao into Thai. The Lao are uncivilized, but it is his noblesse oblige to welcome them into the fold of Thainess, equated with knowledge and civilization. Here, then, is the fusion between notions of national belonging, culture, and civilization; each addresses one facet of the same idea—a great chain of being that places people on a hierarchical scale of inner value.

Urbanity in Northern Thai cities extends from the figure of the ruler (whether physically present, such as the current Thai monarch; historical, such as Mangrai; or transcendent, such as Kham Daeng) downwards. In a similar fashion to the way that the Northern Thai city is constructed in imitation of the heavens—again recalling Condominas' *emboîtement*—urbanity, whether we conceive of it as culture or of sacred power, extends downwards from the central point, controlling and subsiding chaos as it flows.

It is this notion of center-oriented charisma that I seek to explore as the link between past constructions of the *mueang* and modern-day conceptions of culture and power in the city. The *mueang* is a vehicle through which the magico-religious power of the monarch becomes actualized. This is especially salient in Chiang Mai, where the origins of power not only stem from Buddhist sources but have also incorporated to a large extent "animist" notions of power. But what if, as in Chiang Mai's case, the monarch is gone, and with him the sovereignty of the center? Ideas of national belonging propose a flatness where the *mueang* was hierarchical—Thailand's power is absolute up to the border, where it absolutely disappears. How do present-day agents in Chiang Mai see themselves as participating in the construction of the *mueang* as a fountain of charisma? What do they see as centering the *mueang*'s power to provide prosperity in the face of crisis?

3

Mediums

In the previous chapter, I outlined urban power and sacrality as seen through the lens of Northern Thai ritual and myth, arguing that participants in these rituals situate the city as a source of power that extends from charismatic sources downwards. Urbanism, in this reading, was what prevented decline and promised rebirth. But how is such power conceived of today? How does it come to intercede in the present-day haunted and ruinous city? In what follows, I have drawn upon two years of field research conducted on professionals who place themselves as the privileged mediums of this power and show how these intermediaries articulate and mobilize this idea of the urban and bring it to bear upon the ruinous present.

These two groups at first seem quite different from each other. On one hand are the mediums of Chiang Mai's urban possessing spirits who claim to access the invisible powers that make material development (*kan phatthana*) become progress (*khwam charoen*). On the other are those urban planners who seek to capture Northern Thai "culture" (*watthanatham Lanna*) and realize it in the built environment of the city. I argue here that the two groups parallel each other in that they act as conduits for urbanity. But these are not people who would normally draw connections with each other, separated as they are by class, politics, education, and language. The spirit mediums with whom I worked were largely poor, had low levels of formal education, and spoke Northern Thai. City planners were middle-class or wealthy, highly educated, and had strong connections to Bangkok. Yet, much as "emboxed systems" replicated power across many strata, they all positioned themselves as the privileged voice of the city's charismatic power. The members of each group were chosen vehicles through which *charoen* was to take place, a *charoen* that was to involve the resurrection of the lost glory of Lanna to correct the ruinous present time of bad ghosts and empty buildings. As I shall demonstrate, in each case this "lost glory" was seen as something that had to be created anew.

Such a creation of new links to the past should be looked at in the light of Anderson's (1972) seminal study of Javanese power. In Java, part of the way to legitimize a ruler's ability to provide prosperity for his kingdom was to draw connections with other sources of power—past kingdoms, or defeated rulers. Through asserting links to the past, even if such links were not self-evident, rulers were able to imply that they had access to a well of power that would render their actions potent and legitimize their charismatic aura. Such sources of power were also thought to exist in esoteric bodies of knowledge, hidden books of magical spells, or even Marxist texts (Anderson 1972; see also Weiner 2002). I see similar processes at work in Chiang Mai. I argue that the manufacturing of what Rosalind Morris calls "past-ness" (2000, 6) in the present, rather than the preservation of past ways of being, is a new assemblage, one created and adapted to the needs of the present but designed to facilitate the free flow of *charoen.*

Making Rain

In Chapter 2, I described two of the largest in a series of mediumship events held just before the rainy season: the propitiation of Grandfather and Grandmother Sae and the propitiation of the Three Kings statue. Most of these rituals were termed *yok khru,* "raising the teacher," rites in honor of a particular spirit. This "teacher" could be a spirit of the Three Kings, a spirit of the city gates, the spirit of a particularly famous medium, or a lesser tutelary spirit in a neighborhood ritual.

Rain after drought is the most visible sign of prosperity and one associated with Southeast Asian monarchs up to and including the current Thai king, who has added the technological "magic" of irrigation, hydropower, and cloud-seeding projects to older ideas of the king as rainmaker. Urban spirits, as *chao* themselves, also share in this association. During 2006 and 2007, I attended over twenty such rituals, often in the company of Kham. These rituals were scattered across the urban landscape, the larger ones being held at sites with historical significance and smaller ones held at central points in suburban neighborhoods that were the micro-domains of lesser spirits. Interestingly enough, many of these sites of mediumship were also places marked as "cultural heritage" by the city administration, hinting at the relationship between official forms of heritage and spirit belief. Here, I return to the largest of these: the Three Kings monument.

The Three Kings' *yok khru* rite takes three days (for a detailed description of the setup, order, and procedure for a *yok khru* rite, see Manee 1994). There was a loose schedule of events, a morning obeisance to the Three Kings and an afternoon obeisance to the current Thai monarch. But aside from this, individual mediums came and went as they wished. Women, especially older women, outnumbered men, and among the latter, male-to-female transgendered people (*kathoei*) outnumbered heteronormative men.

In my visits to the Three Kings rite in 2006 and 2007, I followed Kham as she prepared for and participated in the ceremony. She woke early, and I met her and Noi in the chill parking lot of a Tesco around dawn. Noi drove her motorbike, and Kham perched on the back with her suitcase on her lap. This old, beaten-up case contained three sets of polyester clothes: a yellow one for the virile king's spirit of Lord Father of the Yellow-Gold Throne; a white set for the ascetic Lord Grandfather of the Hundred-Thousand Golden Pillows; and a purple set for the noble child's spirit, the Small Lord. (For brevity's sake, here I refer to these possessing spirits as "Yellow," "White," and "Purple," respectively.) In a plastic bag, Kham carried fresh purple flowers from her garden and some water for the day. Though Kham did not drink, Yellow and White were known to be avid drinkers and smokers, and she also had a small bottle of whisky, a few fat, handmade tobacco-leaf cigars and a few packets of pickled tea leaves (*miang*). "The spirit asked me to put in an extra one, for you!" She winked at me, knowing that White got a kick out of having the *farang* chew the sour, salty stuff, regardless of (or because of) the fact that it inevitably made me sick.

Kham was a woman in her fifties, loud and boisterous around close friends but often reserved in public. She, like her daughter, was rail-thin and small-boned, with a pale, finely wrinkled complexion and a gigantic smile. She identified herself as Thai-Yuan, the dominant ethnic minority in the Chiang Mai region, and primarily spoke Northern Thai with me. Perched sidesaddle behind Noi on her small motorbike with her suitcase on her knees, Kham seemed an unassuming vessel for long-dead kings.

After we arrived, we greeted the Three Kings with gifts of incense and flowers. Kham moved to the back of the crowd where the mediums were gathered and opened her suitcase. She sat and looked over her costumes. I struck up conversations with other mediums around Kham as she sat concentrating. A plump older woman with a loud squawk of a voice was already possessed; she wore a multicolored pattern of brown and maroon, "A *thewada* [angelic spirit]," Noi leaned over to tell me, "from India. That is why there are so many colors." At this point Kham began to emit horrific retching noises, noises that in another context would cause alarm; here, nobody even turned around. She bent over, shouting as her body ejected her spirit and drew in Yellow's. Then her wrenched-up face relaxed and her tired eyes acquired a lively expression. She tied a yellow turban about her head and pulled on a bright-yellow tunic. "Andrew!" Yellow shouted to me in greeting, "You've come!"

The day then progressed into a long parade of dances. Kham moved in and out of the crowd, spinning and whirling with the other mediums and emerging only to rest. Yellow was replaced by cigar-smoking White, and he, true to form, handed me the promised *miang*. The chill of the morning turned to a comfortable warmth, and then to an oppressive heat. Toward afternoon, the sky began to darken to an angry purple, and I found a shady, quiet spot near the back of the tent where there was a fan and a soft-drink cart. Other mediums sat nearby, also cooling off from the heat. One of these—a large, matronly woman dressed in the purple polyester outfit that marked her as a person possessed by a *chao noi* (lit.: "little lord"), a dead child—came over to us. While possessed, she did not speak, but gestured that she wanted to dance with my girlfriend, who was visiting me at the time.[1] They left to join the whirling cloud of neon-clothed mediums in the center of the rite. Noi leaned over to me: "Don't be jealous. Your girlfriend is very pretty and he wants to dance with her. She doesn't have to, if she is uncomfortable."

A low rumble of thunder rolled over the public square. The mediums began to look around, and one, the *thewada* "from India," leaned back in her chair. She began to stretch her arms up toward the sky. Others also raised their arms and made long pulling motions as if they were physically attempting to draw down the rain. A cry went up, *"Tok, tok, tok* [Fall, fall, fall]" At this point, the purple-clad medium who had been dancing with my girlfriend came back to me. She gestured for me to stand up, then pulled me over to the brass band's singer. She leaned down and made a motion as if she were rubbing cash in between her fingers and then pointed at the singer. A little uncomfortable and confused, I pulled out a twenty-baht bill (worth about seventy-five cents, or just over the cost of a noodle-soup dinner). The medium frowned and shook her head, holding up one finger. I realized that she meant me to give the singer one hundred baht (about three dollars). Obligingly, I did so. She smiled and raised her finger a third time—she wanted me to give the singer *another* hundred-baht bill. The singer gave me an embarrassed smile and a clasped-hands gesture of thanks (*wai*), but I was beginning to feel exploited—here I was being singled out as the only *farang* in the crowd and quite bluntly being told to pay up. I refused; the singer thanked me for my donation; and the medium, still shaking her head in disappointment, led me back to my seat as fat drops of rain began to fall.

It was only later I realized that I, being identified in this situation (as well as in numerous others) as a foreigner and therefore a source of wealth, was being equated with the cloudy sky. By requiring me to give money, the mediums were calling forth actual profit from potentiality—they were making it rain. It is notable that, in this case as well as others where I was asked for money by mediums, the mediums did not ask for donations for themselves, but rather that I donate to deserving others. In doing so, I would be adding to my own stockpile of merit and charisma. The mediums were calling for *khwam charoen* and acting as conduits for it, directing it toward their followers specifically and the city in general, whether it was rain from a cloudy sky or cash from a (presumed to be) wealthy foreigner in a way that contributed money to the needy and virtue to the rich.

In this manner I was incorporated into the performance of the mediums in the same way as Michael Lambek found himself an "actor in the collective poiesis" (2002, 51) in his work with mediums in Madagascar. A drama had just occurred, and I had been drawn into and placed in a central role in it. Lambek introduces the idea that mediums and their spirits offer an "ironic intervention" (2002, 66) of the past into the present, where spirits, in a way acting as characters in a Brechtian play, interact with and comment upon the present situation. In Lambek's case, such interventions acted as critiques of present-day power, affirming the superiority of tradition. Such an intervention is suggested in Chiang Mai at times when, for instance, spirits argued that high-rise construction projects violated Northern Thai building taboos.

But in the Northern Thai case, spirits such as these were not quite an instance of the past coming to critique the present. Rather, premodern Northern Thai spirits (such as the spirit of King Mangrai) were acting as sources of *barami,* voices speaking from higher karmic levels to criticize the action of humans. Thai mediums do not construct a particular form of historiography in the same way as Lambek argues Sakalava mediums do. Instead, even though the medium's spirit came from a commodified, fetishized past, it was a past that was fully in dialogue with the present. As such, the *character* of the spirit—whether ancestral spirit, nature spirit, or historical figure—matters less than its *efficacy.* As with concepts of *watthanatham,* tradition, pastness, and supernatural power are rendered valuable inasmuch as they contain within them the potential to stimulate *charoen.*

I first came to know this group of mediums through Kham and by attending mediumship rites like the one held at the Three Kings monument. Later, I came to know several other mediums of lordly spirits on my own, including Tui, the transgender medium for the ancestor spirit Lord Beautiful Smile, and Mu, whose possessing spirit was a water serpent, a *naga.* Outside of their religious function, the mediums whom I knew were generally laborers—Kham was largely supported by Noi's job at the local Tesco-Lotus superstore but also worked as a day laborer at a tobacco farm. Her activities as a medium were cyclical, with minor consultations occurring throughout the year except for the rainy season, during which possessing spirits were thought to remain sealed in the caves of Doi Ang Salung with their lord, Kham Daeng, observing the Buddhist lent like the auspicious beings they were. Just before this time, there is always a flurry of activity as farmers anticipate the rains, thus reinforcing the connection between mediumship, kingship, and the calling of prosperity.

It was at these *yok khru* ceremonies that the connection between place and spirit mediumship was most manifest. While prominent places, both manufactured (gates, corners) and natural (mountains, swamps) had their own particular spirits, mediums such as Kham, Tui, or Mu invoked the spirits of neighborhoods. At their smaller *yok khru* rites, rather than featuring the melee of dancing mediums, those who lived nearby would line up outside the spirit's personal shrine. Later in the afternoon, after the morning's possession was finished, the supplicants and the medium would share some of the left-over food brought as offerings.

Urban and Buddhist Mediumship

Walter Irvine's look at the transformation in mediumship in Chiang Mai proves useful for investigating the dynamics between urbanity and mediumship. He sees a shift from place-centered, local spirits to national or more charismatically based spirits. In this division, older-style mediums tended to channel spirits of place—*yak* or *phi*—rather than kings or *chao* (Irvine 1984, 318, 320), and new mediums embraced Buddhism more openly than older ones through such practices as donating to temples (319) or abstaining from possession during Buddhist holy days or the rainy season. Irvine argues that, as people move to cities and thereby become more dislocated from particular places, the number of mediums increases and their ritual attention turns toward generating capital for clients rather than toward the forms of prosperity (rainfall, community projects, etc.) of a locally centered rite.

Yet, contra Irvine, this is not a zero-sum shift. For example, any one of the three possessing spirits Kham had in her repertoire could have fit either of Irvine's definitions. While she showed a preference for clients from her local neighborhood and spoke with them about community issues via one spirit, Kham's other spirits' blessings and magical services were geared toward the accumulation of prosperity and wealth, traits that Irvine locates in charismatic mediumship. I found that, for many, the ideas of spirit mediumship as charismatic, decentered power and as place- and community-oriented power did indeed exist, but often within the same individual under different spirits' names and mobilized for different purposes and at different times. In short, Kham saw her spirits as primarily enabling *charoen,* and as such they had their origins in whatever she considered to be an auspicious time or place. What has changed is only what appears to be the source of this charisma—from local spirits to national ones.

In addition to Irvine's separation of nationalist spirits from local spirits, there is also a division between "wild" spirits and urban ones. While most spirits live in the city's center (e.g., city or village pillar) or in the borders of the city (e.g., the walls and gates) and act to maintain these borders, there are also those who manage the areas outside of the city walls and bring this wild power into the city, for example Grandmother and Grandfather Sae. Combined, they present all aspects of the world in proper order: the wilderness tamed, the city maintained, and all paths leading forward toward *charoen.*

This idea of *charoen* as mobility, as in the analogy of climbing a ladder, echoed through many of my conversations with mediums. The idea of facilitating motion was the central theme of the *yok khru,* and many mediums characterized their spirits as having "delayed" enlightenment in order to help others to achieve *charoen.* Indeed, a common blessing spoken by mediums upon receiving a donation was simply, "*Charoen.*" The spirits' *barami,* in their mediums' idiom, renders the potentially prosperous actually prosperous (e.g., the cloud releases its rain or the foreigner gives large tips) much as it renders the potentially dangerous actually harmless (e.g., a busy street has no fatal car accidents despite having fast traffic in narrow lanes). It is the reverse of the "bad ghosts" that plague Chiang Mai's high-rise buildings.

POSSESSION

Kham

Kham, the younger daughter of two, was born in Mae Taeng, a small town to the north of Chiang Mai. She married a man from a lower-middle-class family and moved with him to the subdistrict of San Sai in the outskirts of Chiang Mai. The family, which soon included a daughter, Noi, was poor and lived in a bamboo hut—not yet a house—in the middle of a banana grove. Their life was not idyllic. While Kham and Noi only hinted at their poverty, in her retelling Noi described to me waking up in the middle of the night and seeing the ghosts of the banana grove drifting by the hut, yellow lights in the dark, signs that they were living at the lowest extremity of progress, in a haunted space.

Yet things got even worse after Kham's husband took a mistress. At home, Kham began to experience terrible stomachaches and periods of time when she was entirely delirious, crying out in strange voices. Her husband took her to see medical doctors, but, according to Kham, they told her they did not know what was wrong, only that she did not have long to live. So a person whom Kham described as "someone who knew" took her to see the local neighborhood medium and ask her assistance. The medium told Kham that in her body was living the spirit of Lord Yellow, the guardian of her neighborhood. According to the medium, Kham had been doing things that were inappropriate for a being of Lord Yellow's status, such as eating live animals (e.g., *kung ten,* live freshwater shrimp in lime-chili juice), entering two-story buildings,[2] and having sexual relations with her husband. Her illness was his revenge on her for these impurities. So she stopped engaging in these activities and resisting the spirit's manifestations. As a result, she became a medium.

The transition from lay person to medium was catastrophic for Kham's family. Noi grew frightened of her mother. Then a child of five, Noi said that she would come home to find someone who looked like her mother but who was speaking and shouting in strange, masculine voices. Kham's husband soon left her, taking Noi with him to live with his new wife in Chiang Rai. Kham remained in San Sai as the medium of her old neighborhood.

Noi, bullied by her new step-siblings, had a hard time of it. She returned to her original home seven years later to take care of Kham. Noi went to work at a branch of Tesco selling cosmetics six days a week, and the money from this job went to support her mother. But during the 1990s their fortunes changed again. Kham's old neighborhood became swallowed up by a gated community. As they only rented and did not own their land in the former banana grove, they had no option to fight the sale. Kham returned to Mae Taeng, where Noi built her a single-room concrete structure in her mother's natal compound (*ban*), while she herself rented a single room in a dormitory near her work.

Years went by. Kham and Noi lived off Noi's earnings as a sales clerk and Kham's earnings as a day laborer, along with some small income from her mediumship practice. For Lord Yellow, Noi financed the construction of a concrete shrine in their old neighborhood in San Sai on some friends' land near where Kham had first been possessed by the spirit and located just outside of the new community's walls. This structure was to be a building (*ho phi*) where Kham's possessing spirit could hold court once a year. For Kham's friends and the owners of the land, having Lord Yellow's home there was a serious undertaking. They emphasized to me their own responsibilities toward the structure, that they had to be more morally forthright than they might ordinarily be for fear of offending the spirit. They also expressed concern about keeping their cattle and children out of the structure and their fears about the repercussions should it be broken into and robbed. On the other hand, their donation of land to the spirit's medium would also be something upon which they hoped Lord Yellow would look kindly and reward them with prosperity and wealth.

In 2009, when I last saw Kham, the city had widened the nearby road in order to accommodate the traffic from the new gated community, causing the shrine to collapse after earth eroded away from its foundations. The family who owned the land upon which the shrine stood was shocked and concerned about the effects that this might have on the spirit and quickly offered to pay Noi to refurbish the shrine. Some months later, Noi, Kham, and the family opened a new, larger, and more brightly colored shrine on a new poured-concrete foundation at the same spot. Lord Yellow indicated his pleasure, and all was well.

Kham's story is typical of those told by other spirit mediums to whom I spoke and in fact parallels closely the following life story related by Shalardchai Ramitanon. A middle-aged woman (with marital troubles) has a disease that defies medical solution but is cured when a spirit medium tells her that she is host to a powerful spirit who is causing her grief owing to her neglect of it (Shalardchai 1984, 44). Pattana Kitiarsa likewise describes a woman, Toi, who, after years of marriage, discovers that her husband is having an affair (a "minor wife"). Toi, after having seen her husband with his new lover, falls into a trance and in her delirious state begins to give people lottery numbers or offer them money (Pattana 2005, 216). While a medium pronounces her to be the host of a crashed pilot (a *phi tai hong,* previously described), Toi rejects that diagnosis and instead declares that she has a *thep* (angelic spirit) living inside her (2005, 217). Despite Toi's rejection of her diagnosis, in each case there is a cycle of marital problems, aggressive or strange behavior, illness, and finally the declaration that one is possessed. At the moment of diagnosis, the mysterious disease vanishes (cf. Herzfeld 1986, 110, for a Greek example). Through her recognition that she is possessed and by assuming her role as a medium, Kham, along with her strange and frightening behavior, is cured—it was the *mis*recognition of the disease as medical and not supernatural in nature that was in fact causing the illness.

Kham's possession came at precisely the moment when her hopes were failing and she felt herself powerless. As she faced the terrifying prospect of being single, abandoned, and poor, that prospect was deferred by the spirit's arrival. Scholars working in other contexts such as Sluhovsky (1996), Parle

(2003), or Wolf (1990) have also noted the link between spirit possession and the expression of traumatic or inarticulatable stresses, especially those stemming from radical changes in status—in those cases, puberty, political marginalization, and marriage, respectively.

The spirits' comings and goings have become more predictable since that time, however, and now Kham told me that she could tell when the spirit was likely to come and when it wasn't. Her episodes of possession now did not interfere with her work as a day laborer and could, generally, be relied upon to happen on auspicious days or at *yok khru* ceremonies. Less formal occasions (such as my visits to Kham) were less sure: on many such occasions, the spirit did not "feel like" descending, and by afternoon Kham and I would stop waiting and head off to her garden.

YELLOW

Conflict and Confrontation

I first met Kham and her spirits while attending the ritual to replenish the *sima* stone (those stone boundary markers which in the premodern city ensured the city's sacrality) at Saen Pung gate—the inauspicious southwestern gate, the "ghost gate" from which misfortune flowed. The ceremony took place in a long blue-and-yellow-striped tent on the small strip of earth between Bumrung Buri Road and the city moat, atop land where the city wall had once stood. As in the Three Kings' ceremony, an altar with fruit and pigs' heads was at the back of the tent (figure 7) and a string ran from the altar, in this case encircling the gate's stone that marked the place at which the *sima* was buried. Next to the altar, the brass band shared space with the counter taking donations and selling drinks. The former consisted of banknotes tied on to a "tree," a version of the gold-and-silver trees once given in tribute by vassal kings to their Tai overlords. The tree would now go to the nearby temple (as Irvine notes). While the space in front of the band was reserved for dancing by possessed mediums, this back area was a place for mediums to rest, scout for new clients, and socialize with visitors. Ger, an older medium, tried his luck with me. His approach was direct and forceful. "Three!" he said firmly, leaning far forward and jabbing his finger into my chest. "You have three in here!" I smiled in what I thought was a friendly way, although I had no idea what he was talking about. "Three spirits live in here!" he said again, as he stuck my chest with his finger, "You are the third one!" He motioned for me to put some money on the donation tree. The comment at first seemed disturbing and bizarre, but this is how mediums recruit new

FIGURE 7 │ Offerings to the spirits

FIGURE 8 │ Kham as Lord Yellow

pupils. By convincing me that I contained possessing spirits, Ger hoped to gain a (presumed-to-be) wealthy new student whom he could train. Indeed, he continued to affirm that he saw possessing spirits inside me later, after I had gotten to know him better.

Direct confrontation, otherwise so rare in Chiang Mai, also characterized my first meeting with Kham (figure 8). I had been talking with Noi about the ritual, and she offered to introduce me to her mother, who at the time was possessed by Lord Yellow. I enthusiastically took her up on this offer, but when I met Lord Yellow, he refused to speak Thai with me, in either the Northern or the Central dialect. Instead, he spoke in a staccato, rapid-fire language that neither I nor Noi could understand. I asked Noi what he was saying, and Noi responded: "He is speaking Burmese, I think. I don't understand Burmese, though [neither did Kham]. It might be a heavenly language [*phasa thewada*]." Then, Noi spoke loudly to Lord Yellow: "He doesn't understand what you are saying! We can't speak that language!" Lord Yellow then smiled broadly and laughed, and after that switched into very proper Central Thai—very unlike Kham, who only spoke Northern with me.

I sat down to talk with him, but Yellow was continually evasive in his answers. I asked him what spirit he was and where he had come from, but he just smiled mischievously at me and pointed to Noi. "So! You're going to marry this girl? You're going to live in Chiang Mai? You're going to build a house here?" Questions about the ceremony, or Yellow himself, or ritual were ignored as Yellow bombarded me with sexual innuendoes, leers, and direct questions about how much money I had.[3]

Shortly after this exchange, Lord Yellow fell into a fit of harsh retching noises. He doubled over, paused, and then Kham—the medium—slowly sat back upright, removing her scarf and yellow overshirt. "*Sawat di chao*," she said in a soft, quavery voice, very different from that of Lord Yellow. Her eyes had lost some of Yellow's fiery spark and she seemed tired and confused. Her Central Thai had vanished, and she spoke Northern with a thick accent. Noi introduced me to her mother, who seemed to know nothing about what had been said between Yellow and me.

Why did Yellow act so rudely? Historically speaking, mediumship has often allowed for the expression of opposing sentiments of a village against authorities perceived as being beyond reproach. Somchote Ongsakul describes the response by a famous spirit medium in 1884, when Bangkok began to install a national system of taxation upon the North rather than having taxes collected by local lords. A medium protested loudly, criticizing the (Bangkok-appointed) governor and predicting that "the rain will not fall following the season, and the grain will not grow like it did in the days during the reign of

Chiang Mai's lord" (Somchote 1987, 4). When the rain in fact did not come, the tax was rescinded (ibid.).

M. V. McMorran, citing Gluckman's "rituals of rebellion," supports the reading of expressions of anger in spirit mediumship as times when tensions can be cathartically released, acts that nonetheless reinforce the status quo (1984, 313). Almost thirty years ago, McMorran described female mediums in Lampang forcing men to drink copious amounts of alcohol and then imitate dogs, and argues that this was an angry reaction to the everyday fact of male domination in the village (1984, 312). Showing anger under the protective umbrella of mediumship allows it to be expressed, but not in a way that challenges male domination in everyday life.

But does mediumship really provide an effective space in which to "vent" aggression? Was Kham simply letting off anger that she might have felt toward foreigners? This would imply that expressing feelings means that it diminishes them—not to mention that such rituals necessarily have to have a sociopsychological function. In my own research I also found that, as McMorran suggests, mediumship rituals, like many public gatherings, are often marred by violence, and that mediums, with their habit of expressing what would otherwise go unexpressed, are often at the center of these conflicts. But is such violence ultimately productive in defusing community conflicts, as McMorran would have it? Wijeyewardene cites similar discomfort with a too functional approach to violence: "we cannot assume that these tensions are thereby reduced, we cannot assume [as Durkheim would] that the 'ritual structure' defines or reiterates social structural forms. In fact, because possession and mediumship involve manipulation, they may create new divisions and disrupt where harmony once prevailed" (1986, 161). He cites an example where a medium at a ceremony for a dead woman became possessed by the spirit of the deceased. The possessing spirit then shouted out that the medium had been having an affair with the father of the deceased, throwing the ceremony into chaos (1986, 162).

At a similar ritual, an older medium of a warrior spirit (*phi meng*) began to dance, but the officiating witch spirit (*phi mot*) angrily told her that warriors cannot dance at witches' ceremonies.[4] As the old medium continued to dance, the officiating medium began to kick her, despite the fact that the *meng* medium was the aunt of a local gangster. The gangster then cursed at the witch spirit for kicking his aunt, at which point the medium drew her (ceremonial, but still sharp) sword. The gangster, not to be outdone, went home and got his machete, after which the participants in the entire ceremony scattered, expecting violence. On her way home, the medium, now in her unaltered state, apologized, saying that she had been unaware of what was happening and that her aggressive behavior was caused by the possessing spirit, the *chao*, to which the gangster responded (sarcastically?) that a spirit must have possessed him too (McMorran 1986, 162).

In this story, we see the clash between an attempt to overturn social hierarchy (wherein an older village woman acquires the authority to kick the aunt of a powerful gangster) and the ultimate failure of this action (the gangster threatens the woman). Did such an event allow for the free expression of tensions? Certainly the affair between the medium and the deceased's father was brought to light, but was it cathartic? Such stories of collisions between possessing spirits' explosive anger, the damaged egos of those teased or offended by the spirits, and the political aspirations of mediums are commonplace. Alexandra Denes, working in Surin Province in Thailand's northeast, likewise details a violent confrontation between mediums that in some ways parallels a divide between what Irvine would term "modern" and "traditional" forms. A young male medium channeling a supposedly greater spirit (a "modern" one based on canonical Hindu texts and national origins) grew angry at having to abide by the rules set down by an older medium who was channeling a lesser spirit (a "traditional" one based on local geography; Denes 2006, 371). After the confrontation, the younger medium complained that the older medium's spirit was simply a witch spirit (*mae mot*), a spirit of place and lineage, not an angelic *thep* like his spirit (ibid., 374).

In light of this connection between social conflict and mediumship, Lord Yellow's behavior toward me merits some analysis. When I first arrived, a foreigner speaking Thai with a Central accent and presumably with access to English, Lord Yellow responded in a foreign language of his own. Then, when I asked what he perhaps considered a boring, irrelevant, or undesirable question, he immediately decided to display his penetrating insight and to vocalize what he perceived to be the most obvious cause of my speaking with Noi: Lord Yellow assumed that I, like many Caucasians in Chiang Mai, had come seeking female companionship and cheap housing. At the time I was offended that I could be identified with what I saw as the large number of Caucasian men in Chiang Mai seeking to purchase youth with dollars (or pounds, or euros), but in retrospect I saw that Lord Yellow was demonstrating his acuity, his ability to see through social veils and pretenses to discover the truth. In addition, he was acting in the same way the rainmakers did at the first ceremony I described. That is, he was seeking to produce prosperity—in this case a rich yet young, foreign yet Thai-speaking, husband for Noi who, being in her mid-thirties, had largely passed the age when her peers first got married.

Lord Yellow's initially hostile-seeming response, like his speaking of "angelic language," was a reversal of hierarchy: he had the power to decide what language would be spoken. And Yellow demonstrated to me that, while

I have access to the language of the international community, *he* has access to the language of the heavens, not to mention the power to ignore my questions and guess at my true intentions.[5] He demonstrated to me that his rung on the ladder of *khwam charoen* is higher than mine.

Origins

My later interactions with Kham were much more civil, and as I got to know her and her spirits over the next two years, we developed an easy, comfortable relationship. Even Yellow became comfortable with me. He spoke in a loud tenor voice and was fond of making direct comments and jokes. He also tended to speak in perfect Central Thai, in contrast to Kham or to Grandfather White, another spirit of Kham's.

Lord Yellow wore a bright-yellow shirt, yellow sarong, yellow polyester head scarf, and a giant cluster of yellow flowers behind his ear. While he would not provide an answer for *why* he liked the color yellow, the community of *chao nai* mediums of which he was a part shared a color code, and kings' spirits always wore yellow. Withi's survey of *phi chao nai* in Chiang Mai and Lampang also identifies a color code for the sorts of spirits, but a code that is very different from the one I observed (Withi 2005, 28). He notes white shirts for *thep,* red shirts for soldiers, and yellow or purple for the ghosts of children. In my own work, I identified "Indian" multicolored patterns for *thewada* or *thep,* white for old men (paralleling the white robes of an ascetic [*ruesi*]), green for soldiers or more martial spirits, the aforementioned yellow for lords, and purple for children. With this in mind, I asked Yellow why he seemed to prefer that color. In response, he said, "I am a king [*chao*]."

This was a reference to the Central Thai monarchy. The color yellow was the astrologically appointed color of King Bhumibol Adulyadej, the reigning Thai monarch since 1946. It was especially prominent in the wake of the sixtieth anniversary of his coronation (in 2006), which can be considered the height of monarchical piety in Thailand. In the mid-2000s, the hegemonic appeal of yellow had begun to change. One of Thailand's street political groups, the People's Alliance for Democracy (PAD), had adopted the yellow shirt as a sign of royalist and antidemocratic politics in their protests against Thaksin Shinawatra, and in 2006 the "red-versus-yellow" divide was in its infancy. But during my fieldwork, yellow was still relatively apolitical, and, in sharp contrast to my later visits in 2010, 2012, and 2013, everyone wore yellow on certain days as the color of kings. The other colors used by mediums are self-evident: white is a color associated with ascetics and (non-monk) holy men, and green naturally recalls a military uniform. Yellow, then, links the spirit with the Thai king—both are sources of *khwam charoen* and *barami.*

True to this reading of kingship, Yellow did indeed identify himself as being a king from "ancient times," the same nebulous mythico-historical time in which Kham Daeng ruled. He claimed to have ruled in the North long ago, but centuries after his death he saw that Kham was in need of assistance in Chiang Mai, so he came. I pushed him to discuss historical narratives or his own construction of Northern history, and he described his kingdom as lying in "Chiang Saen, to the north, by Burma." Yellow did not distinguish between when "he" was alive and when he was a spirit—in fact such distinctions did not matter much to Yellow, White, or Kham. (I shall return to this point later.) But first, why the town Chiang Saen? Such a response was not unusual; indeed, while many of my medium informants claimed their spirits originated in and around Chiang Mai, those who cited an outside source for the possessing lords without exception mentioned Chiang Saen.

This invocation of Chiang Saen may seem random: it is, after all, a small town in Chiang Rai Province on the Mekong near the "Golden Triangle" corner of Thailand, Burma, and Laos. However, Kham's invocation of Chiang Saen is an important indicator of how clued in she was to early twentieth-century nationalist constructions of Thai heritage. Chiang Saen is one point on the grand expanse of the development of Thai culture constructed during the early twentieth century and, like the idea of *watthanatham,* was incorporated with some modification into the nationalist narrative. This archaeological trajectory, like so much of Thai nationalism, arrived first via a system for categorizing Thai antiquity developed by late nineteenth- and early twentieth-century scholars and later turned into a Thai-language narrative. The story begins at Dvaravati in present-day Lopburi, center of a Mon kingdom on the fringes of Khmer suzerainty, and continues chronologically through various stages in Thailand's pre-Thai past (Peleggi 2002b, 17). Each place in the narrative— Dvaravati, Chiang Saen, Sukhothai, Ayutthaya, Rattanakosin—becomes a point moving upward in the *charoen* of Thai art until its present incarnation. The narrative is still taught today and makes its appearance in museums, film, and fiction, such as Sanya Phonprasit's *Su Phaendin Mai* (Sanya 1998).[6]

Rosalind Morris' Phayaphrom also traces his lineage along these lines. In an interview, the spirit tells Morris that he "came from Chiang Saen to Lamphun—do you know Wat Haribunchai?—that is where I lived. . . . Then I came to Chiang Mai" (Morris 2000, 153).[7] Phayaphrom, like Lord Yellow, begins at the origin point of Thainess—the place where, according to Thai ethno-nationalist history (e.g., Sanya 1998), the "Thai race" first set foot in Thailand and became a point on Damrong's Thai historical trajectory. Chiang Saen and its Lao dynasty[8] was also the putative beginning point for King Mangrai, founder of Chiang Rai and Chiang Mai. Departing from Chiang Mai, Phayaphrom then went to Haribunchai, the origin point for Buddhism and home of Queen Chamadewi, and ended in Chiang Mai, recapitulating nationalist origin stories and uniting his origins with the origins of the nation.

Yellow, then, draws upon multiple sources of legitimacy. He is a vassal lord of Kham Daeng. He ruled in the original Tai polities of Chiang Saen. He speaks Burmese. These stories are mutually contradictory. Irvine argues that "traditional" spirit mediums often channel the spirits of certain locations or natural features, or even converted malevolent spirits of the wilderness such as Grandmother Sae and Grandfather Sae, whereas "modern" spirit mediums focus more on national figures and heroes, especially those who fought national enemies (Irvine 1984, 317). But Yellow is both. As a warrior king from Chiang Saen, he fulfills the qualifications for Irvine's "modern" medium by drawing his origins at the place where Thai nationalist history and current national sovereignty meet and by wearing the yellow of a king (reflecting the yellow of the Thai king).

Is this simply a poor historical performance by a person attempting to convince me that she knew deep Northern history? Is Kham demonstrating her lack of knowledge about her own region's past? I do not think this is—entirely—the case. Rather, the past, for Kham, exists in the present as a concretion of *barami*. History is teleological. The past exists as potential for the future. It is the story of *charoen*, of becoming. Things that are prosperous in the present and will be in the future exist by forging links between things that are known to have been sources of *barami* in the past. It does not matter to Kham whether or not her story is consistent in terms of dates or places. What matters is its consistency in terms of *barami*.

In this way, Yellow's historical narrative echoes Anderson's examples of Javanese rulers who drew (falsified) connections between their reign and powerful objects of the Javanese past (1972, 12). Javanese rulers surrounded themselves with objects thought to contain power and spread stories about their personal links to various sources of power. Even in the case of entirely contradictory sources of power (e.g., Communism, Islam, and nationalism), the ability to hold these contradictory sources of power together in one person was taken as a sign of one's individual ability to absorb such conflicting forces (1972, 15).

WHITE

Neighborhood Order and Form

The second spirit inhabiting Kham's body was Chao Pho Mon Saen Kham (Lord of the Hundred Thousand Gold Pillows), or Lord White. Kham's transformation into Lord White was remarkable. Behind her battered suitcase, she wrapped a white turban around her head, tucked a purple flower blossom behind her ear, and put on a pair of oversized glasses. As a result, her face, normally the androgynous one of a thin and wiry woman approaching menopause, acquired a craggier look. She aged and simultaneously became more masculine. Yellow's loud and authoritative voice, or Kham's more feminine but often boisterous one, became soft and quavery, like that of a grandfather.

White, like Tambiah's Chao Pho Khao (also meaning "Lord Father White"), was an ascetic. He stressed to his suppliants (as well as to Noi) the importance of maintaining propriety and made none of the loud japes of which Yellow was so fond. This restraint did not extend to all areas, though, and White smoked tobacco and chewed *miang* heavily.

As I sat waiting in a loose line of devotees of Kham's spirits during her annual *yok khru,* I noted that the kinds of questions religious attendees asked White were not the kind I (or, for that matter, Morris or even Shalardchai) was inclined to ask: for instance, there were no questions about origins, no inquiries into relationships between spirits in their spiritual home in Chiang Dao cave (in Ang Salung Mountain, home of Kham Daeng), or other questions of metaphysics. Nor were there any attempts to chart and delineate the cosmology of Kham's spirit world. Suppliants wanted to know about more pressing, personal matters. Could White help a sick family member? Could he bestow success upon a college application? Might he aid in a quest to find a suitable spouse? As McDaniel argues about Thai Buddhism in general (2011) or Evans-Pritchard noted about Azande witchcraft (1976), White's suppliants were interested in the efficacy of magic. White's blessing worked, that was all one needed to know.

White was the tutelary spirit of Nong Khrai Si Sai Mun neighborhood within the larger suburb of San Sai, where Kham had lived before she lost her house. In his role as neighborhood guardian spirit, White held a *yok khru* ceremony on the day appointed for Nong Khrai's restoration—in fact, White's restoration and the neighborhood's were one and the same. In other words, White did not simply protect the neighborhood, he *was* the neighborhood. Through him, and through Kham, devotees could communicate with the invisible essence of the neighborhood, the source of *barami* that undergirds the community (also see Johnson 2012).

This *yok khru* was held in the "ghost hall" (*ho phi*), the structure built by Noi on her former neighbors' land. It was a small building, separate from the main structure of the house and large enough for three people to sit comfortably inside, where there was an altar draped with yellow cloth and garlands of yellow flowers. On the altar were the offerings brought by other suppliants: bananas, dragonfruit, orange and red Fanta.[9] Next to these were two small trees, one silver and one gold, miniatures of the gold and silver trees offered to kings in the Siamese past and recalling the money trees offered by spirit mediums (among others) to local temples. Behind these was a portrait of the abbot of Ban Pong temple, a local monk whose body famously did not decompose upon his death,[10] depicted with a broad grin and smoking a cigar; indeed, White often assumed this very pose during his consultations. On the floor, toward the back, was a throne—a broad chair bearing the inscription "Ban Nong Khrai," which signaled Lord White's dominion over the village.

I arrived early in the morning, bringing fruits and some fried chicken, but Kham had already made the longer journey from Mae Taeng and was possessed by Lord Yellow. He took my food and placed some of it on a large plate, which he offered to the *chao thi*—the guardian spirit of the property. He then showed me around the shrine, indicating the termite mound where an auspicious nature spirit lived and the concrete posts where he had hitched his spectral horse and elephant, ghostly creatures upon whose backs he had arrived in the material world. By this time, three neighbors had arrived—two older women and a younger man. These were White's suppliants, or "children of the ghost" (*luk phi*).

Lord Yellow gave some of the fruit that I had brought to these new arrivals, in order that they "eat it for medicine (*ya*)."[11] The older women were content to sit and talk with Noi, while the young man entered the shade of the shelter to speak with Lord White. He crouched at the entrance while Yellow obligingly took his leave and White descended.

The student offered White a garland of flowers purchased from a vendor on the street, holding them up in front of his face in a *wai*. White returned the gesture before taking the flowers. The two sat for about thirty minutes, speaking in low voices. Lord White, seated on the floor in front of the throne, listened to the student's questions and responded to him in a low, fatherly tone.

Student: I have sent an application in to a technical university.

White: This is a good thing. You are building up your knowledge [*khwam rian-ru*]. But you are worried.

Student: I don't have internal connections [*sen*] there. I just submitted the application, that's all.

White: Ordinary people, they have to have perseverance [*kamlang chai*]. They have to act full-heartedly [*thang chai*]. That is how they can gain knowledge, gain benefits. [You] don't need connections. Grandfather [i.e., White] has connections, too! You are Grandfather's child. Grandfather will do what he is able to do.

(*Student leans down in a deep* wai.)

White (begins to chant): May you be cool and happy [*kho hue mi yen mi suk*]. May you *charoen*. May you build your *barami*. May you get a thousand [*baht*], may you get ten thousand, may you get a hundred thousand, may you get a million (*stops chanting*). After coming here, go to the temple and donate. Don't forget, *na?*

One by one, the other guests spoke with White, each one bringing a token gift of flowers or fruit. White blew on the gifts and returned them. They had now been transformed, Noi told me, into medicine (*ya*); through White's invisible breath, the ordinary-seeming gifts had been transformed into protective amulets. They would fend against sickness, ensure health, or otherwise, in Noi's idiom, grant "completion" (*hai samret*). In addition, he offered the same blessings as he offered the students—coolness, riches, *khwam charoen,* and *barami*.

Suriya et al. (1999) provide another example of such a consultation between a betrayed wife (the supplicant) and a medium:

Supplicant: It's almost time for the birth month. How is the child's for- tune [*duang*]?

Medium: Hmm. . . . The fortune's no problem. There's luck coming, but not a lot. The luck will run out around December.

Supplicant: I would like to ask about my husband and the issue of my husband giving up his mistress—has he given her up?

Medium: He has not.

Supplicant: Has he [*man*][12] been honest?

Medium: I [*ku*] told you [*wa*] he hasn't![13]

Supplicant: When he goes to see her and then comes back he changes his mind. The woman's old. She's fifty. But she likes to dress like a teen- ager, letting her hair grow long.

Medium: The woman won't let your husband go.

Supplicant: Men don't give anything up, huh?

Medium: There's no push [*ken*] for him to give anything up.

Supplicant: Is this about money?

Medium: The woman is giving him money and things.

Supplicant: Is there any way to make her give him up?

Medium: It's [going to take a] very long [time]. It takes some time. . . . The woman who has your [*nu*][14] husband is very clever.

Supplicant: I went to yell at her one day, the next day she [*man*] came to see me at the house, but he wasn't at home, so I yelled at her again.

Medium: I see that it will be hard to separate them.

Supplicant: At first, I saw that she was old so I let it continue. It's better than if he ran after some younger woman [*sao;* lit.: "girl"]. . . . Is he really mine?

Medium: He has to be with you sincerely, in front of your face. He had these women from before. He's a playboy. Who sees him will say that he's harmless, but the minute he's out of the house he does bad [deeds]. . . . [*Here, the medium begins her benediction.*] I call upon everyone to be happy. Whatever happens, have it not be misfortunate. Be rich in Buddhism. Be rich in dharma. Be rich in religion. If we're done here, Father [i.e., "I, the spirit"] will depart. (Suriya 1999, 180–181; translation mine)

Here, the spirit adopts a tone of familiar authority coupled with near-omniscience about the supplicant's problems and thereby leads her to articulate her fears. The spirit removes the woman's doubts (even if he confirms her fears) and may give some supernatural blessing, as Kham did. The medium points to the proper system of social exchange: the man has been engaging in improper relations: he has been cheating on his wife, sleeping with a woman much older than he is, and taking money from his mistress, and the medium seeks to set such transgressions right.

The requests that the supplicants bring to mediums are requests for things from the material world: money, love, and so on. "Magic" monks and mediums offer "this-world" shortcuts to prosperity or magic (cf. Jackson 1998; Pattana 2005), especially during times of stress and change in the Thai economy. As Peter Jackson writes, "The individualistic focus of *sayasat* [the supernatural] may provide a more meaningful and immediately accessible means of expressing and dealing with the anxieties of life among the anonymous competitive masses of Bangkok than more collective religious forms and rituals of Buddhism" (Jackson 1998, 60–61). Such a claim resonates with Irving's (1984) link between spirit mediumship and urbanization, with its increase in landlessness and integration into the market economy.

White's supplicants also offered him a deal. They gave a nominal amount—five baht (sixteen cents) and buried it near one of the mounts' hitching posts. This was a down payment on something more should their requests be honored and they receive what they asked for. In this way, supplicants entered into exchange with forces beyond the social in order to address issues of uncertainty (Johnson 2012). The supplicant offers something of this world—money—in order to receive something from the other world—influence over chaos.

This gift travels via a chain of intermediaries. The supplicants contact Kham, who has a privileged connection with White. But White does not grant these gifts himself. He requests them (*kho hue* or *kho hai* in Central Thai) of "another world" (*lok uen*). Fortune and efficacy flow downwards through connections in the same way that Hanks (1962) envisions power flowing in Thai political systems. Power is concretized upwards and is inaccessible to those multiple levels downwards from it (see Shalardchai 1984). This is the direction and flow of *charoen*.

CONCLUSION

Supplicants to spirit mediums come seeking connections. They try to form a link between themselves and the invisible sources of power they perceive to be directing progress, both material and spiritual. Such an act recalls the Comaroffs' idea of "occult economies" (1999), wherein the hidden actions of the market—especially the present moment of neoliberal capitalism—come to parallel the action of magic and spirits. The Comaroffs present a model of chaos, of new construction and panic. Yet as Kapferer (2003) argues, we should not so quickly dismiss older ways of managing and imagining power when looking at new forms of the occult.

In Chiang Mai, such metaphors of power are expressed in terms of motion. Power is not immediately accessible to individuals, but rather must flow downwards from *chao* along lines (*sen*) of interpersonal connection, of fictive kinship—recall that supplicants term themselves "children of the ghost." In this way, possessing *chao* such as Yellow and White are juxtaposed with evil spirits (*phi tai hong*), beings that cause random violence and disorder in everyday life: traffic accidents, sudden illness, and so on. These "ghosts of bad death" are backflows, bubbles that rise up from lower states of prestige to haunt the present. But by appealing to a source of prestige—these spectral figures of Lanna's past who, as White assures the aspiring student, "have connections"—supplicants hope to triumph over the chaotic ruinousness of the present through activating the charismatic, attractive power of *barami*, the quality that lies at the center of the mandala. As with White, it is the city—personified through its guardian spirit—that intervenes to transform disorder into order. Mediums present themselves as being able to engage with this unknown world, drawing upon sources of prestige.

As Kham stressed when she repeatedly disregarded my questions about origins, sources of *charoen* are fungible. If a thing is efficacious in causing *charoen*, then it is worth calling upon, whether it be a purchased tutelary spirit or the current living monarch. It is in this way that the emphasis on historical authenticity or, as Rosalind Morris terms it, "pastness" (Morris 2000) is misleading. Spirits, monks, and kings are all of a similar sort to the sources of power that lie at the center of cities: all provide *barami* and facilitate *charoen*. Indeed, rather than being entirely "past," mediums are often touted as being exceptionally modern, as when the mediums of Grandmother and Grandfather Sae were described to me as having "nanotechnology more advanced than modern science." In this way, the power of the past is always high-tech.

This being so, it is not surprising that other modern discourses in Chiang Mai follow a similar model, one wherein the invisible but immanent power of the city is called upon to materialize for the purpose of development. With this in mind, I now turn to the discourse of city planners and architects in creating the forms of Chiang Mai's *khwam charoen*.

4

Lanna Style

I pulled my motorcycle off the side road onto the damp grass alongside rows and rows of other bikes. As in the case of Grandmother and Grandfather Sae's rite, I was late. The music had already begun, although the winter morning cool had not quite turned to the heat of midday. In the clearing, underneath a tall canopy of replanted teak trees, a white mat had been laid down as a stage. In front of it sat the guest of honor dressed in white, his hands clasped in a respectful *wai,* a benevolent smile on his face. Behind him was an altar with offering bowls full of flowers and fruits and pigs' heads lined up in a row. Costumed youths milled in a crowd on the mat. Some of them were preparing to dance. The area under the trees looked just like a medium's *yok khru.*

Indeed, it was a *yok khru.* I had talked the day before to a Northern Thai cultural studies student who, excited that I was asking about *yok khru,* had urged that I come to this one. "Those," she had told me, referring to the mediums' rituals I had attended, "aren't so real. This one will be the real thing!"

I approached a cluster of men waiting on the sidelines, much as I had approached mediums resting from the dance at the Three Kings. They were young and were dressed like mediums in turbans, loose-fitting jackets, and flowing cloth sarongs, although their costumes were far more extravagant and expensive-looking than Kham's. I gave one a respectful *wai,* and asked, "Have you [the spirit] descended yet?"

"*Arai na?*" asked the youth nearest to me. "What?"

"The *chao,* has he descended?" The youth looked shocked, embarrassed, and amused all at the same time. I enunciated carefully, thinking my accent might be the issue: "Are you possessed?"

Another young man standing nearby laughed. "He thinks you're a medium!" Some of the others laughed too, but more suddenly became serious and moved forward, shaking their heads.

"No, no, no," said one, switching to English. "This is a show. Dance."

I had assumed, based on the décor, the language used, and the appearance of the dancers, that this *yok khru,* like the many others I attended, would feature possession. The offerings were the same as in the mediums' ceremony—fruit, flowers, pigs' heads. The layout was the same; the altar, the central dance floor, and the dancers wearing the costumes of ancient kings were also similar. But the shocked reactions of the dancers indicated that associations between art and mediumship were unwelcome.

Still, the idea of the *yok khru* here is the same as in the mediums' ceremonies: the followers of the teacher will gain prosperity owing to their association with him. It is just that at this event, "culture," in its museumized form, stands in for the divine. *Watthanatham* becomes the answer to "What insubstantial force will ensure Northern Thailand's prosperity?" Confusing *watthanatham* with spirit possession, as I had done, was an egregious error. I had mistaken educated university arts students for supplicants. By doing so, for these well-to-do students, I was immediately marked as a foreigner. Switching to English was a way of telling me that I did not comprehend what I was seeing.

Such a transformation would seem to follow on the heels of what Weber might have predicted: magical or religious elements change to their secularized form with the advent of modernity (2003). Or, alternatively, one could take a reading from Benjamin: the spirit dance, previously imbued with an "aura" of possessing spirits, now becomes something political, the assertion of Lanna's cultural value in the face of an overwhelming tide of Central Thai and "global" influences. But to read the dance in this light is to ignore the question of what "Lanna" means to those constructing and consuming it. It ignores the magico-religious context of prestige, *barami,* and power. *Watthanatham* and religious power are inextricably linked. As Peleggi writes (2002, 13) and I have already noted, the Thai Fine Arts Department decides upon the locations for "heritage" at places where local residents identify *sak* (sacred power). *Watthanatham* is something urban, something that motivates and calls for *khwam charoen,* and is continually reframed to fit the present. It is sacred power in a secular guise.

This is why my question "Has the spirit descended yet?" was awkward—because I had pointed to the very close similarity between possessing spirits and *watthanatham.* The "cultural" dancers embody the spirits of the past, as do the mediums. In each case, the inarticulate spirit of the past emerges for the direct usefulness and benefit of the present—it creates *khwam charoen* as

Thongchai describes the term, "the sense of transformation into the new age, or modernity, as opposed to the traditional, the ancient, or the bygone era" (Thongchai 2000a, 531). Something from the outside has come in to benefit the present.

Thongchai (2000a, 539) and Peleggi (2002a) describe how elites attempted to *charoen* through the conspicuous consumption of European goods. I have argued that spirit devotees attempt to capture *khwam charoen* by interacting with the spirit world. In the case of Chiang Mai elites, the domestic consumption of Lanna culture fulfills a similar role. In each case, individuals reach, via a medium (consumer goods, a possessed individual, an artist or architect) toward that source of potential power in order to *charoen.*

If both in mediumship and in the construction of Lanna *watthanatham* a well of future-oriented potential lies in Northern Thailand's past, then it is mediums and culture brokers (artists and architects) who are uniquely suited to identify and transform this potential into actual *khwam charoen.* As in the "cultural" dance, the stated contents and purpose may seem quite different—and certainly the actors involved do not see themselves as linked—but the workings of power, potential, and progress remain the same.

In *Orientalism,* Edward Said (1978) points out how Europeans ascribed greatness to the ancient civilizations of the Middle East while simultaneously dissociating contemporary Arabs from this civilization. Representations of Lanna by Thai (both Central and Northern) elite follow the same general model—Lanna *as Lanna* (in other words, as the past kingdom) is portrayed as an advanced, beautiful, and quasi-European place, while current Northern Thailand is considered a rude backwater. Yet the twenty-first-century construction of Lanna and Northern-ness rests as much on Thai concepts of *charoen* as it does on Orientalism. The essentialized, reified Lanna becomes a source of potential power, but one that requires mediation in order to manifest. Like Pu Sae and Ya Sae, the spirit of Lanna must be tamed before it can be reintegrated into the national whole, where it then becomes a source of power.

Marc Askew (1996) and Michael Herzfeld (2006) see such attempts to "revitalize" Thai pasts as a neoliberal erasure of older ways of being urban. In Bangkok, Askew laments the disappearance of the *yan*—an informal community loosely gathered around a central point and sharing a common sense of residence that cuts across socioeconomic class. These *yan* allowed for "different land-uses and activities" (Askew 1996, 194) in ways that are incompatible with a city plan oriented around the dweller as individual. In a similar example from the Chiang Mai suburbs in my own research, Kham farmed garlic and flowers for her own use on a small plot of land[1] informally used by the members of her community for collective agriculture in a way that would be impossible in my own high-rise apartment building or in a gated community.

According to Askew, Bangkok remained more or less *yan*-centered until the 1960s, and only with the rise of the discourse of cultural heritage (*moradok*) did the *yan* decline. Bangkok, then, is not undergoing modernist revision; rather, the city is undergoing *post*modern reconstruction, by which I mean a renovation that highlights the *image* of the premodern past while fundamentally changing the meaning and relevance of "community" to create an urban environment that is oriented toward spectacle—toward the unmooring of signifiers from their signifieds—and toward neoliberal consumption. In Lefebvre's terms, "old 'ways of life' become folklore" (1996, 72) and are stripped of their relevance to everyday life and redesigned for consumption. The new plan is not designed to erase the past, but on the contrary, to make the past more clear, salient, and consumable—at least for the urban bourgeoisie.

Thai urban renewal shares with the modernist movement the desire to bring to light that which is shrouded in unclean darkness. Herzfeld (2006) has worked on the preservation of a poor *yan* near Mahakan Fort on Rattanakosin Island in Bangkok that was faced with destruction in the name of historic preservation and urban beautification. When confronting a city official who claimed that the community was not worth preserving as it did not produce any one coherent product nor was it composed of a distinct ethnic group, Herzfeld, in an attempt to highlight the ridiculousness of the complaint, compared this reasoning with the government's OTOP project, wherein one *tambon* (administrative division at a village level) would produce one product for sale. To his surprise, the official agreed wholeheartedly with this characterization. A true community, according to him, was one that could be summarized briefly as having one coherent ethnicity, religion, and product (Herzfeld, pers. comm.). The incoherence and "messiness" of the *yan*, ironically, was not compatible with a truly historic city.

For the middle- and upper-class Thai community in Chiang Mai, the task of interpreting and mediating this urban potential fell to Chiang Mai's artistic and architectural community. Independent shops, royal projects, private individuals, and even academic departments took up the challenge to adapt and promote this essence. In doing so, they used different terms, most of which were adapted from English: "Lanna Renaissance," "Chiang Mai Brand," or the umbrella term I use here, "Lanna Style" (see Ping 2000; Cummings 2006). Here, the meaning of "Lanna" *watthanatham* is linked to one's understanding of *khwam charoen*. The creation of a new, edited version of "Lanna" would, in the eyes of those seeking to create "Lanna Style," herald a new age of *khwam charoen* and solve Chiang Mai's ruinous present.

CULTURE, PROGRESS, AND EUROPE

On a cool winter night I came downstairs from my apartment and ran into Lung—my nearly seventy-year-old landlord—returning from somewhere with two cups full of red wine. Though Lung liked to drink in the early evenings as he watched the street traffic, wine was a new thing—he normally drank several cans of Chang beer. "Anu,"[2] he said, "you should go across the street! They are giving away alcohol!" He leaned in close to make sure that I got the message: "*Free!*" he added triumphantly.

The event that Lung referred to was a massive party for the opening of a store in a small shopping complex. Modern Dog, one of Thailand's most famous rock bands, was giving a free concert, and a Thai television star was there to act as announcer on a televised tour through the shop. But this was neither a new entertainment spot nor a fashionable boutique; it was the Cotto Tiles Library. Cotto Tiles, a branch of the Thai Ceramic Company, makes tiles for home decoration, and the library was a showcase for Cotto's projects and a place where prospective home decorators could go for inspiration (indeed, the English word "inspiration" was the catchphrase for the party).

The event featured architects working in Chiang Mai. These architects, part of a larger community of architects, artists, and would-be artists living in Chiang Mai, were key players in and symbols of the formation of Chiang Mai's image. They were actively trying to create a "new" Chiang Mai, one that was both the realization of Lanna's promise and at the same time current with global artistic trends and flows.

The Cotto Tiles event was significant in that it lay at the confluence of various forces involved in remaking the image of the city. Here was the city, a private tile company, and Chiang Mai University all calling for Chiang Mai's renaissance—not a rebirth of Lanna as an independent polity, but rather a renewal of the city after the ravages of the 1997 economic crisis. Cotto Tiles was an active promoter of the construction boom in Chiang Mai's suburbs and the city, supplying tiles to many development companies. Also, the choice of venue was in the heart of Chiang Mai's new district— Nimmanhaemin. As Modern Dog played, they were flanked on one side by the Café Nero, an Italian restaurant-cum-coffee shop, on the other by Dai-Kichi, a Japanese restaurant, and in back by the BKK[3] Grill. The architects featured in the Cotto Tiles promotional material and in the posters lining the venue walls were those who were actively producing major high-modern projects in the city: the Mo Rooms Hotel, Yesterday Hotel, Maze Café, and so on. While the group of architects and planners assembled at the Tiles event was not the sum total of architects in Chiang Mai, they represented those aggressively pushing for a new, globally interconnected Chiang Mai. It was to be a new Lanna.

The opening had published a booklet, which they handed out for free along with the wine. It was a guide to Cotto-inspired modern architecture in the cities of Chiang Mai, Bangkok, and Phuket. I quote here my own translation of the Chiang Mai section, entitled "www.Chiangmai: Cultural Delight."[4]

The skyline of the city of Chiang Mai when seen from above, from atop Doi Suthep, for instance, looks like it's not very orderly. But in fact, it's clean and easy to understand [*riap ngai*], and clear. It differs from a big city like Bangkok. From the outskirts into the city below, you will see also that the image that you have seen from the top [i.e., a clear, easy, clean city] is in fact representative of the city.

This is probably the reason why so many people from Bangkok have been able to come to Chiang Mai each year to visit, or to change regions altogether! They are escaping from the poor manners of the capital city. . . . [Or] it might be because the air is free of pollution and cooler in Chiang Mai that makes people from other parts of the country feel the need to come to Chiang Mai and fall under its sleeping spell until they cannot awaken. Or maybe it's because of the various foods, which have tastes that are just right for Thai mouths.

For artists, the old culture [*watthanatham kao kae*] still fills and informs Chiang Mai. Temples and monasteries might be more in number here than [in] other provinces, and the city plan still separates the old city and the new city, showing off clearly the moat and four corners, which are still used in rites and maintained.

There is still too much more left about this city to tell, about the beauty of the Lanna kingdom's culture [*watthanatham*] as well as new trends. People have said that [Chiang Mai] is too much, that you can't possibly see it all, but all of this wouldn't be possible if the majority of people didn't preserve the local habits and culture [*watthanatham*] of the city. But it's not only their [*phuak khao*—e.g., Northerners'] job, because we are all "*khon mueang opayop*" [immigrants, but with a play on *khon mueang;* quotation marks in the original] everywhere we go!

It might be said that one can sometimes buy time, but Chiang Mai doesn't have to buy its slow and easy time. It flows easily, and they [the people of Chiang Mai] are happy to give you theirs.

This description of Chiang Mai assumes it is addressing a Bangkok-based audience, perhaps one that will move to the North and build a house, using Cotto tiles. The reader supposedly feels "hemmed in" by "the capital city," and wishes to move to a purer and cleaner environment, "free of pollution and cooler." The environment is culturally pure as well: the old *watthanatham* is present, embodied not only in temples and monasteries, but also in the walls and gates of the old city "still used in rites and maintained." Despite the "new trends"—of which the booklet itself is a prime example—it is the Chiang Mai people (here set apart as "that group" [*phuak khao*] to be contrasted with "us" [*rao*]) who maintain the local culture. But this culture is not something that will appear foreign to the Bangkok-based traveler: the Cotto Tiles booklet claims that Northern food is "just right for Thai mouths." In short, the "slow and easy time" of Chiang Mai is one that stems from the past. Here, then, is the home of "pastness."

"I Don't Need to Go to Europe"

Strangely, as with Kham's "Burmese" spirits, this "pastness" often coexists with foreignness. But it is not the foreignness that has resulted from Chiang Mai's long association with Laos or (especially) Burma. Instead, many artists and architects with whom I spoke described Lanna as an oddly European place. On one chill November evening there was a large outdoor festival just off Nimmanhaemin Road, very close to the Cotto Tiles Library. As the rock band took the stage, the lead announced that this was the first time he'd been to Chiang Mai. "What good weather!" he announced. "Now that I've been to Chiang Mai, I don't need to go to Europe!"

This remark was not simply about temperature. A new hotel, the Eurana Boutique Hotel, advertises itself as a place offering a fusion of European and Lanna styles of accommodation. At first glance, these two might seem to be irreconcilable: historical Lanna-era travelers' accommodation consisted of a temple floor. But for the hotel's designers, the two ideas "European" and "Lanna" shared something inchoate. Each was a font of *khwam charoen*.

For such a place of "origins" to be likened to Europe bears some analysis. The comparison begins in early twentieth-century nationalist work and centers on the creation and dissemination of the word *watthanatham*. Generally glossed as "culture," *watthanatham* is a Sanskrit-based neologism formed from *watthana*, a synonym for *phatthana*, and *tham*, cosmic law, the Dharma. Culture in the Thai idiom, then, can be translated literally as "development following cosmic law," or "*phatthana* that follows the Dharma." Culture in this idiom is not folk culture. Rather, it is movement toward enlightenment, progress along the path of *khwam charoen*.

The word was coined in the reign of King Vajiravudh (Rama VI; 1910–1925), the era when the Thai elite begin creating and promoting Thai ethno-nationalism. The figure most influential in the forging of *watthanatham* was *luang* Wichit Wathakan, an ambassador and adviser to regimes in Thailand from 1921 until 1962. He was a propagandist and promoter of Thai irredentism and was active in the reigns of the absolute monarchy of Rama VII (pre-1932), the nationalist coup that overthrew him, and the revitalization of the monarchy under Sarit Thanarat (1959–1963). Wichit conceived of *watthanatham* as the artistic, architectural, and (oddly enough) sartorial achievements of the nation that founded "the underlying basis of morals and behavior which led to 'national progress and stability'" (Barmé 1993, 161). Under the nationalist coup group, he diverted attention away from the Thai monarchy and toward the idea of the Thai Volk. As such, his work sought a pure time of Thainess, before outside influences. In this historical recasting, Ayutthaya-era monarchs were stained by "Khmer architecture and rituals" (Thak 2003, 147), and, for Wichit, only in the time before Ayutthaya was Thai society pure. Specifically, he chose the kingdom of Sukhothai, an early contemporary of Lanna, during the reign of King Ramkhamhaeng as demonstrating a period of time when Thai essences were most evident.

Nonetheless, in his depiction of Sukhothai *watthanatham* Wichit sought to find Europe in the Thai past. Rather than presenting Sukhothai as a radical alternative to Western norms, as one might expect from his goal of showing "unadulterated" Thainess, Wichit instead argued that Sukhothai society was already comparable with the advanced industrial authoritarian regimes he admired (specifically Fascist Italy). In his model, Sukhothai and Italy both boasted wide roads, a market economy, and, in his view, the benevolent but absolute rule of a father figure. Indeed, Wichit modeled Ramkhamhaeng explicitly after Mussolini (Barmé 1993, 162).

Furthermore, for Wichit, Sukhothai was "proof" that Thais had been "Western" before colonial influences. Such a comparison focused as much on surface features as on essences: Wichit made much of the fact that the Ramkhamhaeng stele[5] features a Thai script where the consonants and vowels are all on the same line, "western-style" (Barmé 1993, 161); in other words, by writing letters that superficially resembled European alphabets, Ramkhamhaeng anticipated the progress and development that Wichit now saw in the European powers, only to be stymied by the introduction of Khmer alphabet, with its super- and subscripts. By—in Geertz's terms—"imaging" Europe, Wichit sought to bring about Europe's *charoen.*

So, in his writings, Wichit placed importance on the similarity between Thai aesthetic culture and norms from the West, arguing that the latter had been anticipated and predated. In this way, according to him, Thailand's modernization, in both infrastructure and culture, involved returning to the roots of *"watthanatham sukhothai"* (Saichol 2002, 9). Westernization was simply the end realization of Ramkhamhaeng's original dream, making Thailand's modernization something supernaturally foreseen in ancient history. *Khwam charoen*, as Wichit saw it, flowed from a single source, and it was only natural that diversity and divergence would disappear as civilizations headed toward this source.

For this reason, Lanna, for those imagining it as a source of *watthanatham* in Wichit's vein, should naturally appear to be European. In saying this, I do not mean to imply a masochistic valorization of "the West"—recall how Wichit describes Ramkhamhaeng's independent "discovery" of wide streets, single-line script, and market economy independent of any Western influences. Culture brokers often stress Thailand's superiority to the West in cases such as the monarchy's role in politics or religion even as they glorify other aspects of *"farang"* culture (Pattana 2010). Rather, the West represents a misstep on the path to *charoen*, one where individualism and avarice have taken hold.

Here, a deeper look into the construction of *watthanatham* can shed more light on this distinction. While Herzfeld points to the differences between *watthanatham* and *siwilai* ("civilized," from the English), arguing that the former bears the stamp of the national while the latter posits the attempt to emulate the West (Herzfeld 2002, 905), I want to note that, while *siwilai* points toward the achievement of European standards, *khwam charoen* and *watthanatham* point toward a universal goal, one toward which European powers have also moved, however imperfectly.

Just as Phrathepyanmahamuni, the abbot of Wat Phraya Dhammanikaya, predicted the afterlife of Apple CEO Steve Jobs as an enlightened being but a flawed one with demonic passions and characteristics (*Bangkok Post*, August 20, 2012), so Western powers appear more progressive—but in a way. For many Thai activists with whom I worked, as well as Thai academics (cf. Chatthip 1991), "globalization" (*lokaphiwat*) presented the challenge of mitigating economic and technological success derived from "international" (*sakhon*) sources with "Thai" values. To return to the ladder analogy, things that are on a higher rung tend to look alike, as there is only one ladder. Thus, the progressive parts of Chiang Mai's culture would naturally appear European. But certain aspects of global or European culture indicate, for these activists, that the rung on which Europe sits is not as high as Europeans might think. The challenge lies in determining which aspects of international cultural trends are truly *charoen*, and which are false steps on the ladder of *charoen*.

Women, Europe, and Lanna

Chiang Mai–based historian and social critic Nidthi Eoseewong claims that Bangkok's writers and artists have created the idea of "Lanna" that Northerners consume today. The term he uses is evocative in Thai—*chat fun*—literally, to "organize the dreams" (Nidthi 1991, 182). The story Nidthi references in his article is that of the film *Sao Khrua Fa,* a reinterpretation of *Madame Butterfly* that replaces the original story about a US naval officer's doomed romance with a young Japanese woman with one about a Bangkok soldier and a Chiang Mai woman. The two fall in love, but the soldier eventually returns to Bangkok, leaving the poor Northern girl pregnant and alone, after which she kills herself by leaping to her death from the top of a waterfall. Yet for Nidthi, the aesthetics of the film are far more important than the plot: the artistic director and writer of the film freely invented Northern language, costume, and the image and décor of the city, without reference to Northern dialect (*kam mueang*) or the city of Chiang Mai at all. Ultimately, for Nidthi, *Sao Khrua Fa* is an important marker showing how ideas from the metropole have the power to rewrite the aesthetic of Chiang Mai.

Nowhere is this historical rewriting more apparent than in the National Museum. It presents Lanna history in a series of dioramas as the kingdom progresses upward from its roots in rock paintings and hill tribes, skipping over the Burmese period entirely and resuming the narrative with Kawila, the ruler appointed by Siam after Chiang Mai's restoration in the late eighteenth century. But the display culminates in the image of Dara Rasami, one of the nearly one hundred wives of (Central Thai) King Chulalongkorn (r. 1868–1910), who was elevated to the status of Great Consort when she gave birth to a daughter (who died as a child). However, the figure of Dara Rasami now becomes recast as a proto-European figure (see Hong 1998 for other examples of the recasting of royal consorts). She wore her hair long (similarly to Western women and in contrast to late nineteenth-century Central Thai practice). In addition, Thai-language sources at the time were full of allegations that Queen Victoria wanted to adopt Dara Rasami as a daughter (support for which is not found in British records; Woodhouse 2009, 73–74). While in the nineteenth century these rumors might have fed into fears of British expansion, here I explore the significance of their repetition in the present through how they are displayed (in places such as the museum dedicated to Dara Rasami to the north of Chiang Mai) as evidence of Dara Rasami's cosmopolitanism and elegance. It is certainly a strange end to the narrative of Lanna history, as though the struggles of the polity have culminated in the image of a pseudo-European woman locked in a subordinate marriage to the Central Thai Chakri dynasty.

Tribes, Invention, and Lanna

In addition to the National Museum, the Old Chiangmai Cultural Center (OCCC) is another site where "Lanna" *watthanatham* is expressly displayed: the OCCC's slogan is "The Magic of Lanna Kingdom." The center was created in the 1970s by Kraisri Nimmanhaemin, whom I cited in regard to Grandmother and Grandfather Sae and who lends his name to Nimmanhaemin Road. The OCCC hosts *khantok* performances, dinners oriented toward tourists and featuring Northern Thai and "tribal" dance performances. The Northern Thai anthropologist Manee Phayaomyong describes the *khantok* as follows:

> Lannathai is a region that developed along with art and culture from ancient times [*boran*], and used to be the kingdom of Lannathai from the eighteenth to the twentieth Buddhist centuries (AD 13th–15th c.). There was King Mangrai who was the first king of the Mangrai dynasty, and many other developments [*phatthana*], such as government, religion, arts, culture [*watthanatham*], resting, eating, ordination, marriage, etc. The remnants of these are things that we should study in earnest and have more people who are interested in them get others to write in many languages for study and to be an example for researchers. Here, I am speaking of the *"khantok,"* which is one part of the arts and one part of the tradition [*prapheni*] of the *khantok dinner,* or the tradition of the *khantok* of Lannathai. (Manee 1994, 228; translation mine)

The *khantok* is expressly an invented tradition, one that is the result of *phatthana* and that exists to promote Lanna (or, as Manee writes, "Lannathai," unifying Northern and Central Thailand). For Manee, it exists in order to entertain visiting guests and encourage them to develop an interest in the region—its explicit invention does detract from its authenticity or importance to *watthanatham.*

An aspect of the *khantok* that Manee does not describe but is starkly visible in its performances is the emphasis on hill tribes. The dinner is divided into two sections: one for Northern Thai, Central Thai, Shan, or newly invented dances; and the other of which takes place out of doors and introduces the various tribes of the mountains surrounding Chiang Mai. Hjorleifur Jonsson (2005) describes the OCCC's *khantok* as replicating the divide between lowland and highland groups (and the subordinate status of lowlanders in this divide), contrasting the indoor, air-conditioned lowland dance performances accompanying dinner with the outdoor, post-dinner tribal ones (2005, 71–72). But here I wish to stress the association between the two. It is an association replicated in many places in Thailand, from depictions of Northern Thais in "longneck" Karen (Kayan) costume to the nickname "Maew" (Hmong) given to Northern-born Thaksin. In the national imaginary, Lanna culture contains within it, albeit at a subordinate level, the tribal, the (imagined-to-be) primitive. Here, Lanna appears as a product of what Louisa Schien (1997) terms "internal orientalism": Chiang Mai as subordinate, female, tribal. But all orientalisms are not created equal. How Chiang Mai is interpreted by Bangkok (or, indeed, how local elites interpret Lanna) is deeply influenced by notions of *watthanatham, barami,* and *khwam charoen.* Chiang Mai is subordinate, backward, but also in some sense united with Bangkok and full of progressive potential.

These tropes continue to be relevant in popular media today. In the romantic comedy film *The Memory* (*Rak Chang;* Haeman 2006), a careless superstar crashes on his way back from a vacation in the popular tourist destination of Pai, just to the north of Chiang Mai.[6] Having lost his memory, he is taken in by a group of hill tribesmen (who speak in a sort of Northern Thai-ish patois) played for laughs as bumpkins with blackened teeth. The star is pursued by an ambitious tabloid photographer who ends up up falling in love with him.

The Memory may be a light romantic comedy, but it shows a great deal about this first "raw" image of the North and how it is "cooked." Northerners, aside from their tribal stand-ins, are entirely absent from the movie. Northern *symbols,* if not *people,* are present in the film—outside of the city. Northern dress, speech, and rituals become those of the film's hill tribes. The tribesmen wear Karen-esque outfits but speak in a quasi-Northern accent and decorate their festivals with the long white banners (*tung*) that mark a Northern Thai temple ceremony. But the North is not depicted as entirely a land of barbarism: when the hero finds a café in Pai, he makes a point of asking the owner if she is a Northerner, to which she replies, "No, I'm a Bangkok person! [*pen khon* Krung Thep]." The exchange is orphaned from the preceding or antecedent parts of the conversation—it exists simply to explain existence of the café (a symbol of cosmopolitanism) and the woman's urbane manners and Central speech. The relaxed, urbane atmosphere of the café emerges from this combination of Northern and Central—the natural world of the cool Northern mountains and the cultivated urbanity of Central shopkeepers.

Maurizio Peleggi notes the way in which Bangkok Thais mimic Western tourists on their visits to the "backwater" provinces such as Chiang Mai and Pai (Peleggi 1996, 437). But, as I have argued, the North is not only backwater. As we saw in Wichit's valorization of Northern culture as being quintessentially Thai, in the logic of nationalism the untouched, allochronous, primitive space contains within it the kernel of authenticity, something (as Cotto Tiles suggests) "just right for Thai mouths." It is raw potentiality. For instance, Sao Khrua Fa embodies both backwardness (in her naïveté) and cultivation (in her beauty). In other words, Khrua Fa's raw charisma is natural, inherent, as opposed to something learned. Only with refinement can the true potential of such charisma be realized, a trope that echoes the drive to "improve" upon Lanna.

As in the case of the dancers, the repetition of and sensitivity toward such representations pervaded many of my informants' discourses, especially those of Northern Thais who were actively involved in Chiang Mai's artist community. For example, I was once drinking with a group of Thai, Northern Thai, and European artists (and their friends) at a large house/studio in Chiang Mai's fashionable Mae Rim suburb. The house (a poured-concrete, brightly painted, avant-garde–style place) was at the edge of a rice field. Joe, the Central Thai owner and a friend of mine, had moved to Chiang Mai several years before after being an actor and artist in Bangkok for many years. He rhapsodized about how he was now a farmer (*chao⁷ na*) and how he loved to stand in his rice field and gaze at the mountains. In the spirit of friendly, slightly drunken mockery, and knowing Joe's elite tastes (and therefore how unlikely a farmer he made), I asked him where his buffalo was at that moment. Joe responded, laughing, that *he* was in fact the buffalo; but his friend, Dao, a Northern woman roughly my age who ran a flamenco school in town, took offense at the joke and switched between English and Thai as she chastised me: "*Khwai man phaeng wa* [Buffaloes are fucking expensive]! Thai farmers don't use buffaloes! Buffaloes come from the Philippines, not here!"

Obviously I had hit a nerve somewhere—a white foreigner making fun of a Thai person for being a farmer (notwithstanding Joe's own joke to that effect or the obvious incongruity of a wealthy Bangkok painter imagining himself a farmer) had violated what Herzfeld (2005) terms "cultural intimacy": I had presumed an "insider-ness" and was quickly reminded that I was no such insider and had no right to be speaking about Thai buffaloes.

Dao's claim that Thai buffaloes were nonexistent is, of course, patently false, especially in the North or Northeast—I (and she, presumably) saw them daily on the side of roads, being led to and from rice fields by local farmers, or occasionally ate them with Northern-style *lap*. What is significant is the fact that it was Dao—one of the only Northerners at the party—who displayed sensitivity toward my characterization of Joe as a buffalo-driving farmer. In that crowd of mostly Bangkok-born, elite university-educated artists, mockery of Northern Thai customs and language as being backward and uncivilized "buffaloes" was commonplace. By closing the borders of Thainess against me by switching into English, Dao was presenting the North, both to me and to Joe, as being more industrialized and *charoen* than we all thought we knew it was. In short, she was advocating the ideal image of the modern North, one she had a hand in promoting through her school. I had damaged the *barami* of the North by suggesting a "raw" Chiang Mai. In other words, I had pointed to the current state of things—a state Dao wanted to make me understand was not the true North, but rather, that farmers plowing with buffaloes were only a temporary glitch in the trajectory of *charoen* that was the North's destiny.

Chiang Mai as Europe

The Eurana boutique hotel in Chiang Mai claims on its Web site that it offers a blend of both European and Lanna styles—hence its name. Each, for the hotel, is exotic in its own way; yet they are somehow complementary. Similarly, the Yesterday boutique hotel, catering both to wealthy youth from Bangkok seeking Chiang Mai's night life and to foreign tourists, traffics in nostalgia: the lobby is decorated with antique appliances, old photographs, and the like. The Thai-language Web page features computer-animated menus scattered around sepia-tinged Western-style rooms, implying that the "yesterday" the guests will experience is not that of their parents' Chinese or Thai backgrounds but rather the "yesterday" of old American films (Yesterday 2009). Chiang Mai is transposed onto a *farang* past, becoming other both in time and in place to the Bangkok-based visitor.

As with the "tribal" motif, the casting of Chiang Mai as the *farang*-influenced past is also reflected in Thai films. In *The Letter* (*Chot Mai Rak;* Pa-oon 2004), the heroine, Dew, flees from the violence of Bangkok, where her bon vivant friend has been murdered, to the teak-paneled, mist-shrouded idyll of Chiang Mai. This Chiang Mai—represented by a small town on the Burmese border—with its fresh coffee and air so cool that, as Dew says, she "doesn't have to use air-conditioning" (and which, incidentally, allows her to wear fashionable, long, foreign-cut winter trench coats) is inhabited by silent old people who are only audible when she speaks to them, and then speak only in polite, slow Central Thai. Indeed, nighttime scenes of "Chiang Mai" in the video invariably have the actors dressed in ski hats and heavy winter coats huddling around a fire—a long way from the scenes of nightclubs and office buildings that represent Bangkok.

In Chiang Mai, Dew meets Ton (Tree), a quiet employee of a royal tree-planting project.[8] He is genuine, kind, and unsophisticated—he doesn't know how to use e-mail and doesn't own a cell phone—a contrast to Dew's promiscuous friend in Bangkok. Ton has spent his entire life in Chiang Mai but does not speak Northern Thai, not even with his fellow employees.

What is significant here, as in *The Memory,* is the absence of the Northerners themselves and their replacement by innocent, pure, uncorrupted Thais like Ton. In the former example, the figure of the Northerner—what in earlier times had been the figure of the "Lao"—has been transformed into the hill tribesman. In *The Memory,* for instance, the Lanna region consists of cute, clean cafés (run and patronized by Bangkokians), roads winding through green mountains, and tribal villages. In the promotional materials for the "Yesterday" hotel, Chiang Mai is depicted as a nostalgic, quiet, and more specifically *solitary* space to reflect. In *The Letter,* Chiang Mai provides a place for Dew to take on the role of foreign expatriate—a person of an altogether different nature from that of the allochronous, elderly people who shuffle around in the background. Indeed, when Dew marries Ton and moves from the tree-planting project to Chiang Mai, the ruin she has inherited from her step-grandmother suddenly changes from a dark-teak structure inhabited by large tokay geckoes (an animal considered particularly repulsive) to a clean, high-tech mountain home with bright colors, computers, and the like. In other words, in order for the potential in this place of good weather and good raw materials to be realized, Dew had to appear and bring modernity to it.

The casting of Chiang Mai as a pseudo-European allochronous space is the descendant of Wichit's formulation of the North as the repository for that aspect of Thai *watthanatham* which has been lost in modernizing Bangkok. Chiang Mai becomes home to the potential of a developed, evolved Thailand: it contains the utopian basis for what Thailand might have become had misfortune (blamed either on an abstract idea such as "politicians," "greed," "globalization" or on other outside factors) not drawn it astray. Chiang Mai is therefore a place where the Bangkokian tourist or expatriate can imagine a different Thailand: one that is undoubtedly in the past but possesses the potential of a greater *charoen* than Bangkok; one that looks European but is in fact more Thai than Thailand.

The erasure or othering (as hill tribe or provincial) of Northerners in this image is not a contradiction to the "more Thai than Thailand" image. Rather, they become savages (noble or not) who are too embedded in the cultural wealth of the region to recognize its worth. They exist surrounded by potential but are innocent to the ways in which it can be refined and utilized. It is those from the capital city who are able to recognize what is of value. This is why the coffee-shop owner is a Bangkokian; in other words, while the North contains seeds of *charoen,* one must come from a place that already is *charoen* in order to recognize the fact.

This echoes official state and royal ideology in Thailand: recall how the Thai queen was so impressed by Karen silversmiths that she "gave" them patterns for their silverwork. Here, the "raw" pattern is too unsophisticated; rather, what is needed is a dose of civility. Northerners-as-tribes are living amid the potential for advanced *watthanatham,* but for this potential to be transformed into real *charoen,* a greater person must realize this. Such a trickle-down flow of *watthanatham* parallels Lucien Hanks' model of Thai power: just as those with money and status are best positioned to understand and articulate merit (Hanks 1962), so those from the city are best able to understand and articulate *watthanatham*. It is those professionals to whom I now turn.

ARCHITECTURE

Lanna Modern

The ASA's 2007 conference focused on the future of the Lanna Style trend in architecture. An assumption behind the meeting was that Lanna-themed architecture had reached a crisis point. After Lanna Style had been the dominant trend in the 1990s, promoted by the wave of academic interest in Lanna at Chiang Mai University as well as by the Ministry of the Interior in Bangkok, architects grew bored with it. At the conference, a panel of young and stylish architects assembled on stage. They were preparing to discuss their proposals for redesigning the future city when Sulak, an older architect, leapt up from the front row and grabbed the microphone. He held it close to his mouth, causing his voice to boom out across the lecture hall. The moderator made a perfunctory motion to take the microphone away from him, but the older man persisted, proclaiming:

> I have been tricked [*lok*] by my teachers! They should have told me that I have only three options: to study abroad, to go to work in Bangkok, or to be a teacher. But instead I tried to be an architect here in Chiang Mai. It's a trick! It's so hard to find work, and what work you do find doesn't pay! Now people always use modern styles [of architecture]. Who knows Lanna-ness [*khwam pen khon* Lanna] or Thainess more than we [those born and educated in Chiang Mai]? We have had seven hundred years to develop architecture; why do we now have to follow trends from *farang?* Local architects don't do anything for the local society!

After this interruption, the moderator reclaimed the microphone and Sulak sat down. Sulak had pointed to the fault lines running through the ASA. His rhetorical "Who knows Lanna-ness . . . ?" was barbed as, of the architects seated on stage, a distinct minority were Northern, most had been educated in Bangkok, and Central Thai was the language of the seminar. His accusation that the architects simply followed Western styles had weight, as those on stage were the voices of Chiang Mai's new avant-garde—an avant-garde that recast "Lanna" in terms of concrete, metal, and glass, with teak and gold accents. In calling for local autonomy and an emphasis on a Northern essentialism, Sulak had echoed the voices of urban activists, provincial officials, and academics involved in local cultural movements. His model of "Lanna-ness" would be one where local artisans and local architects re-created a shaded village of teak-walled stilt-houses with crossed gables (*kalae*).

The panel convened, ignoring Sulak's comments, but they hung there in the background, marking stark contrasts between the two points. The moderator followed Sulak by discussing "Lanna Brand" (in English) as a new alternative to "Lanna Style." Wit, a young architect known for his redesigned shop-houses with bright pastel interiors, groaned with frustration. While he did not look at Sulak, his comments seemed directed toward him: "Lanna is a boring topic! Lanna architecture is a metaphor for Thai people. The surface is first, the substance is second.[9] [You say that you] want Lanna? Put a *kalae* [crossed gables] on it. Finished! Modern? Traditional? It's all the same!"

Tong, a young architect I came to know quite well, piped up, again indirectly addressing Sulak. "*Khwam pen* [the essence; something-ness] reflects the life of people in that age. . . . Look at the space, the function, the culture [*watthanatham*] of that time period. It's up to the owner to decide how he wants to be. Are we modern [using the English word] or Lanna? We're not modern. We're Chiang Mai people [*khon* Chiang Mai]. The designs that we're doing will reflect this time in our history."

Tong was echoing the frustration felt by many in Chiang Mai's artistic community in their attempts to resist the orientalized, allochronous image of Chiang Mai in such representations as *Sao Khrua Fa* or *The Memory*. Instead, he advocated a distinct "Chiang Mai," one that was not "modern" but also was not allochronous. Indeed, Tong argued passionately against using the term "modern" or its Thai equivalent, *thansamai* (up-to-date), to describe his works. Yet when one was looking at some of his projects, it became hard to imagine exactly what was not "modern" about his architectural style. The structures were reminiscent of those of Alvar Aalto in their glossy concrete surfaces. He specialized in long rectangular tubes of concrete, with one or two of the walls consisting wholly of plate glass. Interior surfaces were often bare glass and concrete polished to a green-gray shine, with raw metal or wood highlights. They had a cool, high-tech feel to them, offset by occasional strips of dark metal or wood set into the poured concrete. Glass-topped tables increased the spare effect; simple woven area rugs warmed it. We continued the conversation in one of his cafés, on an upper floor looking down on to fashionably dressed diners below through the plate glass, Tong was adamant: his work was *not* modern.

What, then, did "modern" mean to Tong? Did he mean a certain architectural period? A particular trend? Neither, he responded. Instead, he described "modern" in terms very like those of Sulak or Aek (at the provincial cultural office).

When I think of "modern," I think of those concrete boxes. There's no feeling in them. There's no *art* [*using the English word*]. There is no connection with the place or with the *watthanatham* of the city. I want Chiang Mai not to be considered *phumiphak* [provincial], but instead *buriphak* [a play on the term "provincial," replacing *phumi*—land—with *buri*—city]. Too many people just follow foreign trends. What people do in Japan or Germany isn't right for Chiang Mai. But we need to create a new Chiang Mai architecture, one that reflects Chiang Mai-ness. [*Referring to those like Sulak*] Why can other people do it and Chiang Mai can't?

Even though he is criticizing Sulak, Tong echoes some of Sulak's points. He rejects "modern" as something that rejects past ways of being or is derivative from foreign trends. Instead, he maintains that he, in his own way, is channeling Chiang Mai-ness (*khwam pen* Chiang Mai), articulating the new zeitgeist of the city. I repeatedly challenged him on this point. "So what is the connection," I asked him on several occasions as we toured his new and past buildings, "between this [building] and Chiang Mai-ness?" Tong responded enthusiastically but often grew frustrated with my skepticism. "It is a *chill-chill* [*using the English word*] space." "It is *sabai* [relaxed]. *Relax* [*using the English*]."

As we stood in front of one of his buildings, a raised wooden and concrete structure that was to be a Japanese restaurant and a coffee shop, I asked him:

AAJ: What makes this place "Chiang Mai" and [another nearby tropical-lounge-designed coffee shop] "in *farang* style"?

Tong [*sighing*]: Do you think that *farang* are the only people who live in air-conditioned buildings and drive cars?

AAJ: Of course I don't think that, but I meant to say . . .

Tong: Lanna cannot be a *frozen form* [*using English*]. Nowadays Chiang Mai people don't live in traditional buildings! Those were good in the past, they let the breeze in. But now they are too hot! Roofs made of leaves were natural. But they let the rain in! Chiang Mai people now, they turn on air-conditioning and want concrete walls and [solid] roofs.

AAJ: This building here [the Japanese restaurant /coffee shop structure]. Why wouldn't you call that modern [*thansamai*]?

Tong [*smiling*]: I don't like to call this a modern [*thansamai*] space. We are Chiang Mai people. Our architects [*referring to himself*] are Chiang Mai people. Our builders are Chiang Mai people. Chiang Mai is a city of culture [*mueang haeng watthanatham*], and you can see it reflected in our work [i.e., here].

AAJ: But where?
Tong [waving a hand toward the structure]: Everywhere.
AAJ [peering closer at the structure]: Where?
Tong [frowning]: Maybe you have to be a Northerner.

In this exchange, Tong could not understand why I couldn't see the *watthanatham* in his work or why I seem determined to link his work with other international trends. When I described his concrete blocks as "modern," Tong rejected my assessment. "Chiang Mai" cannot be "modern," as "modern" for Tong implies a break with the past. Instead, he sees his own work as somehow continuing a Chiang Mai zeitgeist, something unique but never static. In doing so, he rehashes ideas about Thai *watthanatham,* and by passing off as "cultural" the very concrete squares that he criticizes in other places, displays the "crypto-colonialism" (Herzfeld 2002) of his own concepts of culture and modernity. He maintains, like Wichit, that his architecture was always latent in the North, that its realization here is the result of a natural process of becoming.

Tong, like the other architects in his community, sees himself as the privileged medium of this becoming, articulating the past for the benefit of the future. He was not alone in this. Tong's projects were key sites in the growth of Nimmanhaemin Road, a locale of rapid expansion in Chiang Mai's western edge. The editor of a popular Chiang Mai magazine raved, "I have lived around Nimmanhaemin Road for ten years now and I have felt impressed by the prosperity [*charoen*] and diverse [*chiwit chiwa*] growth of Nimmanhaemin Road—it's the one place to live in Chiang Mai!" (Punna 2009). During my fieldwork, the road became a place to see and be seen. Local celebrities (such as the comic Udom "Nose" Taepanich) lived along the road, and Japanese restaurants and Italian coffee shops proliferated there. Joe, the artist who fancied himself a farmer, spent his weekends on Nimmanhaemin and brought his work down there to sell, along with many other artists. Chim, the woman with the bead shop who feared her gated community, also lived and worked on the street. In other words, it was the center of Chiang Mai's bourgeois urban community.

Possessed by Chiang Mai

Joe, like Tong, felt at home on Nimmanhaemin Road. He was born in Kanchanaburi Province but moved to Bangkok when he was still quite young. There, he attended college and afterwards became something of a socialite, forming relationships with people in the Thai television and film industry while working on his art. But then something happened.

"I started having pains in my ribs. I had no idea why, but it was getting impossible for me to breathe. I went to the doctor, but he couldn't figure it out. Only after talking with a friend who had moved out to the countryside [*tang changwat*] did I realize that it was because I wasn't breathing in fully. The air in Bangkok was so bad. My body realized it before I did—I was taking short, shallow breaths. Like this [*gulps*]. Then I knew that I had to get out of Bangkok, or I might die." He moved to Chiang Mai with his partner to a house in the suburb of Mae Rim, an area popular with wealthy Central Thais, and used his land there as an art studio and a place to entertain guests. "Here," he said about his new life, "I can finally relax. Here, it's like Bangkok, but without all of the bad points. ["Like what?" I asked.] People are nicer, slower. People in Bangkok have no manners. They are only concerned with themselves. Here, you have culture, civility, it is easy to live [*yu sabai*]."

Joe's discourse oddly mirrors Kham's. He has a pain in his chest. He knows that it might kill him. He visits the doctor, who cannot help him. It is only through consulting with another who has had similar problems that he recognizes the true source of his pain. He accepts his affliction as a problem with his orientation to space and adopts the same lifestyle as the friend in order to correct it. Joe also contradicts himself. On many other occasions, he openly mocked Northern Thais as "buffaloes" and as "not knowing what to do with the city." In other words, Joe presents himself as being the person who knows, who can make the most out of the potential that the city has to offer. He alone (and other artists in his community) has the cultural capital to make Lanna into what it should be. He is the one who can properly see and guide Chiang Mai toward *charoen*. He is the farmer who knows how to properly use the power of the buffaloes.

Building Lanna Community

Nimmanhaemin Road, for Joe, was where this development was made manifest. Noise was constant, as if growth itself was a noisy business. Construction began on new high-rises along the street at eight a.m. and lasted until late in the evening. After work, in the late-day heat, there was a brief lull, and the sound of jackhammers changed to clanking dishes and occasional Shan-language songs coming from builders' compounds next to construction sites. At ten at night, live music from the bars along the street competed with the sound of drunken patrons. Haphazard boom-time zoning patterns contributed to the chaos. One older resident, a schoolteacher who had lived on the street for nearly fifteen years, complained to me that the neighboring bar had put a live band five feet from her bedroom window. The bars wound down at two or three a.m., occasionally spilling brawls, arguments, or motorbike races out onto the street. In the dead of night there were a few short hours of silence, briefly interrupted by the howl of a stray dog or the cry of a rooster from a Shan workers' compound.

These workers were building a new high-rise compound to be called the "Punna." While the site itself was unremarkable,[10] billboards for the construction were placed at each major intersection in the city. Attractive Caucasian[11] women dressed in long coats strolled out of their ads with the confident, if slightly ambiguous slogan in English, "Lock and Leave." The designer, though, saw more than just another cosmopolitan space in his project. Rather, the Punna was to be a key point articulating Lanna, with its international destiny of *charoen.* He boasted that it was going to "transform Nimmanhaemin into Thong Lor"—a fashionable section of Bangkok. The project was to be a pivotal point in Nimmanhaemin's becoming. The project's Thai-language statement read:

> "Punna"[12] in the ancient Thai meaning means *"mueang,"* or "community" and is the basis for the name "Punna Residence," arising from [a combination of] the atmosphere of the Lanna community [*chumchon Lanna*] mixed with the way of life of modern people [*yut mai*—"of the new time"]. These combined to create a community [*chumchon*] of modern people [*khon thansamai*] who have convenience, comfort, style, and safety that you can be confident of, with the generosity of the people of Lanna. (Punna 2009)

The English-language statement is also illuminating:

> Punna is a Thai Lanna word meaning town, or community, something which the creators of Punna Residence firmly believes [*sic*] in building. Punna Residence aims to create a community for people who wish to enjoy comfort, convenience, luxury and security in their live [*sic*]. (Punna 2009)

In the first description, the designer highlights the "Northern" aspects of Punna life and the fact that, by living there, one can be part of the Lanna community—a community that, it should be noted, is in the Web-site text mutually exclusive with being "modern": the site specifies that the Punna will take the Lanna way of life and "blend" it with a modern one (*thansamai,* the same word that figures so prominently in Mary Beth Mills' ethnography [1999]).

For Tong, Joe, and the Punna developer, Nimmanhaemin is a crucial step in Lanna's becoming. They reject suggestions that Chiang Mai's growth alters what they see to be the essence of Northern Thai *watthanatham.* Rather, growth realizes it. Just as Wichit imagined Sukhothai as prefiguring Fascist

Italy, so Nimmanhaemin was always latent in Chiang Mai. Indeed, Tong and Joe both rejected the claims of anti-sprawl NGOs as attempting to prevent Chiang Mai from achieving *khwam charoen*—as Tong put it, placing Chiang Mai in a "frozen form." As Wichit would have it, it is alteration and change, not stability, that are at the root of *watthanatham.*

Lanna and Royalism

While Nimmanhaemin's development came from various national and international large businesses (like Tong's company and the Punna developer), the state was not exempt from actively trying to mobilize *watthanatham* for the sake of *charoen* in Chiang Mai. Thaksin and his local allies in the political and business community planned to turn a large part of the Doi Suthep/Doi Pui national park into a kind of Lanna Disneyland, a "Chiang Mai World. " This would combine four major attractions. First, Thaksin proposed to build a night safari, modeled on Singapore's tourist attraction.[13] Second, the Chiang Mai World project would feature an elephant camp where tourists could ride elephants and see elephant shows. Third, there would be a new cable car climbing the peak of Doi Suthep to increase tourist traffic to the temple. Fourth, Thaksin proposed a floral exposition, a shrine to the Thai royalty. The whole project, in theory, was to be a refurbishing of Chiang Mai's tourist industry, one that would attract wealthy foreign as well as Thai tourists to the area, increasing income by moving the industry away from thrifty backpackers and toward wealthier spa-going Europeans, Chinese, and Japanese (characterized by the Tourist Authority of Thailand as tourists "with value [*khun kha*]").

The Chiang Mai World project encountered stiff opposition from many local groups. Some opposed Thaksin's proposals on a larger scale, such as northern chapters of the People's Alliance for Democracy. Other concerned groups included academics and activists who were worried about overdevelopment in the Chiang Mai area, especially near the peaks of Doi Suthep (home of the city's principal temple) and Doi Kham (home of Grandmother and Grandfather Sae), which were protected forest areas. On a practical level, anti–Chiang Mai World groups attacked the amount of water the projects would drain from the mountains' aquifers, the symbolic effects of the proximity of these projects to the sacred peaks, the scale of corruption in the projects' administration,[14] and the wear and tear on the city's infrastructure that masses of expected tourists would inflict. Ultimately, they argued, the local population would reap only the disadvantages of the projects and see none of the benefits. Such protests were harbingers of the conflict that would oust Thaksin in 2006 and that continue to divide the country to the present day.

Despite the increasing opposition, Wilangkha's jungle on the slopes of Doi Kham was cut down, the Night Safari was built (and opened in February 2006), and Royal Flora Ratchaphruek begun. Extensive sections were slashed out of the jungle on Doi Suthep, ostensibly to control wildfires blamed on hill-tribe minorities but rumored to be in preparation for the as yet unbuilt elephant camp and cable cars. It was in the midst of this construction, just two months before the opening of the Royal Flora Ratchaphruek site, that the Thai military under General Sonthi Boonyaratglin (and, it is widely rumored, at the behest of the king) instigated their coup d'état. Though the elephant camp and cable car were scrapped and the Night Safari sidelined in importance,[15] Ratchaphruek went on as scheduled, albeit with a makeover from the new government.

The expo opened in 2006, right on schedule. As the place became a rallying spot for yellow-shirted royalists, it quickly lost whatever association it had with Thaksin. My object here is to examine Ratchaphruek and its central Lanna-style "Golden Hall" as it was perceived by my informants and those working at the site. I see it as a pilgrimage destination, a place that had quickly risen to a central position in the construction of Chiang Mai's *barami,* and had just as quickly been abandoned. As such, it is a potent example of the construction of potential fortune and potential ruin.

During the time the exhibition was open, I visited Ratchaphruek three times in the company of local tourists (once with Fah, a middle-aged woman from Fang district and her American boyfriend, Bruce; once with Maew, a graduate student at Chiang Mai University taking her family around Chiang Mai from their home province of Udon Thani; and once with Noi, Kham's daughter, in addition to talking with a number of visitors from Chiang Mai and elsewhere about their experience). After the exhibition had closed, I regularly visited the site and talked with employees and local sightseers as the Ministry of Agriculture attempted to figure out what to do with it.

To create Ratchaphruek, the ministry invited investors from some of the largest companies operating in Thailand, including the Boonrawd Beverage Company (Singha Beer), the Thai power company, Toyota, and others, as well as several nations—Iran, Kenya, Japan, the Netherlands, and Turkey, among others—to build gardens, as the department invited, "to express respect for HM the King or highlight historic links between His Majesty's royal activities [between these activities and just what remained unspecified]" (Royal Flora 2007).[16] For Thai audiences, the international pavilions reinforced the idea (continually reiterated in royal-related news) that the king was revered internationally as well as in Thailand: these pavilions were smaller and subordinate to the royal one, and each was required to show its relationship to the king's activities. Here, the king was presented as a source of knowledge and merit extending to a worldwide network.

The site was named after the national flower (*Cassia fistula,* the "Golden Shower tree"). I was told that this flower had been chosen because its color is the hue of both Buddhism and the king, and because the tree's flowers bloom all at once, which is intended to represent the spiritual and royalist unity of Thais.[17]

The center of the site was the Golden Hall,[18] a shrine built of teak (figure 9). Its architect told me that the Northern style with its Burmese influence was perfect as a symbol for the project: "The Lanna style *ho kham* has its inspiration from Burma, you know? That's what makes it so perfect for the project. Here, in the heart of the region, we have a building that combines all of the elements that comprise Lanna: from Thailand and all the provinces of the north and Burma as well. We wanted it to be a symbol to unite Suvarnabhumi,[19] especially Burma and Thailand, where there's been so much strife."

A shrine for the king in "Lanna style" as a unifying image for the entire region may at first appear incongruous—why should the Burmese and Lao care about the Thai monarch? One interpretation would echo Wichit's proposal for an ethnic unity for all Tai groups (including Shan, Lao, Dai, etc.) under the

FIGURE 9 | Golden Hall of Ratchaphruek

aegis of Thailand. But more than such a call for ethno-nationalism, these were images for the royalty, touted as the center of Theravada Buddhism, the religion of Burma, Laos, and Cambodia as well as Thailand. In this way, ethno-nationalism and Thai irredentism fuse with the divine right of a Theravada Buddhist king—the architect implies that Theravada Buddhist Burmese, Laos, and Cambodians would naturally feel drawn toward the figure of the Thai king as a demigod (see Jackson 2010)—indeed, the Ratchaphruek Web site addresses him explicitly as "a devaraja, a divine king."[20] For those visiting the shrine as a site of pilgrimage, the shrine of the king in Lanna style reinforces the notion that Central Thai power remains ascendant. Just as in Condominas' idea of *emboîtement,* where the city replicates the heavens and the village replicates the city, Ratchaphruek's pavilion was a reminder that Bhumibol was the true source of *barami* for the North.

Ratchaphruek officially opened on the first of November 2006. For those in Chiang Mai, the opening was heralded by a flood of Thai tourists: based on figures provided to me by the Tourist Authority of Thailand, while foreign tourist numbers decreased from 2005 to 2007, presumably owing to fears about the coup, Thai tourists increased to three times the amount of 2005. Especially in and around the streets that cater to Thai tourists, such as Nimmanhaemin, new condominiums and hotels attempted to cash in on the boom with names like the "Chiang Mai Flora."

Yet the proposed images often differed from the reality. While promotional materials depicted a cool, misty mountain paradise, echoing *Sao Khrua Fa,* the midday temperature often broke thirty degrees Celsius. The exhibition's namesake flower, a yellow blossom echoing the color of the tourists' shirts, failed to appear on the plants in the exhibit owing to the heat. Farther off, in Mae Hong Son Province, tourists flocked to view the yellow flowers on the slopes of mountains, but in the hot Ping river valley, these plants remained dormant and had to be chemically dosed in order to coax out a brief blossom for the crown prince's visit. Visitors had also been enticed by the picture of a field of tulips in the Dutch exhibit, which was intended to be a draw to the international gardens. These tulips were dutifully planted but subsequently died in the heat. A new crop was planted for the prince's visit, but after these also died, the actual flowers were replaced by a giant poster of tulips.

The heat and the crowds were the primary complaints of the people I talked with both in and out of Ratchaphruek. After midday the wide-open thoroughfares and plazas thronged with people became unbearably hot. As the asphalt paths in the exhibition were too hot to walk on even in the evening, tourists stayed on the tram or hid in the scant shade provided by trees flanking the path. The large, open-air theater (featuring tribal dances), lake, and fountain remained mostly empty, but the plaza in front of the royal pavilion, the *ho kham,* was flooded with visitors, tourists standing there to take pictures before heading inside to the shade.

Each of these miscalculations involved planners from the Ministry of Agriculture having relied too heavily on their fantasy of a cool, misty Chiang Mai. As the rock-band singer who exclaimed, "Chiang Mai is so cold we don't need to go to Europe," or the films *The Letter* or *The Memory* imply, Chiang Mai is a cold place. This image becomes powerful: when discussing rumors of a planned outdoor ski resort in Chiang Mai during a conference in Washington, DC, one Thai university student from Bangkok cited her superior knowledge of Thailand by telling me that this sort of project wasn't as ridiculous as it sounded. Snows, according to her, were common in Chiang Mai[21]—a statement that is, of course, false (but I, the foreigner, was in no position to tell her, the Thai national, this).

Many Chiang Mai residents were given free tickets by their employers, valid for a certain month, and for my first trip I accepted one of these from Lung. In fact, nearly all my middle-class informants in Chiang Mai had received a large bundle of these from friends, work, or family and were eager to dispense them to anyone who seemed interested. Many of them had not been to the exhibition and were not planning to go but were very interested in having me go and visit. On giving me my ticket, Lung spent nearly thirty minutes lecturing me about the marvels of the exhibition. "They have nearly four hundred *rai*[22] of flowers!" he said, then went on to tell me about all the work engineers and planners had done to design the exhibit. Finally, he added, "and make sure you see the tulips!" After I returned, Lung questioned me about my experience, then confided that he hadn't in fact gone himself and didn't plan to, as seeing it on the TV was "good enough."[23]

On the highway to the exhibition, blue signs directed tourists toward the site, which was roughly twenty minutes away, at the base of Doi Kham. Buses left the city from large hotels or the new Tesco Lotus shopping center, but from other spots (such as the city center or Kat Luang market) one had to take a private taxi. The road to Ratchaphruek from the highway was lined with footpaths and banners depicting the royal family, although the footpaths led from the park to nowhere, extending alongside the road to the highway—not a place where one could walk. In front of the entrance, large letters displayed the name of the site in Thai: "Ratchaphruek 2549."[24] One road headed out toward the Night Safari; a second led to the Doi Kham temple; and the central route led into the floral exhibition, passing manicured lawns and artificial hills. Prominently displayed near the entrance was the slogan: *Rak pho, pho phiang* ("Love Father [the king]. . . . Sufficiency").[25] This was a reference to the Thai king and his Sufficiency Economy Philosophy (SEP: *sethakit pho phiang*), a call following the 1997 economic crisis that emphasized self-reliance and drew upon notions of Buddhist economics (Keyes 2013). Critics (Walker 2010) argued that SEP discouraged social mobility and misrepresented rural livelihoods, although criticism of SEP inside Thailand was muted owing to the country's harsh lèse-majesté laws.

Once one had parked and was inside, one had to stand in long lines: first an entrance line, then one to board the tram or private electric car. All told, on my trips the initial waits lasted an average of two to three hours. Visitors packed the entrance area, the majority of them wearing yellow shirts with "We love the King" emblazoned on them (figure 10).

As later events would dramatically prove, the yellow shirts were far more than a fashion statement.[26] Royal astrologers had predicted that yellow was a prosperous color for the king, and as such the choice to wear it became a display of piety, as anthropologist Pattana Kitiasara has argued, especially when coupled with the booming Chatukam Ramathep amulets that had become popular that year (Pattana, pers. comm. 2007). According to Pattana, wearing the shirt and the Chatukam amulet were a way in which middle-class or

FIGURE 10 | Crowds of tourists arrive at Ratchaphruek

lower-middle-class Thais could directly involve themselves with the nation and with magical means of bolstering their luck. At a time of political crisis and a growing sense of economic malaise, a means by which Thais felt they could take concrete action was in this public display of Buddhist faith and monarchical sentiment.[27] (The costume was to change dramatically, however, when the yellow shirt became associated with the PAD in later 2007 and 2008.)

Back in the main square of the exhibition, we piled onto the electric tram, which wound back and forth around the country pavilions. The tram conductor roughly allowed time enough for an introduction to each pavilion and added a sentence or two, occasionally poking fun at the problems of the exhibition, for example: "To the left we have the Dutch pavilion, and look at all the lovely tulips! Look at all those tulips! No, it's just a photograph, ladies and gentlemen, no tulips here. . . ."

The passengers on the tram on each of my trips during the park's opening uniformly stayed seated, glancing to either side as Iran, Turkey, or Kenya rolled by. On all of my visits, the day was simply too hot to walk on the asphalt roads winding in between gardens (later, during my trip with Fah, after she and Bruce had left and I was alone, I braved the heat and saw the country pavilions in turn). But shortly thereafter, the tram emerged from the maze of country-specific pavilions to reveal a dramatic view of the royal *ho kham* with the green backdrop of Doi Kham. Here, the visitors sprang to life and left the tram to head over the bridge to the royal pavilion, many pausing to take a picture in front of the pavilion. In each case, my informants did likewise.

The hilltop temple of Doi Kham visible behind and above the *ho kham* and the floral exhibition showed the differences, at least aesthetically speaking, between the two sites. The *ho kham* was made of dark teak, the chocolate-cinnamon color contrasting with the bright white, unpainted statues of religious creatures (guardian *yak*, lions, etc.) dancing outside it. The stark whiteness of the statues echoed the aesthetics of another new Northern pilgrimage site, Wat Rong Khun in Chiang Rai Province, designed with the same style of realistic yet uncolored statues in the same blinding white (a color notoriously requiring a lot of labor to keep clean in the sooty, damp Chiang Mai air). In contrast, the part of Doi Kham—home of shrines to Camadevi, Wilangkha, Wasuthep, and Grandfather and Grandmother Sae—that was visible to the exhibition was the gigantic concrete Buddha, simply made and brightly painted, with its bright-red lips, yellow robe (the paint chipping and cracked from the weather), and a pleased-looking smile. The contrast between *ho kham* and the Buddha was dramatic: the first showed Lanna and Lanna-style aesthetics as imagined by Chiang Mai's "educated" classes; the second, religious aesthetics as imagined by others in the local population.

The *ho kham* was a space devoted to the current monarch—indeed, while the entire exhibition was space devoted to the monarchy, the *ho kham* was the part where the monarch's presence and *barami* were most manifest. As such, this was the centerpiece for visitors: whereas the gardens, with their open plazas and bright sun, were only moderately crowded even during the height of the exhibition, and the country pavilions remained largely ignored, the *ho kham* was, for most, according to tourist surveys filled out by visitors leaving the park, the sole stop they made in the place. It was not only the symbolic heart of the exhibition, for the majority of visitors it was the exhibition itself.

I made this stop in a group of Thai visitors on each trip. In the pavilion, the first floors were devoted to the king's royal projects and to art devoted to the king. The former included irrigation projects, agricultural projects, hill-tribe development projects, and the king's SEP theory. It was a simplifying and largely imagined picture of rural life. For instance, one artist, having painted a portrait of a hill-tribe woman harvesting coffee, claimed that it was "[p]resented from the angle of Thai hill type people from the far areas, who live in peace, simplicity and happiness by following the advice of the King's speech concerning the sufficiency economy," implying that the tribes' poverty was a result of a conscious choice to abstain, and that their frugality was a demonstration of their royal piety. Outside the gallery, in the hall devoted to the sufficiency economy, posters explained not only the concept but also the various applications of the theory to different professions. A poster detailed the application of SEP to teachers, academics, business people, farmers, and so forth, each exhorting the individual not to reach beyond his or her means, and to realize his or her role in society.

But the center of the exhibition was not this display of royal development projects. The *ho kham* was a shrine, not a museum. Above the SEP exhibit was the teak structure of the *ho kham*, its walls lined with paintings evoking a Buddhist temple, and at its center, a tree fashioned from various precious metals, designed after the gold and silver trees presented to Siamese kings as tribute during the feudal period (figure 11). This particular one had leaves of copper, gold, and platinum, representing the progression of royal thinking during the sixty years of Bhumibol's reign. This tree was at the center of Ratchaphruek—the primary gift to the monarchy from the Ministry of Agriculture. Observation of and controls over visitors were at their height here, at the center of *watthanatham*'s disciplining gaze. After moving around in a long line to the entrance and removing our shoes, we climbed the stairs into the main hall. Inside, a red carpet lined the walls, and staff with megaphones chastised anyone who stepped too close to the carpet.

This room was the primary objective of those visitors with whom I attended as well as the site where the true purpose of the exhibition was shown. Noi removed her shoes and crowded into the sea of yellow-clad tourists, shuffling in front of the massive gold, copper, and platinum tree. She sat on the ground, hands folded in a *wai,* then bent forward in a manner similar to the respectful gesture she would have made to any other sacred image. She then had me take her picture in front of it, just as she had me take her picture in front of the *ho kham* outside. Here, at the center of Ratchaphruek, she was part tourist and part pilgrim, having come there not only to showcase her ability to identify and consume images but also to "brush against *barami*" (*chom barami*).

The connection between the monarchy and supernatural power is explicit in many circles, and certainly was with Noi. In the same way as other sources of *barami* such as famous monks, spirits, or images of the Buddha, stories abound of miraculous happenings associated with the king: for instance, amulets sold or given away by the palace showing the king's image that supposedly protect soldiers from bullets, the national lottery's selection of the number 999 on the king's birthday in 1999,[28] even the king's supposed ability to stop or cause a rain shower (Handley 2006, 436). At Ratchaphruek, the monarchy, dressed

FIGURE 11 | Tourists inside the Golden Hall

figuratively in Lanna style, has created another pilgrimage site, another place where royal *barami* is emitted and available to supplicants. At the point in time when it opened, in the wake of a coup and economic crisis, the place became a source of pilgrimage and comfort in a time of anxiety. Yet ironies were brewing. The site that was intended to be a demonstration of Thaksin's grand vision had turned into the rallying place for a group that would turn out to be anti-Thaksin. And, finally, that site which was to be a booming, "sustainable" tourist draw for the North closed its doors on January 31, 2007. As the hot season drew near and the low tourist season began, the flowers continued to be watered and the grounds taken care of but visitors were barred. Later, in 2010 and 2011, Ratchaphruek reopened in a more limited capacity as a center for royal-related activities and assemblies. But in the hot season of 2007 its future was uncertain.

During this time in early 2007, I sat for several days at the front desk of the exhibition, talking with tourists and the workers at the desk and occasionally wandering around the mostly empty site. The international exhibits and much of the other exhibits were closed and untended, and stray dogs from the neighboring area had crept in. Many of my informants in Chiang Mai city were doubtful about the future of the site, saying that no one knew what was to be done about it and no one wanted the responsibility of paying for its maintenance. The new font of *khwam charoen* had become a ruin. But despite the wild dogs and weeds, the site retained its function as a site of royal pilgrimage.

On a hot day in March, I sat with Phetch, the day manager at Ratchaphruek. The weather had turned hot, anticipating the scorching months of April and May. We sat at a table under some umbrellas, acting as gate guards for those visiting the site. Attendance in those days was usually between ten and thirty people, some having travelled some distance to get there, others from the neighborhood seeking an early-morning walk. For Phetch, her assistant, and me, this meant plenty of time to talk.

During its construction, many anti-sprawl groups had targeted Ratchaphruek as a place of corruption , framed either in terms of the English loanword *khorapchan* or the more direct "inappropriate, ugly" (*mua*). After Thaksin's ouster, when the site became more explicitly tied to the monarchy, these criticisms became more muted, but privately many still pointed to the abandoned site as a place of waste. Trying to get at these issues, I asked Phetch how she would characterize Doi Kham in the past, before Ratchaphruek's construction.

Phetch shrugged. "Nothing was here."

"What, though?" I pressed. I was playing dumb. At that point I knew quite well that the site had been converted from a national park to the floral exhibition, but I was interested in Phetch's response of "Nothing."

"Was there forest? Farmland?"

"Exactly!" she responded. "It had no value [*khun kha*]. Now, look around yourself!"

She pointed across the square to the green artificial hills rolling in front of the naturally formed peak of Doi Kham. In the foreground was a strip of perhaps thirty small concrete stalls, of which four were open. The national and corporate gardens were abandoned and withering in the heat, and walking on my own through them I had seen stray dogs building dens in the brush. But Phetch was pointing past all of this to the main approach to the *ho kham*, which had been newly lined with dark-green plants better able to handle the heat. Pointing out the ruined edges as I had was to miss the point, according to Phetch. The heart, the shrine to the monarchy, was still there.

As if to reinforce Phetch's point, as we were talking about the shrine we were approached by a well-dressed older Thai woman. "I am *very* impressed!" she began. "Do you know, we just went to Buckingham Palace in England and they charge twenty pounds to get in! But it was nothing compared to this! Those countries think that they have so much, but they don't have anything to compare to here." Concerns about corruption, the loss of national park land, and the sheer waste of all that space now home to weeds and stray dogs were swept away by the united image of a grand, developed spectacle in the heart of the North. Again, Chiang Mai had become Europe, only a Europe purged of its faults—for instance, Europe charges visitors money to approach the centers of royal prestige; Lanna does not.

Here, Ratchaphruek is, on a larger scale, what condominiums such as the Punna are: contested symbols of *charoen*. Indeed, in the case of Ratchaphruek, it is a site where a new source of supernaturally conceived prosperity has been founded, yet one dressed in the style of a past age. The past (the Lanna-style *ho kham*) and the future (e.g., the king's development projects), are both rendered as mutually commensurable ideal types—echoing Choke's comment about Chiang Mai's urban aesthetics, "The future will go back to the past." For many of the visitors, like the wealthy woman who had been to London, Ratchaphruek was proof of Chiang Mai's entrance into the realm of developed, *charoen* places, and her comparison to Buckingham Palace recalled royalists' emphasis on the Thai king's seniority over other monarchs (at the time of this writing, in 2013, he is the longest-reigning living monarch). For the developers, and for those for whom Ratchaphruek was a positive symbol, it became, like the Inthakin pillar, a font of *barami* and a place where the revitalization of

Chiang Mai was possible—a revitalization that fused the nation (the place was a government-funded and -run site), Buddhism (the *ho kham* was designed after a temple and a Buddhist *yak* guarded the site), and the monarch.

When the woman left, Phetch went on to tell me how Ratchaphruek was to be the vanguard of a new Chiang Mai, one that would have its roots in a more aesthetic way of being. In this, she echoed Joe and Tong. "You have development to the north—there is Mae Sa and Mae Rim," she said, referring to Joe's home neighborhood, a fashionable suburb with a number of five-star resorts and houses. "You have development to the east—there is Bo Sang [a tourist attraction involving umbrella making and other handicrafts], and to the west you have Doi Suthep. But here, to the south, you don't really have anything. Now that we have built this [Ratchaphruek and the Night Safari], it has *charoen.* It is balanced—it is *pho phiang* [sufficient, referencing the royal 'sufficiency economy' edict]."

For the manager and the architect, Ratchaphruek would be a symbol that would bring "balanced" prosperity to the area, help to ease border tensions with Burma, and ultimately place another sacred site on Chiang Mai's map. And, indeed, this last is what happened. On Thai-language posters distributed by the city, Ratchaphruek's *ho kham* took its place next to other sites of religious pilgrimage: Doi Suthep temple, the Inthakin pillar, and a statue of Khruba Siwichai. Ratchaphruek, for city officials and visitors such as Noi at least, was not secular space. Rather, it was a point on a trajectory linking the *barami* of Lanna's past to the present and the *barami* of the Thai king to the North.

THE MALLEABILITY OF LANNA

In each of Chiang Mai's shopping malls, there is a section devoted to Lanna-style goods. In one, the *kat mueang* ("city market," using the Northern Thai term for "market" instead of the Central *talat*), a vendor described to me her *temari.*[29] A *temari* is a traditional Japanese hand ball originally made from kimono scraps for children to play with, but the vendor was selling them as "Lanna-Thai *temari*"; indeed, a *temari* presented as a product explicitly marked as "Japanese" would not have been allowed to be sold in the section, as the managers insist that *kat mueang* products must be "Lanna." What, then, made these *temari* Thai or, as she suggested, "Lanna?" "I am Thai," the vendor explained, "and I am living now in Chiang Mai. So when I make these *temari,* I make them in a Thai way [*baep* Thai]." She did not elaborate on what "a Thai way" was; instead, she simply reiterated that she was indeed a Thai person and, although originally from the south, was now in Chiang Mai. In this case, it was ethnicity—*khwam pen* Thai—and the fact that the vendor lived in Chiang Mai, not any connection to tradition or a specific stylistic invention, that removed the national "Japanese" label from the *temari* and made them, according to her, a Lanna art form.

Such an explanation—"Thainess" being something invisible yet available simply by articulating that it exists, runs very close to Kasian Tejapira's characterization of "the postmodern of Thainess" (Kasian 2002). Kasian characterizes Thainess in its "fossilized form" as "ripped away from its traditional social contexts, deprived of its aura and turned into a free-floating signifier which can then be commodified by goods of any nationality" (Kasian 2002, 215). However, Kasian's analysis implies a previously existing pure state of Thainess—a creature must have once been alive in order to end up a fossil. But "Thainess" and "Lanna *watthanatham*" both are recent inventions, and whatever aura existed before (fetishized as the supernatural power of the city, for instance) was a continually changing entity.

While the *temari* vendor's specific explanation might have been forced owing to her need to highlight the "local" aspects of her products in order to obtain a stall in the Kat Mueang, other vendors offered similar explanations. Nu, a woman who sold higher-end clothing in a mixture of Lanna and contemporary or contemporary Asian styles, explained the process of negotiation between being local and being cosmopolitan: in order to sell goods in Kat Mueang, "you have to have something to do with local products and local culture. But if we were to sell people things that were in a very local style [*phuen mueang dip dip*—lit.: "raw"], they wouldn't like it so much, so we have to mix things together [*prasom prasan*]. For instance, we might take a Lanna pattern or cloth and make a *kimono* out of it, like that. Here is just such a thing [she flipped through a rack of clothing]. And here are some local cloth patterns and we've made a Chinese-style blouse out of it."

Nu's products anticipate the fact that her customers—by her estimates half *farang* and half Thai "from another province"—are not actually interested in "raw" goods, but rather want something similar to what they know or what they expect: in Dennison Nash's terms, they must show "compatibility with metropolitan dreams" (Nash 1977, 38), or, in Nidthi's terms, they present an image of difference (Nidthi uses the term *khwam pen mueang nok*—"foreign-*mueang*-ness") which is different, but not too different from what the (Bangkokian) consumer expects (Nidthi, in Nathakan 2001, 14). But these alterations, according to Nu and the *temari* seller, can be made "Lanna-style" without damaging the content of "Lanna" or showing divisions between "Lanna style" and middle-class aesthetics. In this way, these new inventions are examples of *watthanatham* in its sense of a progression and orientation toward the assimilation of foreign and new goods. They highlight the unproblematic way in which invented traditions become read as "Lanna."

In these examples—the new construction boom of places such as Tong's new Lanna (but not "modern") structures, the Punna, film representations such as *The Memory,* and the Ratchaphruek exposition—as in the *temari* case, "Lanna" becomes cast in a certain way. Northern Thailand becomes a rung on the ladder of *khwam charoen.* For instance, Tong and the Punna developer see calling their constructions "Lanna" as a claim to their cultural authenticity and as a call to a pure, innocent state—a fresh start on a faster path to *charoen.* The plasticity of *watthanatham* (as both Wichit and the *temari* vendor demonstrate) allows it to be used to legitimate their desires for Lanna's commensurability with other discourses—be they international or national. And this is precisely what the National Museum and Ratchaphruek do: erasing a complicated and often contrary Northern Thai history, these nationalist recastings of Lanna adopt the Central Thai nation and monarchy as the destiny and ultimate realization of Lanna. Lanna, according to these readings, has always been waiting to become modern, to become Thai.

5

Rebuilding Lanna

The folk music duo Mai Mueang (Northern Wood) set up in the central night market every weekend as well as in their own restaurant to the north of the old city. The performers adopted a blend of American country and Northern Thai music styles—a blend not unfamiliar in Chiang Mai (see Ferguson 2011). The lead, Thiraphon Bunyaphonhom, sang in a soft, clear voice in a blend of Northern Thai and Central, with music that combined American folk tunes with Northern Thai instruments or melodies. The lyrics interspersed classic love ballads with songs about the disappearance of Northern culture. Jane Ferguson (2011) has written about Northern Thai folk music and argues that its tunes and themes approach Northern-ness from a point of similarity with American country and bluegrass music, distancing the listener and the musician from the other genres of Thai country music such as the more upbeat, dialect-heavy *mo lam* or *luk thung* music popular outside of the "educated classes" (and that Noi and Kham favored). Where Mai Mueang's songs differed from the folk music of Jaran Manopetch was in their focus on loss and displacement rather than celebration of the North's purity or innocence. For example, the song "Doi Suai, Nam Sai" (Beautiful Mountain, Clear Water) goes as follows:

The top of the beautiful mountain, bearing [the weight of] tall buildings.
The women of Doi Tung don't wear the striped skirt [*sin*].
Watthanatham is disappearing.
Lord Mangrai, your descendants have forgotten to pray to you. . . .

Those who come only think of profit,
Those who go escape to battle the jungle,
[The newcomers] destroy *watthanatham*.
[They] destroy Lanna.

As Thiraphon's lyrics indicate, architecture is the battleground for how best to realize Northern Thailand's transformation. She builds on a thirty-year tradition of protest against tall buildings in the city, especially buildings such as the Punna that stood close to religious or historical sites. This struggle began in 1985, when the first high-rise condominium building went up on the banks of the Ping River at the same time as the city gates were renovated. Response from local civil society was swift.[1] The building was denounced as *mua*—ugly, inappropriate—and the gates were blamed for the increase in AIDS in the city (Thammakian 1985; Thanet 1993, 91).

When ten new condominium projects were begun in 1989, opposition to the construction reached a key point. Anti-sprawl activists joined forces with monks and spirit mediums to perform a cursing ritual on the builders (Morris 2000, 274). The group's complaints were manifold. They included environmental (overuse of water, the blocking of airflow) and social concerns (anomie, loss of solidarity), but also concerns about the traditional hierarchy of space: as sacred things were properly above profane things, to build living quarters where people would sleep, eat, defecate, have sex, and the like looming above the spires of Buddhist temples or animist spirit shrines—or indeed merely above the heads of any passersby—was an affront and potentially dangerous (ibid.). The rite itself played upon similar juxtapositions of pure and impure—it was an active violation of taboos and the direction of the ensuing misfortune at the condominium builders. In the ritual, the ashes of those who died a "bad death" (*hong*) were exhumed and taken to the governor's mansion (Morris 2000, 275).

The conflict between condominium construction and opposition to it continued through the 1990s, reaching a peak during the administration of Thaksin Shinawatra (2001–2006). Thaksin's proposed "mega-projects" like Ratchaphruek suggested a new era of development for the North. In response, local academics such as Somchote and Sarasawadee Ongsakhul and Thanet and Duangchan Charoenmueang, as well as NGOs such as the Love Chiang Mai group, held seminars, published books and articles, and held protests against these and other projects, calling for a return to "Lanna" as a model of urban development superior to either Central Thai or Western models (Duangchan 2005).[2] Their lobbying led to a city planning ordinance that prevented the construction of tall buildings next to religious structures[3] or historical sites.[4]

The rationale behind this, according to Pornsuk, a city planner with the provincial government, was that a tall building next to a temple or the city wall would destroy the *watthanatham* of the city. "It would show that Chiang Mai people don't care about Chiang Mai's identity [*ekkalak*]." As she indicates, ideas of sacrality are not confined to the formally religious realm. As Peleggi describes (2002), planners searching for locations of cultural heritage often identified places of sacred power. In short, planners unified the magical with the nationalist-historical. Possessing *sak* and possessing *watthanatham* ultimately pointed to similar destinations.

But there was something deeper at work here than simply an attempt to stymie Thaksin's construction projects. If, as Pornsuk maintains, "Chiang Mai people" no longer cared about Chiang Mai's "identity," then why should they be affected by their disappearance? Her concern reflects another dimension, one that welds magico-religious notions of height to the ostensibly secular *watthanatham*.

An example of this merging of sacred and secular came during a conference between Japanese architects from the historical city of Nara and Thai architects concerning cultural heritage and tall buildings. The conference focused particularly on mountain peaks. For the Japanese architects, the problem lay in urban residents not being able to see the peak from the city center. Their solution involved a steady increase in the allowable height for buildings as one approached the peak. This would enable a person standing in the city center to see the mountain from any point and still allow for a large number of tall buildings around the city. The Thai architects in the room praised this plan and agreed that not being able to see Doi Suthep (although they specified *prathat* Doi Suthep—the spire of the temple, not the peak of the mountain) was their chief concern. But despite their praise of the Japanese solution, they proposed its exact opposite—namely, that buildings would rise in the city center but grow shorter, not taller, as they approached the peak.

In other words, despite their open expression of agreement with their Japanese colleagues, Thai architects were obviously not concerned about being able to *see* the temple from the city center. Rather, their principal concern—unvoiced in the conference but spoken in private afterwards in reference to the Japanese plan—was about profane space rising higher than sacred space.

"It is simply not appropriate [*mai mo*]," one architect told me. "Chiang Mai people are Buddhists." I protested that so were many Japanese, but he maintained that in the process of building near the mountain, "something" would be lost [*sia hai*]—society would break apart, the weather would turn hot, and the city would fall into ruins.

Urban design NGOs maintained that the key to saving Lanna was in its built environment, ensuring the proper growth of the city—a growth that in its basis had to be "Lanna." This paralleled other emphases on "culture"- or Buddhist-based approaches to development in Thailand (see Sulak 1992). It is a form of the same editing and reification that leads to the dismissal of opposing voices in favor of a "prefabricated past" (Herzfeld 2010, S265) that Michael Herzfeld describes elsewhere in Thailand (see also Herzfeld 2006).

During the late 1990s, in the economic boom that preceded the 1997 crash, this pressure was sufficient to induce the provincial governor[5] to issue a statement that buildings in the old city must "draw out the identity of Lanna-ness [*ok ekkalak khwam pen Lanna*]." In practice, this meant the application of crossed gables (*kalae*) to all buildings (figure 12), regardless of their architectural style.

There is nothing unique about this idea that national cultural sources must act as gatekeepers against the corrosive elements of globalization. Similar

FIGURE 12 | Examples of crossed-gable *kalae*

movements occur across Asia, from Vietnam's prohibitions on Western-derived "social evils" (Robert 2005) to Singapore's emphasis on the continuity of "Asian Values" (Zakharia 1994). In Thailand, this opposition to a vaguely defined "globalization" was institutionalized by the Office of the National Culture Commission. The ONCC stated that one of its core duties was to "[become] familiar with, [then selectively] choose [aspects of], and build upon foreign culture that is spreading in Thailand. The effects of this cultural exchange, [with the added caution of] scrutinizing and protecting against [possible] change, [will alter foreign culture] so that it is appropriate [to] the way of life of Thai people and the stability and safety of the nation" (accessed May 2010; translation mine). The charge of unmitigated acceptance of foreign values gained political cachet as well. After the 1997 economic crisis, Thai civil society[6] was badly frightened. International monetary networks had collapsed; the Thai baht and IMF reforms were widely recognized as exploitative (Pasuk and Baker 2010). In Bangkok, *watthanatham* was seen as the solution, with the king's SEP chief among these new cultural barriers against the effects of global capitalism. In Chiang Mai, SEP was widely disseminated and promoted among local NGOs. Opponents to the Thaksin regime used SEP as a means to cast Thaksin's globalization-oriented policies as un-Thai—as simply seeking *kan phatthana* without giving due attention to *khwam charoen*.

"WE HAVE NO SPIRITS AROUND HERE"

Anti-sprawl activists in Chiang Mai launched an aggressive campaign of promoting Lanna "local wisdom" (*phumpanya*) in the late 1990s and early 2000s against globalization and unchecked capitalism. From those neo-Marxists who follow the "Community Culture" school to those royalists who follow SEP, the revival of Lanna is a way to correct these flaws and relocate them in a more spiritual, purer, more "Thai" place. Just as, for Tong, the invocation of Lanna allows him to give cultural authenticity to something seemingly "global," so the invocation of Lanna allows local activists to adopt a stance that mirrors Western anti-globalization movements while setting itself apart. As in the links between Lanna and Europe I have detailed, one remakes Lanna into the proper image of *khwam charoen,* the Europe *that should have been.* In the cases upon which I draw upon in this chapter, this idea of Lanna is then deployed against the kinds of nationalist readings I have already described. To ensure the proper flow of *charoen,* one must revisit, revise, and edit the cultural archive of Lanna. One must remove those elements that are unenlightened or unknowingly foreign in order to get at the real progressive essence underneath.

Peter Jackson addresses this attention to the "image" of *charoen* by referring to what he calls the Thai "regime of images" (2004), a term he uses to refer to the Thai state's attempt to manage which images were seen by foreigners and which Thai people were permitted to see. As Jackson writes: "public discursive activity conducted under the regime [of images] is not directed toward the seeking out of the genuine essences of representations or discovering the truth of statements. Instead, it works to construct and uphold the relationally determined prestige or *barami* [charismatic power] of representations and statements" (Jackson 2004, 204).[7]

I would take the emphasis on spectacle a step further than Jackson does. On one hand, the effort to manage images extends, as I show here, far beyond the state. On the other hand, the logic of such an editing has its roots in magico-religious ideas of efficacy. As premodern urban planning recalled the *barami* of the Hindu heavens, so the current process of image production attempts to conjure a "Lanna Renaissance" by selecting some elements, denying others, and manufacturing still others (such as the *khantok*) out of whole cloth. My assumption that an undesirable element of "old" *watthanatham* had remained, just as I assumed that mediumship was going on in the teak-grove dance, was a sign that I did not understand the meaning of the new "Lanna" and that I had been distracted by its retrogressive elements.

A good example is when I was trying to make contact with the medium of the local spirit of Chiang Yuen neighborhood just north of Siphumi corner. There was a large spirit shrine in front of a square, well-kept and well-maintained, with a sign reading *San chao pho ban chiang yuen* (The Shrine of Lord Father of Chiang Yuen Neighborhood). The shrine was larger than Kham's—a white concrete structure roughly big enough for a person to stand in. Whether or not the spirit currently had a medium, someone around the neighborhood had to know about who took care of and maintained the shrine. I had previously asked around without any luck, but then I saw an old man cleaning the square. Excited, I called out to him (excerpt from my field notes):

AAJ: Excuse me, Uncle! Hello. Are you taking care of this shrine?
Uncle: [*No response*]
AAJ: I have come here because I am interested in spirit shrines [*san chao*] in Chiang Mai. Is this a spirit shrine [as I point to the sign that says "spirit shrine"]?
Uncle: [*No response*]
AAJ: I'm sorry to have disturbed you. Do you know what this place is? Do you know the history [*prawattisat,* the academic term for "history"] of this place?

Uncle: [*Looking up for the first time*] History? You should go to Chiang Man temple [the first temple in Chiang Mai and the first stop on historical tours of the city]. That's a lot better than here. There are many *farang* there. They have written things in *farang* language. [*He says this despite the fact that we are speaking Thai together. He then proceeds to give me directions back into the old city.*] Keep going until you see all the things in *farang* language.

AAJ: Oh, yes. I have been there, but today I'm interested in this place. I am interested in protective spirits of neighborhoods [*chao pho suea ban*].

Uncle: Spirits? We have no spirits around here.

AAJ: What about this place? It says on that sign *guardian spirit* of Chiang Yuen neighborhood [chao pho *ban* Chiang Yuen].

Uncle: No, we don't have them. Chiang Man Temple is that way [*again, he gives detailed directions*]. Keep going until you see signs in *farang* language. There are *farang* filling that space [*tem pai mot*].

AAJ: I will go. But first I am interested in this place right here.

Uncle: This place has no history [*ni mai mi prawattisat loei*]. [*He gives me directions to Chiang Man Temple again*]. Just go right through there. You can get a guesthouse and everything.

AAJ (*frustrated*): I have a house here. I am doing research [*tham wichai*] on community spirits. Not on the history of the city as a whole. Not on temples.

Uncle: Oh, I see. Well, if that is the case, I think you should go right over there into the old city. It's right there!

AAJ: What's right there?

Uncle: Chiang Man Temple. It has all the history.

What is striking about this man's response was his refusal to acknowledge to me the existence of the spirit shrine *in which he was standing*. The more I asked about it, the more I asked about it, the more he cast me as an outsider and suggested that I go where other *farang* have congregated, in a place of acknowledged "history"—indeed, at the beginning of this "History 1." Spirit shrines and spirit mediums had no part in how he conceived the "history" of Chiang Mai in the conception that he wanted me to understand. I, being in that space and time, was matter out of place, and he took it as his task to put the foreigner with the foreigners and history with its source. I, by being in a spirit shrine, speaking Thai and asking about spirits, was attempting to read a history of Chiang Mai that was not compatible with his conception of how Chiang Mai's history *should* be read.

Lanna Consumerism

The conflict over how to manifest Lanna properly also emerged in the debate over the Mandarin Oriental Dhara Dhevi hotel and its copious use of temple imagery in its grounds and guest rooms. The hotel was decorated in the style of a Lanna-era town (albeit incorporating stylistic elements from across the Tai region). Hotel areas were decorated in the manner of Northern temples and palaces, and the resort paid local villagers to handcraft much of the décor. They also hired villagers to use buffaloes to plow the central enclosure of the hotel. While Joe Cummings (2006) describes the Mandarin Oriental as a key player in the preservation of "Lanna," the provincial government was less enthusiastic. Yet it was not the colonial or racial tension involved in having wealthy (assumed to be *farang*) tourists sipping cocktails while viewing allochronistic Thai laborers at work with buffaloes that concerned them. Aek, the provincial cultural officer, described to me an encounter between the regional government and the hotel:

> The Dhara Dhevi uses things from the temple in the hotel, so this is an example of the Thais selling off their culture for money.[8] This Dhara Dhevi, the Office went to go talk to them, and to go tell them that these things aren't really appropriate for a hotel. The Dhara Dhevi replied that they wanted foreigners to know that Thailand is a Buddhist country,[9] which is indeed a good thing, but these are symbols that *mean* something. Like having lions [*singha*] in front of a building. You can't have that and have it not be a place where people go to pray [*wai phra*]. A foreigner might see that and then go and put *naga*s in front of their house. It's not appropriate. Like the Chedi hotel [another luxury hotel in the city center]. Does it have a real *chedi* [Buddhist stupa] inside? They use these symbols just because they are good-looking [*suai*], but *do they know the consequences* of using them?

Aek, as a government official in charge of culture, was a staunch promoter of nationalist and royalist readings of culture and history. He presented the struggle as one between naïve but well-meaning "Thais" against greedy forces "from other nations," with only the figure of the monarch and the talisman of culture standing between them. But what I found interesting about these particular statements of Aek's was his prediction of apocalyptic "consequences" that would ensue should cultural symbols be misused.

I asked Aek what these consequences might be. Without answering my question directly, he began to talk about the recent craze for Chatukam Ramathem amulets. These were a series of amulets that gained sudden popularity in Thailand in the mid-2000s owing to their purported powers to protect and to ensure wealth. The fad for the amulets had led many temples to mass-produce them. Their power came from two angelic spirits—Chatukam and Ramathep (occasionally fused into a single spirit named Chatukam Ramathep)—from a famous temple in Thailand's south. After telling me that sales of these amulets were diminishing the power of Buddhism by promoting superstitious beliefs and capitalism in the temples, Aek sighed: "It's not like in the past, when we didn't have so much foreign influence in Thailand. Then, if you needed a bicycle you could just ask your neighbor. . . . [This was a time when everyone] was following the sufficiency economy according to the royal proclamation."

This turnabout struck me as strange. Aek was explaining the Chatukam Ramathep amulet boom in terms of Western influences in blatant disregard of the long history of marketing and selling Buddhist amulets and charms in Thailand (see Pattana 2005 and Jackson 1998). By ascribing "capitalist Buddhism" (*phuttha panit*) to Western influence, Aek was editing the archive of Thai religion and removing "superstitious" elements by calling them "un-Thai" and "un-Lanna." By labeling them foreign, Aek was maintaining that true Thai *watthanatham* eschews such practices.

What at first glance appears to be a non sequitur—the fusion of "Western influence" with superstition— makes more sense when viewed in the light of Thai conceptions of power. As Pattana argues (2006), Thai political discourse differentiates between worldly power (*amnat*) and the transcendent, moral power characterized by *barami*—the power that mediums channel and that is embodied in the Thai monarch. Worldly power enables prosperity, development, technology—in short, *phatthana*. Transcendent power enables wisdom and progress—in short, *charoen*. In what Pattana (2010) terms Thai Occidentalism, the former quality becomes associated with the West and the latter with Thais. Hence, for Aek, magic, with its focus on worldly power and prosperity, naturally was seen as "Western" in the sense of oriented toward greed and accumulation rather than toward transcendent wisdom.

But what did this have to do with the "unintended consequences" of the Dhara Dhevi's architecture? Why did Aek suddenly change the subject? I asked him, and he, frustrated that I seemed not to be picking up on the association between Western consumerism and Chatukam Ramathep, offered me a nonanswer: "We just tell people the teachings of the Buddha, about doing what is right, and thinking about the consequences."

For Aek, the Dhara Dhevi's décor would cause disaster for a reason he could not articulate exactly. But in trying to do so he brought up nationalism, the risk posed by globalization, and an assertion of a certain kind of revisionist Buddhist belief. The perceived undermining of Buddhist symbols, as in the cases of the Dhara Dhevi or the Chatukam Ramathep amulets, is something

Aek identifies as foreign, or at least foreign-inspired, a feature that resonates with Kasian's Thai "postmodern." For Aek, the risk posed by the Dhara Dhevi reaches across all levels of Thai society.

The push for Chiang Mai's "educated class" to create and change architecture and urban space to become more "Lanna" was especially prevalent in the mid-2000s, in the wake of economic and political crisis. Peleggi suggests that the growth of manufactured past nostalgia in Thailand reflects an anxiety about the future of the country and the future of Thainess—in other words, as Thailand's future becomes less certain, there is an urge to revitalize that inchoate quality that could in turn revitalize the country (Peleggi 1996, 434). The concern over the promotion and reconstruction of *watthanatham* make this linkage more than explicit, recalling the Office of the National Culture Commission's goal to "revive" and "improve" *watthanatham.*

In *Lanna Style,* William Warren defines Lanna as "a subtle blend of many ingredients, some of them stretching back into the realm of legend, others of comparatively recent discovery" (Ping 2000, 14). Lanna Style, then, is always inherent in the landscape: old elements are "legend," while newer elements are themselves not really *new,* but "discovered." Something that is discovered has always been present, latent. It is the opposite of an invention—one "invents" or "creates" art, whereas one "discovers" nature—the invention of tradition is the discovery of what was already there.

CREATING LANNA SPACES

Potentiality

As the old man in the spirit shrine indicated, *charoen,* then, requires the jettisoning of those elements that appear backward in order to arrive at the true potential of *watthanatham.* In other words, not everything local is "wisdom." But, just as the mandala state was assimilatory, so is this idea of culture. As the cannibal spirits of Doi Kham were sources of raw power that had to be subjugated by the civilizing power of the Buddha in order to provide the city with the natural resources it needed to *charoen,* so raw potential exists within this archive of Lanna but has to be disciplined, refined, and tamed by an outside source.

City planners and urban civil society (by which I mean groups such as the ASA-Lanna, the Urban Development Institute Foundation, and Chiang Mai University) proposed new projects in order to make urban space more "Lanna." Here, I detail three projects that were particularly provocative and inspirational for these and related groups. The first of these was a revitalization of

Northern-era public squares; the second involved Lanna-era building taboos (*khuet*); and the third was a system of spatially oriented temples (*thaksa*). All of these were argued to be elements of Northern city planning that had fallen into disuse. Advocates claimed that their revitalization would be a key element in leading to Chiang Mai's success, and their neglect a reason for the city's languishing.

For these groups, a return to Lanna was also a move away from capitalism and consumerism. Designing Northern space in a Northern way, it was thought, would move Northerners away from globalism, consumerism, and capitalism. The advocacy of pre-Ayutthaya Thailand as a space of primitive communalism carries great appeal among many on the Thai Left, perhaps most famously Chatthip Nartsupha (2000, 1991), the advocate of the "Community Culture" school of thought.[10] As Thongchai (2010) shows, Chatthip ironically veers quite close to the writings of right-wing Wichit in his valorization of ancient Thai ways over corrupt modern ones. Finally, as Aek indicated, the issue of consumerism became politically heated during my time in Chiang Mai, as many (though not all) NGOs singled out Thaksin as the salient force behind consumerism in Thailand.

Khuang

Khuang is a Northern Thai word for an open space used communally by members of a certain group. Temples and housing compounds had their own *khuang,* and on a larger scale, cities and capitals had special plazas for ritual functions as well. Duangchan Charoenmuang, of the Urban Development Institute Foundation and the Social Research Institute and a professor at Chiang Mai University, argued that, as space becomes more individualized in Chiang Mai, areas of public use such as the *khuang* are widely disappearing in favor of privately owned, commercial space—shopping malls, high-rise condominium buildings, and so on (pers. comm.). Planners with concerns about public life and public space (like Duangchan) therefore have turned toward proposing open, publically owned sites for social gathering, ones explicitly rooted in a "Lanna" spatiality.

The main space that many of these planners wished to re-create was the central square of the city. The *khuang* of the capital city—*khuang luang*—existed at the intersection of the city's north–south and east–west axes and was the social heart of the city (Withi 2005, 49). In Chiang Mai's early days, this central point was the home of the Inthakin pillar and the royal palace, thus placing spiritual and kingly power at the central point of the city. Remembering that the Inthakin pillar was a gift from the Hindu deity of kingship, Indra, this is hardly surprising: royal, religious, and urban power were all the same thing. In essence, this central point, in the supernatural idiom, would be the fountain from which the city's merit flowed. In the modern-day planners' vision, a revitalized center would be the center of Chiang Mai's symbolic and social network from which the city's culture would pour. Yet the central problem with re-creating this scenario in a planning office was how to decide exactly where that point would be.

Geographically, a central point is difficult to determine. Chiang Mai does not have four main roads forming a cross in the middle like the ideal Hindu-Buddhist city (Duncan 1990).Instead, two roads meander out from one northern gate toward the two southern gates. One of these roads never reaches its destination—it ends near the city center. The east–west axis road is also not a straight line, bending to avoid a temple in the center-west of the city. The city, then, has multiple "central points." Of these, five were proposed to receive a full renovation and anointment as the *khuang luang* by the ASA-Lanna architects (also see Karuna 2002).

The former resting point of the Inthakin pillar, the "city navel," is a temple that lies next to the old governor's residence (now a museum) in the center-north part of the city. The temple itself advertises its status as the heart of the city, but such a claim appears to go unheeded. It has been split down the middle by a busy road, its stupa cut off from its Buddha images by a line of traffic. The abbot of Doi Suthep was reportedly in favor of reestablishing the temple and closing the road, but other clergy confessed to me that they saw this as a bid for power by a Central Thai monk, one not associated with the Northern Khuba movement.[11]

With the "city navel" burdened by temple politics, many planners turned toward the market in the center of the city, Kat Klang Wiang. The original site of Kat Klang Wiang is now buried behind a row of shop-houses, only marked by the spirit shrine of the city's founder, Mangrai, who was struck by lightning and killed while standing in the market square. However, the *name* Kat Klang Wiang has been taken up by a privately owned market specializing in high-end tourist goods, Northern-style coffee shops, and jazz music that lies several blocks over.

While the title of Kat Klang Wiang has been eagerly adopted by planners as a place of urban spatiality (albeit a private space, as opposed to Duangchan's ideal *khuang,* a public space) and reconstructed near the original site, the spirit shrine, with its association with mediumship and lower-class religious practices, has been removed and now stands in a side alley a block away from the market. The Kat Klang Wiang contains all the elements that Chiang Mai's educated classes associate with *khwam charoen:* international food (the market has Italian and Japanese restaurants), coffee (a new branch of Waawee Coffee borders both the lawn and the main street), and jazz. Indeed, these last two elements tie the space back into the figure of the current Thai monarch, who has championed coffee production in the North and whose love of jazz caused an appreciation for it to be nearly mandatory among educated royalist Thais.

Yet the spot ASA-Lanna architects most favored for fixing the central *khuang* was the Three Kings monument. While I have discussed the monument's role in spirit mediumship, in what follows I shall examine the way in which planners proposed to remake the square.

First, however, why was the square not already a *khuang?* Bordered on three sides by busy roads and blistering hot during the day, but full of break-dancing youths, musicians, and vendors during the nighttime weekend markets, the square functions as a gathering place for markets and festivals, although the relocation of the provincial government offices to a distant suburb neatly removed the opportunity for mass public debate or protest at their doors. As this space—a large central square near (if not directly in) the center of town—already existed, what needed to be done by architects to improve it? The ASA-Lanna's proposals were unified: the square had to be made more "Lanna" and to show an increased connection with "the land."

One proposal was to raise the entire square so that the traffic would pass underneath it. On top would be a three-tiered garden, with the Three Kings monument at the highest point. This, according to the architect, would be in keeping with the idea of the mandala, the mountain-like shape of Borobudur in Indonesia, and the natural shape of the palm tree. The invocation of these disparate symbols placed Chiang Mai not only in a regional cultural and Buddhist context but in one that was reflected in the natural world around it, as well as evoking the international idea of cultural heritage sites. Ironically, for a project advocating public space, such a structure would eliminate a great deal of the open space currently used for vendors, rituals, or foot traffic.

Another proposed restructuring of the Three Kings monument was to put sunken plazas running north to south and decorate them according to the season. This minor change would have a profound impact, as, according to the architect, the "true Chiang Mai people" (*chao* Chiang Mai *thae thae*) have "almost forgotten the beauty of seasons" and the value of their own *watthanatham* owing to the corrosive influence of consumer space. Having a more colorful central space, and one that changed with the seasons, would "fix the *wiang* [older term for walled city] and fix the lives of the people who are inside of it, giving an open space without the need for commerce." The architect also makes it clear that this was not to be an image of a static Lanna; rather, "not only do cultures that reflect authentic values [*tang doem*] but also contemporary cultures could be pursued."

These architects provide a clear image of a once pure people drowning in a sea of commercial interests, at risk of losing their *watthanatham* owing to rampant consumerism. The cure lay in the rebuilding of the *wiang,* the old city. Indeed, the drive for public space on the part of Chiang Mai architects was undertaken in the hope that such space would somehow lead to a social transformation in the city—a growth of civil society and an increase in participatory democracy—that would mirror a perceived as utopian Lanna past. New architecture would become the solution to consumerism: by consuming in new ways, goes the logic, we become anticonsumerist.

Duangchan elaborates this connection between architectural revitalization and utopian realization. She characterizes Chiang Mai's past as being one of especially tight social relationships owing to the availability of public space:

> The way of life of the ancestors of the Chiang Mai folk gave the opportunity for people to have the time to meet together all of the time. Walking [instead of driving] together and riding bicycles down the orchard road made people on the same route greet each other and built a sense of family. It also created a close-knit bond and the feeling of being a community together [*khwam pen chum-chon diao kan*]. The ability to share various thoughts often increased the feeling of being a community, and everyone helped to improve their community in order to make it better. (Duangchan 1998, 14; translation mine)

Duangchan goes on to claim that, in the past, Chiang Mai's residents did not try to trick people in order to make a profit, and they respected ancient sites such as the *khuang* and did not destroy them (1998, 150)—a claim that chooses to ignore the history of structural modifications to the city such as destroying the northeastern corner of the city wall and opening a new gate in the northeast. Indeed, as Askew (1996) argues, the very idea of a valued, unalterable heritage in Thailand dates from the late twentieth century, not from "the way of life of the ancestors."

But to focus on the mismatch between imagined past and actual past is to miss the point. Instead, following the logic of Duangchan and the architects already cited, parts of past knowledge, such as the *khuang,* must be adapted to the present and reintroduced.

Thaksa

This idea of transformation is perhaps best expressed in the magico-religious idiom: the *barami* of the exemplary center will cause it to *charoen;* its denial will cause it to crumble. But this emphasis on magico-religious explanations is not always left implicit. Other urban activists were pushing for an explicitly religious revival of urban space by incorporating into the suburbs a system of temple-based spatial organization.

As already detailed, the urban layout of Chiang Mai and its city walls had spiritual significance in early chronicles as well as in present-day spirit medium and *suep chatta* practice. Each corner and gate is inhabited by a different spirit; but according to Somchote's reading of Sanguan's Tamnan Mueang Nuea (see also Sanguan 1972; 1969), each corner and gate also has jurisdiction over a certain aspect of Chiang Mai's fortunes, a system called *thaksa*. The word itself is Pali, meaning simply "border" or "boundary" (Phra Maha Sanga 2004, 33). These fortunes are, in clockwise order beginning from the "head of the city," the northern gate:

1. *Det mueang* [the might of the city]—*chang phuak* gate
2. *Si mueang* [the splendor of the city]—*si pum* corner
3. *Mun mueang* [the foundation of the city]—*tha phae* gate
4. *Utsa mueang* [the persistence of the city]—*ka tam* corner
5. *Montri mueang* [the adviser of the city]—Chiang Mai gate
6. *Kalakini mueang* [the doom of the city]—*ku hueang* corner [Note: Between Chiang Mai gate and *ku hueang* corner lies *saen pung* gate, the "ghost gate."]
7. *Bariwan mueang* [the follower of the city]—*suan dok* gate
8. *Ayu mueang* [the lifespan of the city]—*hua lin* corner
9. Finally, in the center, *Ketu mueang*—the city navel and Inthakin pillar

During the past ten years, the key point of controversy regarding the *thaksa* of the city was whether or not this system extends beyond the city walls. Somchote claimed to have discovered evidence of a system of directional temples for Chiang Mai similar to Bali's. He argued that this extended the palladium and capacity for *charoen* of the city out to the suburbs. He and his spouse, the local historian Sarasawadee, invoked this system at first in order to protest the expansion of the superhighway—the "ring road"—to Rin Kham corner, at the intersection of Nimmanaheminda and Huay Kaew Roads. The widening of the road meant expansion over the land belonging to Wat Chet Yot, built in 1455 by King Tilokarat for a famous visiting monk. What Somchote and Sarasawadee (and the monks of Chet Yot) found particularly offensive was the routing of a sewage pipe through the temple's lotus pool.

While Sarasawadee did mention the temple's long history as one reason for its preservation, it was suburban *thaksa* that became her primary focus in its defense. She argued that Chet Yot was a key node in the *thaksa* of Chiang Mai and as such had special importance for the historical preservation of Lanna.[12] Sarasawadee based her argument on a palm-leaf text from Wat Chai Siphumi, a large temple on the northeast corner of the city (Sarasawadee 1992, 20). This text argues that in the renovation of Chiang Mai under Tilokarat, each direction was assigned a different temple to oversee each auspicious facet of the city's *thaksa* outside of the city walls, in the city suburbs. These temples were, in the order that I have listed them above: Wat Chiang Yuen, Wat Chai Siphumi, Wat Bupparam, Wat Chaimongkhon, Wat Nantharam, Wat Tapotharam (Ramphoeng), Wat Suan Dok, and Wat Chet Yot, with Wat Chedi Luang occupying the center position (figure 13). Sarasawadee and Somchote's argument continues to add that, as pillars sustaining the future and fortune of the city, these temples are still vital spots in maintaining Chiang Mai's spiritual legacy—a fusion of *watthanatham* and supernatural power.

Others have opined that, while the efforts to preserve Wat Chet Yot have merit, the system of *thaksa* that involves temples is simply a promotional effort on the part of the author of the chronicle of Wat Chai Siphumi. Indeed, one Lanna Studies academic (whom I shall not name here) hinted darkly to me that "no one has ever seen this manuscript! Somchote supposedly took it and hid it!"—implying (but not openly saying) that Somchote and Sarasawadee

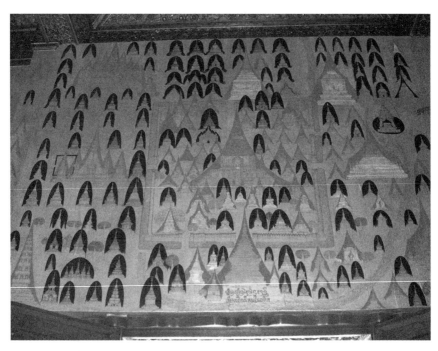

FIGURE 13 | *Thaksa* system in suburban Chiang Mai

invented the whole story. I have no evidence to support or deny this claim, but I introduce it here to show the level of vitriol the debate generated.

These arguments reached their peak in a collection of rebuttals to Somchote and Sarasawadee published in 2004 called *Mai Mi Wat Nai Thaksa Mueang* (There are no temples in the *thaksa* of the city), which focused on the fact that each of the temples supposedly tied together in this system were built at different times, for different purposes, and in many cases are only generally located in the direction to which they were supposedly assigned (Duangchan 2004). Others in the volume chose other elements of the *thaksa* debate to criticize: for instance, Thanet, in the same volume, bemoaned the attempt to commercialize Lanna's past or to manufacture aspects of Lanna history for the benefit of the present (Thanet 2004, 114).

Claims about *thaksa* arise in unexpected places in the English-language literature as well. For instance, in the online material collected in preparation for a popular book on Chiang Mai, the Chiang Mai-based, English-language publishing house CPAmedia makes Sarasawadee's claims for each temple that, for instance, "Jaeng [corner—*chaeng* in my orthography] Ku Ruang influences the city's misfortune [by which they mean *kalakini mueang*]. It is associated cosmologically with Wat Rampoeng" (CPAmedia site 2009).

In my visits to each of the temples associated with the *thaksa* system, I noticed that *thaksa* was fiercely promoted in some places and denied in others. Visiting Wat Buppharam on Tha Phae road, I noticed a large painting in the *wihan* (temple hall) depicting the stupas of each temple featured in the *thaksa* system arranged in their proper positions at the city's cardinal points. An older monk described the system to me, precisely following the points laid out by Sarasawadee and Somchote, and then offered me a relativistic explanation: "But it's all really a matter of belief. Some people believe in these things, some people do not." In contrast, in Wat Ramphoeng, the abbot angrily denied the *thaksa* system as a self-promotional effort espoused by arrogant temples, even though his disciple, to whom I had been speaking the minute before, affirmed the existence of *thaksa* as an auspicious boon for the city of Chiang Mai and a source of the city's supernatural power.

In short, with *thaksa,* we see either the invention or the "discovery" of tradition (Hobsbawm and Ranger 1983). In either case, before Somchote and Sarasawadee began their campaign for suburban *thaksa,* no living people knew of such a system. While the academic argument revolved around whether or not there had ever been such a system, I find the speed with which it was taken up by many temples and advocates very compelling. Tradition's validity or invalidity was not the point. Indeed, *watthanatham,* it seems, does not have to be authentic in order to "work."

Khuet

Duangchan and her organization rejected the calls for *thaksa* but advocated resurrecting another aspect of Northern Thai magico-religious belief for the benefit of the present, namely, *khuet,* a system of taboos largely concerning space in the old city (see also Mala 2008; Charuphat 2007). She defined *khuet* to me as: "things that people knew about in the past." In the future, according to Duangchan, it is the knowledge from the past that will solve the problems Chiang Mai is facing in the present (2004, 158). As she wrote: "Our society has looked down upon local wisdoms [*phumpanya*] and no longer believed in them. Not until this society faced economic crisis [in 1997] did people review their thoughts and revive local wisdom. Examples can be seen from the violation of the *khuet* that led to the recent severe flood problems" (2005, 16). In a similar vein, she observed that "in the past" Chiang Mai was a place of kindness and neighborly love, a situation that has been changed by an increase in gangs, suicides, the loss of public space, and because "people who live there have lost the feeling of being owners of the city" (2004, 112).

What needs to be restored, then, is the feeling of being a community, of owning one's city and remembering lost knowledge. One ironic aspect of this statement is how closely it mirrors the advertisements for the Punna residence: while Duangchan fiercely opposed the growth of high-rise residences in the city, and especially near the slopes of Doi Suthep, both she and the high-rise condominium developers claim that what Chiang Mai needs now is a return to the wisdom of the past and the sense of community that existed in the past.

According to Duangchan, high-rise buildings violated *khuet* in that they loomed over religious sites, placing the secular world above the sacred. They offended spirit shrines and historical monuments, offenses that would ultimately lead to a loss of social cohesion in the city. Social isolation in single-dweller apartments would lead to suicide and increases in teenage pregnancy and social disunity. The narrow sightlines provided by tall buildings would also limit the effectiveness of political protest. Pressure from civil society groups eventually led to the passage of a city planning law prohibiting tall buildings from being located next to "religious or historical sites" or near to Suthep mountain. The law had limited impact, as construction firms maneuvered around some of the regulations (for instance, one hotel next to the city wall sold a meter-wide strip of land in front of its doors), were grandfathered in, or simply ignored the prohibition.

Regarding *khuet,* Duangchan described the prohibitions as "things that are good advice—for instance, if you build a house out of new wood and old wood, that is *khuet.* Why? Because the new wood will change shape at a different rate than the old wood and your house will break apart! It is also *khuet*

to build your house with one wooden post buried inside a termite mound."
She finished by asking rhetorically, "Now, why would that be?" For her, *khuet*
taboos are common-sense proscriptions based on ancient trial-and-error and
created to preserve harmony in infrastructure (the house). For instance, it is
khuet for pregnant women to go to the toilet at night. Why this is so is not
specified in the text, but Duangchan reasons that at night a woman might slip
and fall and perhaps injure her baby (Duangchan pers. comm.). According to
one palm-leaf text (Buntha et al. 1996), greeting someone who is eating meat
is also *khuet*—the director suggested that this was to prevent people from self-
ishly doing so just to be invited to share the meal. Ultimately, for Duangchan,
khuet has a rational function.

Prawet,[13] another academic, NGO head, and urban-sprawl opponent,
echoed this sentiment. For Prawet, *khuet* "is a code of life that teaches us how
to successfully live together in a society—it addresses social issues like teen
pregnancy, drugs, and so on. The curse of *khuet* is that if one violates *khuet*,
one will not *charoen*." He provided more examples of how forward-thinking
"Lanna wisdom" was: "Today, the nuclear family is the organizing principle.
It's not a tight-knit society; people largely look after themselves. But in the
past [*samai boran*], we emphasized a person's responsibilities towards other
people, which in a way is very like today's idea of human rights."[14] Here,
Prawet claims that the present way of doing things (in terms of the nuclear
family) has forgotten the superior past way of doing things but then suddenly
implies that the past way of doing things anticipated the progressive aspect of
the present (e.g., human rights).

For reference, Prawet, Duangchan, and others drew upon a collection of
palm-leaf descriptions of *khuet* compiled by Buntha et al. (1996) and published
during the first wave of anti-high-rise activism in Chiang Mai. What emerges
from Buntha's collection is a system that is primarily concerned with boundaries, directions, and hierarchies, especially as they relate to architecture. As
one would expect from a Lanna-era text, *khuet* here is primarily concerned
with temporary houses, temples, huts, and agricultural structures like grana-
ries. Most rules are negative (e.g., "it is forbidden to do X"); a few are positive
(e.g., "X is an auspicious thing to do"); but almost all are concerned with the
mixing of the old and the new or with attention to spatial orientation.

Some examples include:

- The building of a new house that faces south near an old one that faces
  north is not good, it is *khuet*. (Buntha et al. 1996, 69)
- If you have a small old house that you expand to make wider than
  before, it is not good, it is very *khuet*. (Buntha et al. 1996, 77)

- There are two kinds of "dead houses" in which one shouldn't live. The first is an abandoned house that hasn't had people living in it and then one comes and builds upon that house.[15] The second is taking old wood from lots of different houses and combining them to make a single house. These aren't good, they are *khuet*. (Buntha et al. 1996, 81)
- Even if [your] homes and cities are doing well, if [you] have a market that sells things in the city for a long time, and behind that market is an abandoned space, this is not good. It will cause the city to not prosper [*charoen*], because that space will become a home for ghosts. Ghosts of violent death, *hung* ghosts, *phong* ghosts, and *phrai* ghosts will all live there because they will come to eat the food that is in the market, like raw meat or raw fish. It will make it so that you cannot eat the food. The ghosts will trouble the entire city, making people and beasts suffer much. (Buntha et al. 1966, 12)
- Cities, temples, monasteries, house compounds, gardens, or homes are well. If one is going to build a home [*huean*] around there, do not build it right next to a river, or build it next to a large or small road, or build it in the sightline [*sai ta*] of a temple, or in the sightline of a giant [*yak*, e.g., a spirit shrine]. Doing that is not good, it can be *khuet*. (Buntha et al. 1996, 1; all translations mine)

The penalty for a violation of *khuet* depends on the scale of the offense. While minor offenses trouble only the offender, larger ones affect the neighborhood and, in the final two cases, the entire city (*khuet mueang*). It was this last point that was emphasized by anti-sprawl advocates with whom I spoke: for them, *khuet mueang* was an example of Lanna-era social responsibility toward good city planning. For instance, a prohibition against filling in old wells was interpreted as a precaution against flooding; the flooding that routinely menaced Chiang Mai was, according to this logic, a result of filling in the swampy area to the north of the city. In this way, the vagueness of the punishments described in Buntha's text—most often "the city will not *charoen*" or "the city will suffer [*dueat ron*]"—reinforces urban activists' tendency to see *khuet*'s violation in the present.

Patcharee[16] was another urban activist in Chiang Mai who made *khuet* a centerpiece of her anti-sprawl argument. When I first spoke with her, I made the mistake of mentioning my research with Kham and other spirit mediums. "Andrew," she told me, "you have to be very careful with these mediums. Maybe some of them are real, but many of them are liars and drunks. I thought you were serious about doing research on Chiang Mai's *watthanatham*. It would be better if you spoke with some old residents of a community than these spirit mediums." Patcharee was thus pushing me to accept the secular and the Buddhist aspects of *watthanatham* and to exclude the animist and supernatural explanations for *khuet.*

Stymied and rather angered by her response, I returned to her some days later with references to animist spirits and *khuet,* both taken from my ethnographic work as well as from texts. In light of her previous dismissal of spirit cults, I asked her about the explicit references to spirits and ghosts. She was not to be shaken. "Each one of these [references to spirits]," she explained to me, "is really about a real problem that people had. Maybe it was a disease. Maybe it was conflict in the society. *Khuet* was a guide to tell people how to live peacefully together. Ghosts were just how people from ancient times [*samai boran*] explained conflict."

The functional explanations given by urban activists and proponents of *khuet* as "local wisdom" differ from those given by lay people. Tiamrat, my neighbor, a woman from Lamphun in her mid-sixties, provided a more structural reason for *khuet.* I asked her if she knew the word, and she responded. "*Khuet?* Yes of course. It's things that you shouldn't do. Suppose you were to touch me on the head. It's not appropriate, because you are younger than I am. That would be *khuet.*" Tiamrat made no attempt to dismiss or downplay *khuet* or to provide a culturally specific narrative (e.g., *khuet* as "Lanna wisdom") or a functional reason why certain things are *khuet* and others are not; instead she gave a structural explanation: there is a hierarchy of high and low embedded in hierarchies of age and the body, and to violate these (e.g., by having a young man's hand touch the highest point on an old woman's head) is to violate the way in which the world is ordered. I asked Tiamrat what might happen should I touch her on the head. She still refrained from replying with a "disenchanted" explanation along the lines of what Duangchan or Patcharee provided—for example, that society would frown upon the disrespect shown to the wisdom of the older generation. Instead, Tiamrat simply said that she would get sick.

Ya Pu was an older devotee who spent her days at Chet Yot temple. I asked her to give me an example of *khuet,* and she described the fate of one hapless youth who had positioned himself above a guardian spirit:

> I saw a guardian spirit [enforce *khuet*] once. There was a youth, younger than you, who had come to the temple for a temple fair. He was right over there, by that spirit shrine. He didn't know what he was doing [i.e., he was drunk and/or acting foolish] and climbed on top of the tiger statue over there [pointing to a plaster statue of a tiger]. Suddenly, he jumped up and climbed that tree [pointing to a large tree next to the shrine]. Not in the manner of a person! Not like

a person! Faster than a person could do it, he went up, making sounds like an animal. He was up in that tree for several hours. The guardian spirit had entered him. He was doing something he shouldn't have done—climbing on top of that statue—and it possessed him. When he came to [lit.: when he knew himself], he was so frightened he wouldn't come down!

The youth acts in the same way as Tiamrat suggested would invoke supernatural retribution: he, a young man, places his body above something more sacred; he climbs on top of the dwelling place of a spirit and calamity results. The boy inverts high and low, and the once friendly guardian spirit turns vengeful. Ya Pu identifies inappropriate and disrespectful behavior as the root cause of the boy's possession, but it is notably disrespect and a lack of religiosity toward guardian spirits—not toward age, propriety, or Lanna culture. It is the dismissive attitude toward guardian spirits, the treatment of possessing spirits as mere superstitious, irrational belief, that Ya Pu describes to me as *khuet*. In short, Ya Pu sees rationalist attitudes such as Duangchan's, not high-rise buildings, as the source of *khuet*.

While those promoting localist architectural revitalization like Duangchan, Prawet, and to some extent Tong took pains to gloss *khuet* as functional standing reserve, older people such as Tiamrat and Ya Pu referred to *khuet* in a holistic, cosmic sense: *khuet* refers to the violation of boundaries that keep the universe ordered and in line, and as such it cannot be separated from other elements such as health, happiness, and luck.

But such interpretations as those of Ya Pu or Tiamrat fail to gain traction as *watthanatham*. Instead, *watthanatham*, in the examples I have provided, is, like *khwam charoen*, a fundamentally forward-pointing concept. As such, it can be deployed against globalization but, as in Prawet's discussion of "human rights," must always *anticipate* and *preempt* globalization. In this way, it allows for a globalization that is always unquestionably local.

REVITALIZATION

In these examples taken from Northern Thai civil society, Lanna, once transformed into "local wisdom" or "culture," becomes thought of as a source of potential progressive knowledge, albeit one that requires editing and alteration to be rendered commensurable. In this way, Lanna becomes a spirit: a force arising from the past to ensure *charoen* in the future. But, like a spirit, it is invisible. It requires mediation in order to be realized in the present.

For instance, Tong sees this intangible, invisible quality of Lanna as what separates his glass-and-concrete structures from those of other international architects, rendering his "Lanna" and theirs simply "modern." The Punna developer sees in his project a new way of bringing back ancient Lanna forms of sociality through building a high-rise residence/shopping complex. In Ratchaphruek, we see the *becoming* of Lanna as a part of the Central Thai royal body, a central node in Theravada Buddhist networks, a claim to "sufficient" tourist development, and a marker of Thailand's superiority in the construction of royal shrines. In the *khuang, thaksa,* and *khuet* debates, we see the revitalization of senescent cultural practices for the creation of a more utopic, less consumerist, more Lanna society.

In these ways, we can see the construction of *watthanatham* or "local wisdom" as a technology in Heidegger's sense. In *The Question Concerning Technology* (1977), Heidegger defines "technology" not as a material thing but as a way of seeing through which previously ambiguous things and places become conceived of as having calculable value. For instance, a forest becomes thought of as timber, a source of clean water, a hunting ground for wild animals, a tourist destination, or even just a place for aesthetic reflection. Each of these ways of seeing ascribes a particular tangible benefit (e.g., "lumber," "reservoir," "park") to a previously unquantified place—"forest." In a similar way, civil societal ways of looking at *khuet* see a source of some benefit rather than simply something that *is.* Wichit sees the seeds of Thai independence in a past that anticipated and predated the West, while Sit mines the Lanna archive for those elements which would impute a primordial anti-Communist spirit to the North. But why must all referents point toward something authentically "Lanna?" Why can there be no critique that does not reference the past?

Michael Herzfeld characterizes Thailand's lack of formal colonialism as "crypto-colonialism" (2002). As its neighbors were being colonized by English, French, and Dutch powers, Siam adopted European norms internally rather than having them directly imposed by a colonial state. Therefore, culture and politics are "aggressively national[istic]" but at the same time "suited to fit foreign models" (Herzfeld 2002, 901). But the constructedness of such a change cannot be spoken—to question "Thai culture" is to be "un-Thai" (Herzfeld 2002, 904). In my own experience, I received severe reminders of this when I was reprimanded by Tong for asking just where Lanna was in his work, when mentioning my work with mediums to Patcharee, when pointing out dead grass and wild dogs in Ratchaphruek, or when Aek reminded me that the desire for Chatukarm amulets came from the West.

Such a process haunts Thai postcolonial writing (Thongchai 2010). While the *attributed source* of Lanna "local wisdom" must be putatively "local," at the same time, the *value given* to such practices ("wisdom") is always dependent upon outside hierarchies. *Khuet* prohibitions on buildings overlooking holy sites are touted by Chiang Mai's civil society as "local wisdom," but ideas hard to reconcile with bourgeois lifestyles or the modern city—spirit mediumship, for instance—are dismissed as "not meaningful."

The search for an authentic Lanna, one that can compete with Western models of urban development on the West's own terms, falls into the trap of mistaking "localized elements of the West . . . as connoting authentic non-Western identities" (Thongchai 2010, 251). In their zeal to create a sustainable, livable, and progressive city—unarguably a worthy goal—Northern Thai civil society, like Thai anticolonialists before it, recasts, edits, and alters the archive of Northern Thai cultural practice.

Here, I shall return to the idea of *charoen* as a ladder. This idealized Lanna is a place several rungs up, past the missteps of Bangkok and the West. In this sense, Lanna is a *place of desire,* not what exists on the ground or even existed in the past. It lies in the future, farther up on the ladder of *charoen.* But from the vantage point of the current, haunted, ruinous present, it is out of reach. Those who are constructing these narratives of an idealized past "local wisdom" or *watthanatham* imagine this higher level and project their fantasies—those already informed by their own desires for modernity and bourgeois life and *khwam charoen*—on this higher rung. In reaching it, one can surpass the primitive past, the ruinous present, and the false steps taken by Bangkok and the West.

Conclusion
The City Doesn't Have a Future

"The city doesn't have a future," was Bon's judgment when confronted with Chiang Mai's crumbling architecture. Surrounded by new construction, he confided to me that progress in Chiang Mai was in a state of crisis, unable to move forward and threatened by bad architecture and malignant ghosts. By fusing these two elements, Bon had united the discourses of the mediums and urban planners into a unitary narrative: the failure of *charoen*. Now, I wish to return to the empty space that exists at the center of Bon's sketch of Chiang Mai.

Bon sought to convince me that Chiang Mai is in a state of collapse—that it is crumbling, just like the buildings he showed me. It crumbles, empty at the center, just as a mandala would crumble in the absence of its ruler. But others in the city—Kham, Tong, Duangchan, and all those who are seeking to revitalize the urban spirit(s) of Lanna for the future—saw themselves as uniquely suited to fill this void. Here, then, the discourse of spirit mediums and that of planners come strangely to mirror each other. Each group becomes the means through which the mandala will be revitalized. Each sees itself as the vehicle through which the golden past will be translated into the golden future, bypassing the ruinous present.

James Scott, in his recent and provocative book *The Art of Not Being Governed* (2010), argues that the cultures of "Zomia," the Southeast Asian highlands of which the mountains ringing Chiang Mai are a part, were formed by people escaping coercive state projects. His characterization of an almost monolithic control-hungry lowland state has been criticized by some anthropologists working in the area as overly reductionist (cf. Jonsson 2010). But here I wish to take up his remark about the lowland state's assimilation of highland people—to use the Chinese idiom, "cooking barbarians" (Scott 2010, 273). Indeed, what more are the stories of Grandmother and Grandfather Sae, Wilangkha and Chamadewi, or Chao Luang Kham Daeng and In Lao than tales about wildness tamed through the power of lowland charisma? Although Scott largely focuses on the coercive powers of lowland states, he also mentions their charismatic, attractive potential. Like the man of prowess in Lucien Hanks' early study of Thailand (1962), and like Geertz's (1980) theater state, urban centers at their ideal level were concretions of symbolic power. In times of prosperity, those on the periphery would be drawn closer to them; in times of hardship, this power to attract would wane.

But as I show in Chapter 1, this power is invisible; it rests on abstractions such as progress (*khwam charoen*), possessing lordly spirits (*chao nai*), or culture (*watthanatham*). And these powers all have their home in the city. Southeast Asian conceptions of urbanism (in contrast to Williams 1973 or Simmel 1950) designate the city as the center of both intellectual *and* moral superiority. It is the apex of the ladder of *khwam charoen.* But as doubt regarding *charoen*'s forward progress arises, so does the feeling that the charisma of the city is waning. Haunting forces creep in, forces that are unassimilated, wild, and barriers to the forward motion of *charoen.* As I argue, the very notion of what it means to *charoen* is thrown into doubt. That these outside influences are blamed on ghosts by some, on Burmese invaders by others, and on an abstract "consumerism" by still others is immaterial—in all cases, the invaders are signs of the failure of this power. In every case they create the need for revitalization; and in every case the power requires a medium through which to act.

Possession by the place-based lordly spirits of the city was one such path toward revitalization. The cults of Kham Daeng and Theravada Buddhism were powerful discourses of progress, sources of charismatic power (in the idiom of *barami*) with which potential subjects could identify. In the twentieth century, spirit possession has been sidelined by mainstream sources of authority in the secular and Buddhist realm. Yet along with the breakdown of progress, the sources of progress in the nation, in orthodox Buddhism, and in the monarchy are questioned. Possession becomes a source of potential, one that urbanites turn to as other discourses fall into doubt. As such, spirit mediums flourish as the city expands (Irvine 1984).

Another expanding discourse was that of Northern Thai cultural heritage, especially as it concerns physical space in the city. After the boom and bust of the 1997 financial crisis, a return to "Lanna" was increasingly the thing that was to save the city, at least from the perspective of its "educated classes." This was not to be the Lanna of Kham Daeng, however. Instead, this was to be an edited version, one commensurable with but independent from perceived-to-be Western forms of culture. Lanna was to be a new Europe, remade without its flaws. By becoming mediums of Lanna's spirit, architects and planners were to enable Lanna's innate *khwam charoen* to manifest itself in the present. What is constant between these varied "new" ways of urban revitalization and mediumship is the idea of the city as a vehicle through which potential (*barami, watthanatham*) can be converted to prosperity (*khwam charoen*) as well as a stage upon which this power to convert is displayed. The conflicts and divides within this community show how ruination leads to increasing contestation over the "right" way to access *khwam charoen*.

I use the term "stage" intentionally. Clifford Geertz presents the idea of the Balinese "theater state," a political system in which emphasis is placed on spectacle, on the presentation of the exemplary center as the source of divine prosperity and order (1980, 13). The king, at the center of the Balinese mandala, "ensured its prosperity—the productiveness of its land; the fertility of its women; the health of its inhabitants; its freedom from droughts, earthquakes, floods, weevils, or volcanic eruptions; its social tranquility; and even . . . its physical beauty" (ibid., 129). The conspicuous display of charisma and repetition of charismatically effective forms—for instance, the heavens in miniature—assured his subjects of their continuing prosperity. It is not hard to see the parallels with Bon's dire prediction about the future of Chiang Mai. "The king" in Geertz's sense means more than simply the Thai king or the faded Lanna monarchy. Rather, "the king" here is a source of *barami,* a source of that power which impels forward motion and the assurance that further rungs of *charoen* are in fact reachable. Sovereign power assures progress; but with political and economic crisis, with a loss of faith in the forward motion of modernity, cracks appear.

The parallels between magico-religious notions of *barami* and secularized *watthanatham* should not be surprising. Magico-religious interpretations of power and progress haunt, in Derrida's sense (1993). The more fervently they are covered up or denied, as Patcharee denies the trustworthiness of spirit mediums, the more ostensibly secular constructions of culture, history, or progress take on magico-religious characteristics.

While Geertz adduces a Balinese emphasis upon the preservation of a steadily declining glory, in Thailand this idea of continual decline is replaced by a call for progress, for *khwam charoen,* a quality that combined global notions of development with Buddhist ideas (Thongchai 2000). Thai ideas of progress became profoundly assimilationist. For instance, King Mongkut (Rama IV, r. 1851–1868), faced with the influx of European astronomy, embraced

European calculations in order to prove his own superiority vis-à-vis court astrologers (Thongchai 1994, 46). But Mongkut also presented himself as possessing astronomical knowledge superior to that of the Europeans: after being presented with a model of the earth as round—a model to which his advisers reacted with skepticism—Mongkut responded that he had already determined the earth's spherical shape years before the Europeans had suggested it to him (Thongchai 1994, 38). In this way do "foreign" ideas become assimilated to a larger, absolute idea of progress rooted in Buddhist understandings of *charoen*. Mongkut, having more *barami* and therefore more *charoen* than the European dignitaries *and* his court astrologers, claims his superiority to both. The king readily adapts the newly acquired knowledge of astronomy into a framework—not necessarily of Siamese astrology, but of *khwam charoen*. He perceives that the European knowledge has *khwam charoen* and adapts (and positions himself) accordingly.

The political model of the exemplary center has disappeared (see Thongchai 1994). But just as Mongkut's idea of astronomy is one that assimilates both European astronomy and Siamese astrology into a hierarchical system of knowledge based on qualities of *charoen,* so Lanna urbanity takes "new" discourses of heritage and culture and fuses them into the idea of the exemplary center. The city is still the site of center-oriented notions of progress. Even despite nationalist rhetoric valorizing an essentialized "Thainess," this quality becomes located in (ancient) cities, not in the countryside. In the discourse of both spirit mediums and architects, something—be it spirits or cultural heritage—reemerges to fill the void at the center of Bon's map.

In this way, while the *content* of such urbanity might be highly variable (e.g., possessing spirits or cultural heritage), in each case, the city is the vehicle through which the potential of the past is actualized into *khwam charoen*. Just as the raw and violent power of Grandfather and Grandmother Sae is converted by mediums to cool air and clean water for the city, so the (perceived to be) rude and backward potential of Northern Thai practice is converted by culture brokers to civilized, quasi-European *watthanatham*. Successfully converting this power ensures that one's development is permanent, wise, and lasting (*charoen*), as opposed to hollow, temporary, and fleeting (simply *phatthana*). The city in Northern Thailand is a vehicle for creating progress from potential. But in its current state, doubts have arisen as to its ability to do so. The city is haunted, not by its past, but by its present.

NOTES

INTRODUCTION

1 *"Khwam"* renders the verb *charoen* a noun. If we translate *charoen* as "to prosper," *khwam charoen* would be "prosperity."

2 The direct Thai translation of "mandala" is *monthon,* but *mueang* is a far more commonly used term for such states.

3 Louis Wirth brought Simmel's idea of the city as generative of a fundamentally different "mentality" to the American context, arguing that the urban mode of life entails increased specialization and differentiation among individuals, but that these roles and categories are "tangential" (Wirth 1964, 16) to each other. In his view, because interactions are so fleeting, individuals are fragmented into enacting many such roles, each of which, however, contains only a segment of the self.

4 Most Thai pronouns are gender-neutral. The teacher could be male or female— Bon uses the Northern Thai/Lao *poen.*

CHAPTER 1: Progress and Its Ruins

1 The Thai word *farang* refers to white foreigners, regardless of their national origins (which are often assumed to be English, Australian, or American). I will henceforth use the term *farang* without translation. The maid's killer does not enter the story. His identity as *farang,* and the maid's identity as Burmese are entirely extraneous to the plot.

2 This man was in his late fifties, Northern Thai, and a resident in an urban high-rise.

3 Nidthi Eoseewong has written about the "Lanna woman" as a fetishized object (1991). The image, stemming from Chiang Mai's colonized status vis-à-vis Bangkok, is one of an elegant, slow-speaking, but naïve woman as opposed to the brash worldliness of (masculine) Bangkok. I address this subject in more detail in subsequent chapters.

4 She could not sell the house and recoup her losses, so she kept it in the hope that a visiting family member might use it.

5 The "reinvention" of Northern Thai heritage and its fetishization by Central Thais and Northern Thais themselves are subjects about which I and other authors (Nidthi 1991; Morris 2000; Johnson 2010) have written extensively elsewhere.

6 My interlocutors at first generally identified the ghosts as unspecified *phi.* When I pressed them about what sort of *phi,* they would go on to identify the former person—e.g., "the ghost of a girl," "the ghost of a suicide." When I then asked about the specific variety of ghost, the term *phi tai hong* emerged, without exception.

7 I searched local newspaper reports but could find no record of such a suicide.

8 The term "Shan"— Thai-Yai in Siamese (Central) Thai, Ngiao in Northern Thai, or Tai in their own language—refers to a group of people in northeastern Burma and parts of Northern Thailand who practice wet-rice agriculture and Theravada Buddhism. Shan are linguistically, religiously, and historically very close to other Tai groups such as Lao, Northern Thai, or Siamese Thai. See Amporn 2008.

9 As of late 2013, the academic community was still divided on the use of the name "Burma" versus "Myanmar." Here, as I primarily deal with Thai interpretations of "Burmese" as *khon* Phama rather than with events or people actually in Burma/Myanmar, I have continued to use "Burma"/"Burmese."

10 Many members of "hill tribe" (*chao khao*) communities in and around Chiang Mai have a limited form of citizenship that renders them able to remain where they are but unable to move freely around the country, and with more limited civil rights than full citizens. Those who enter from Burma are often placed in refugee camps along the border. But Aong was one of the many Shan who, owing to religious, cultural, and linguistic similarities, are able to blend into Thai society more easily and therefore manage to live without any sort of official documentation. As such, they are subject to arrest and deportation but also employed in a large number of low-wage jobs. "Shan" is not a recognized hill-tribe minority group, but shares similar histories with groups such as the Karen with regard to conflict in Burma and migration to Thailand.

11 I have no way of verifying Aong's story. While the shooting had made it into the newspapers, traffic accidents were so commonplace that they often went unreported.

12 *Mo phi,* literally "ghost doctor," denotes someone who specializes in dealing with malevolent spirits. These are often monks, although the practice is frowned upon by the national Buddhist administration (*sangha*) as being overly superstitious. Non-monk *mo phi* are also often portrayed as villains in films, where they capture evil spirits to use for nefarious purposes (cf. Nonzee 1999).

13 Here, I repeat my interlocutors' stories of migrants fully aware of the tales' often racist character. I do not wish to be understood as supporting my interlocutors' ideas as facts, but rather as analyzing the figure of "the Burmese migrant" as it exists in the imaginations of those relating these stories.

14 Somboon described it as "Burmese," although he admitted not speaking Burmese.

15 Somboon did not know what the people were charged with or what happened to them, nor did he seem to care. Drug suspects in Thailand—often unfairly seen as synonymous with illegal migrants—were, during the Thaksin era, subject to harsh extralegal punishments, and Thaksin's "war on drugs" claimed over 2,500 extralegal killings within three months (Pasuk and Baker 2006, 162).

16 *Lok* compares less accurately with the English "haunt" than with the Japanese *bakeru*, "to change," as in *bakemono*, "monster," a thing that has deceptively changed from its true form (see Foster 2009, 6).

17 Some interlocutors hung up yantras or carried a Buddha amulet as a precaution as well, but such practices are common among most Buddhist Thais regardless of a fear of ghosts. Unlike the case in Mills' villages, they are purchased ("rented") individually at temples.

18 Mills (1995) prefers to translate "modernity" as *thansamai*. *Thansamai* literally means "equal with the times" and might be compared with the English "up-to-date." *Charoen,* as I explore here, has a quite different meaning, one that implies knowledge and wisdom.

19 *Laeo* provides past tense: "Already developed/ already progressed."

CHAPTER 2: Foundations

1 A pret (Sanskrit: *preta*) is a Buddhist "hungry ghost," an individual condemned to being reborn as a mouthless spirit perennially hungry, and *yak* (*yaksha*) are boar-tusked giants, most of whom are violent and malevolent, but some of whom become powerful guardian spirits.

2 The city in question is the Lawa town built on the site where Mangrai would later found Chiang Mai. This story is obviously an allegory. In choosing the pre-Tai city, the chronicle situates the narrative in mythic rather than historical time. See discussion below on Northern Thai history and stories of *Chao Luang Kham Daeng.*

3 Here, one should note the close connection between Indra and kingship in Thai Buddhism.

4 *Tai* refers to the larger linguistic/ethnic group, whereas *Thai* refers to the Thai nation-state or Siamese language.

5 The present-day province of Nan was occasionally independent of Lanna, although is now certainly in the North.

6 The identity of both the residents of Hariphunchai and the "Lawa" is a hotly contested issue. Here, I follow the admittedly simplistic model of Buddhist Mon cities and animist rural Lawa populations presented by Sarasawadee (2005). Divisions based around ethnicity as opposed to lifestyle or religion would likely be secondary, following Leach (1973). Indeed, Scott argues that the very term "Lawa" stems from the Sanskrit *tamilawa,* or "non-Buddhist" (Scott 2010).

7 The name "New City" refers, not to Chiang Mai's newness vis-à-vis Haripunchai, but rather to the fact that it was Mangrai's second attempt at city building, his previous attempt at Wiang Kum Kham having been destroyed by a flood.

8   Seri sees Lanna's vassalization by Burma as something of a very different nature to that of its later vassalization to Siam. For Seri, the same status is "slavery" on one hand and "freedom" on the other.

9   The revolt's grouping together of Thai and Chinese into a common enemy of Northerners and Shan proves a counterexample to Thai nationalist suppositions of a unitary ethnic consciousness linking Lanna and Siam (Seri 1966; Sit 1980).

10   While this might seem to be a contradiction—a symbol of Northern resistance and a symbol of Bangkokian dominance next to each other—it is no longer. Instead, Siwichai and the Thai king, Bhumibol Adulyadej, are both signs of *barami* more than they are of their respective polities. The juxtaposition reminded me of seeing conservative Americans in my hometown in southern Virginia flying Confederate and American flags together without feeling that these two symbols contradict each other. In the American case, both flags represented something free and rebellious (an interpretation that would be hotly refuted by many of those for whom the Dixie flag was a symbol of slavery). But in each case, the former opposition has been subsumed under a common underlying idea of unity: their high status in terms of merit, charisma, and *khwam charoen* equate Siwichai and Bhumibol just as, for conservative white Southerners, notions of independence and rebellion bring together Dixie and the Union.

11   TAT data show 54% of visitors as Thai. Other significant groups include Americans (8%), Malaysians (4%), British, Japanese, German, and French (3% each). The data are based on hotel occupancy and reflect somewhat of an atypical year, given both the Floral Exposition for the King in Chiang Mai (2006–2007) and the military coup of 2006.

12   I use this word to refer to a generalized time before the influence of European powers accelerated in the mid-nineteenth century, acknowledging that Thailand did not in fact have an "official" colonizing power.

13   Other Thai words function in similar ways. Bangkok and other large centers are termed *krung*. *Krung* is never used to refer to Chiang Mai but only to centers of Central Thai authority—Bangkok, Ayutthaya, and Thonburi. *Krung*, to Chiang Mai residents, means a place marked by modernity, bustle, activity, and size over and increasing that of Chiang Mai itself. While a *mueang* is a center in the wilderness and a place where religion, art, and politics reach their peaks, the *krung* is a node in a *world* network, where cosmopolitan forces and international influences mingle. A *krung* is a metropole—a usage exemplified by the term Krung Rattanakosin, in reference both to the city of Bangkok, Rattanakosin Island (site of the royal palace and center of Bangkok's government), and the monarchy.

But here are multiple meanings: city, state, and king. As Thongchai notes, the word *krung* was used prior to 1914 to mean a polity. In this formulation, it is the capital city with its embedded ruler that defines the country, and not its geographic scope (O'Connor 1990). Such boundaries only become significant during the late nineteenth and twentieth centuries, and as a result a word formerly meaning "region" or "area"—*prathet*—becomes used to represent "nation-state" (Thongchai 1994, 135).

14 I mention this group in the Introduction: the "great Thai," as they are called in Thai, of Burma are also called "Shan" in Burmese, and simply "Tai" in their own language.

15 "Lawa" itself is an unstable ethnic category, at its roots simply meaning "non-Buddhist" (Scott 2010, 254). Today, the term "Lawa" has become defined to mean a largely assimilated ethnic group in the region. The Mon, in contrast, were and are lowland Buddhist wet-rice cultivators and maintain a strong presence on the Thai-Burmese border region. Linguistically, Mon and Lawa are both in the Mon-Khmer group.

16 Stories of the Buddha's travels in Northern Thailand remain popular myth.

17 The conch is a symbol of Vishnu and signifies righteous rule.

18 And, though the chronicles do not mention this, presumably a population.

19 According to different texts and oral stories, Chamadewi was alternatively believed to have been born in Lopburi but stolen from the cradle by an eagle, or mystically conceived by Wasuthep. Other versions have Wasuthep sending for an adult Chamadewi in Lavapura. Yet in all cases, the giant of the mountain calls upon the power of the city to build Haripunchai.

20 The reason for women and transgendered individuals being mediums is generally ascribed to their penetrability. Men normally have "hard souls" (*khwan khaeng*) and do not accept inhabiting spirits as easily as women or gay men. Peter Jackson has written extensively on Thai gay and transgender identity (Jackson 1996).

21 The use of masculine/feminine pronouns in describing mediumship is problematic. The medium is male but the spirit is female (in most examples of mediumship, this situation is reversed). Thai and Northern Thai third-person pronouns are gender-neutral (*khao* and *poen* being the most common, respectively), but mediums will speak with the gendered language of whatever spirit they are channeling. They are likewise generally treated as the gender which they are performing, so in deference to this, I use the gendered pronoun of the *spirit* rather than the vessel.

22 Rosalind Morris, in *In the Place of Origins* (2000), delivers a detailed analysis of the relationship between media and mediums in Chiang Mai.

23 As McDaniel 2011, Terwiel 2012, and Pattana 2005 note, popular Thai Buddhism interweaves multiple threads of practice and belief. Attempting to separate out "animist" or "Buddhist" or "Brahmin" aspects prove unfruitful, even if orders such as the Thammayut attempt to do so.

24 Cambodian ritual in Central Thailand is also considered "more powerful," as is Shan magic by Northern Thais.

25 In popular Thai film and history, Burma is typically cast as the principal villain (see Pavin 2005 and my discussion in Chapter 1).

26 Turton translates *kham daeng* as "golden," whereas I translate it as "copper."

27 It is worth noting that the common Northern term for king—*chao*—is identical to that used for higher spirits and gods.

28 Ngammueang and his city-state of Phayao fades from the historical record along with the rise of Sukhothai and Lanna. He is present in the statue as he is present in the Yonok Chronicle, but he remains a somewhat subordinate figure in the

history and historiography of the region. Phayao plays a key role as the home of Kham Daeng in Chiang Mai's "History 2."

29 The mediumship, dancing, drinking, and many other aspects of the ritual distinguish it markedly from middle-class worship of Central Thai monarchs. See Stengs 2009.

30 The figure of Chamadewi undoubtedly raises the question of queenship in Thai ideas of *barami*. While most possessing spirits are male and most Tai rulers were kings, queens were not unheard of. Female spirits can also be sources of *barami*, although they are more often associated with popular religion and magic (*sayasat*) (Johnson 2012).

31 I.e., during the reign of Chulalongkorn, Rama V. This era was marked by rapid modernization and a centralization of the absolute monarchy.

32 Numbers refer to chapter and page. Translations and references are from the online English translation done by Pasuk and Baker and posted at http://pioneer .netserv.chula.ac.th/~ppasuk/kckp/chapters.htm (accessed June 2009).

CHAPTER 3: Mediums

1 Daena Aki Funahashi was taking a break from her own work in Finland (Funahashi 2013) and visiting me at my field site.

2 These are a combination of Buddhist and animist prohibitions and serve to illuminate Chiang Mai's hybrid religious world. With regard to two-story structures, entering such a building would force Yellow to be spatially underneath beings to which he was spiritually superior. Such an inversion of high and low would, in Northern Thai cosmology, have profound consequences, disrupting Yellow's power and causing him to become angry. See my discussion of *khuet* in Chapter 5.

3 Yellow here is behaving quite like Morris' informant (2000).

4 "Witch" and "warrior" spirits are variations on the forms of possession that I describe here. In each case, they are dominated by older women. I use the term "witch" here as a translation of *mot*, and "warrior" to describe the *meng*'s more martial character. *Meng* is the Northern Thai word for Mon—significant in light of Kham's connection between spirits and Burma.

5 After several months, when it became plain that romance was not to bloom between Noi and me, Yellow admitted to me he had made a mistake, saying that, while at first he had divined that Noi and I had been married in a previous life, now he saw more clearly that she and I had been siblings.

6 *Su Phaendin Mai* was an attempt to create a "new epic" in Thai literature, one that narrated the migration of Tai peoples down into what is now Thailand. In writing, Sanya rehashes old and discredited theories (e.g., Dodd 1996) and reinforces notions both of Chiang Mai as allochronous, "pure" space, and Bangkok as the inevitable product of a "Thai" process of *charoen*.

7 Morris connects this medium's spirit to a poet by the name of Phayaphom from the late nineteenth century. An alternate reading of Morris' spirit medium's

possessing spirit would be one stemming from Northern Thai history. A famous palm-leaf text describes the adventures of *phrachao phrom* in Chiang Saen (Manit et al. 2002)—here, I should note that, like *phrachao*, *phaya* is a title meaning "Lord," so the difference between *phrachao phom* and *phaya phom* is negligible.

8   As I have discussed, in the *tamnan* many older Northern lords have the name "Lao" in their titles. The meaning is unclear, although Cholthira interprets it as meaning "Lawa" (1991, 70).

9   Red or orange Fanta was the preferred soft drink of the spirits, as it was bright and colorful (unlike Sprite) and not overly dark and gloomy (unlike Coke or grape Fanta). Few Northern spirits "drank" dark liquids, unlike the Central Thai practice of propitiating Rahu with black objects.

10 The body was preserved in a *rong kaeo*, a glass case where it is worshipped today. Whether or not it is in fact a waxwork model, as is found in many other temples, is irrelevant. Kham, Noi, and many others believed it to be the actual corpse. Non-decay as a marker of sacredness is something that flies in the face of traditional Buddhist teachings about non-permanence and the decay of all things (see Klima 2002). Here, it is an example of the—as Shigeharu Tanabe puts it when speaking of gender—"multiplicity and inconsistency" (Tanabe 1991, 183) present in religious discourse. As McDaniel argues (2011), the religious lives of Noi and her fellows are not structured by pure Buddhist doctrine, but rest on more vernacular systems. For one local abbot whom I asked about such inconsistencies, there was little problem: while he admitted that occasionally temples accepted things in which he held little faith (such as wax monks), he argued that such practices strengthened belief in Buddhism and, in that respect, the good outweighed the bad.

11 Recall the connection between the term for "medicine," *ya,* and its earlier meaning of "magic."

12 *Man* is an extremely familiar third-person pronoun. Here, it refers to the close relationship between husband and wife and also between spirit and supplicant.

13 Here, the spirit is using extremely familiar terms. This is a break from *pho*, "Father," that he uses earlier, and here his use of familiar language shows his anger. The resultant feeling would depend on dialect and the nature of this particular spirit–supplicant relationship, but it might be equivalent to "Damn it, I already told you he hasn't!" Kham's spirits were often studiously polite, with the exception of Yellow's initial outburst toward me; but such rude familiarity was not unheard of, especially among "wilder" spirits.

14 Here, the spirit (and the supplicant) uses pronouns that place the supplicant at the level of a child with respect to the spirit—*nu* is the pronoun that children use with adults.

CHAPTER 4: Lanna Style

1   This was Kham's (and the community's) garden plot, not to be confused with the large agro-business tobacco plantation where she occasionally worked.

2   *Anu* was my nickname, a shortened version of "Andrew."

3   BKK is the airport code for "Bangkok."

4   The title was in English, although the text was in Thai.

5   The Ramkhamhaeng stele is the (likely forged) monument upon which much of Thai scholars' knowledge about Sukhothai is based. Wichit unquestionably invented parts of Sukhothai that he wished to highlight, but whether or not the stele itself is a fake is hotly debated (see Vickery 1991; Wyatt 1991; Mukhom 2003).

6   Pai becomes another central point for tourism in the North, both national and international. For international circles, it is a sort of hippy destination, full of folk music and backpackers. For national circles, the image could not be more different—Pai is a cool, trendy, and luxurious spot for wealthy Bangkokians to explore the Northern mountains. For another film example of the wealthy Thai interest in Pai, see the 2009 film *Pai in Love* (Tanit 2009).

7   The word for "person," *chao,* and "lord," *chao,* differ in ways that the Royal Thai General System of Romanization does not express. "Person" begins with an aspirated *ch,* a long *a* vowel, and a flat tone (similar to the English *chow*); whereas "lord" begins with an unaspirated *ch* (similar to an English *j*), a short *ao,* and a falling tone. There is no link, or even rhyme, between the two in Thai.

8   The significance of Ton as a royal employee in the North should not be lost, given the focus on the king's role as a conduit for *charoen.*

9   *Pak pen aek, lek pen tho:* literally, "Mouth is one, numbers are two."

10 The Punna site was also the location of the story about the laborer's ghost that I recount in Chapter 1.

11 At the time of my interview, the building, out of seventy-five total units, housed forty-six Thais, four British, three Korean, and two Japanese residents, with twenty rooms remaining empty.

12 The development group romanizes the word *punna,* although I would write *panna.* The term means "thousand [*pan*] rice fields [*na*]" in the same way that "Lanna" means "million rice fields." Central Thai would alter the word by aspirating the initial *p* in order to keep the same meaning.

13 This is a nighttime zoo, more conducive both to a Southeast Asian climate and to the nocturnal schedules of many mammals.

14 A common complaint was that contracts were handed to Thaksin's allies without being made available to other vendors in the city.

15 The Night Safari, as another Thaksin megaproject, is also an interesting study. In 2006 and 2007 it was administered by Plodprasop Suraswadi, a political ally of Thaksin, but its future is continually thrown into doubt. After over three hundred animal deaths and two escapes (of Canadian wolves), foreign governments refused to send more animals to the project.

16 http://www.royalfloraexpo.com (accessed May 2007; now off-line).

17 Thailand's Muslim, Christian, and animist populations are presumably left out of this supposed unity.

18 *Ho kham,* a Northern Thai and Lao term for the dwelling place of a king.

19 "The Golden Land," a term taken from accounts of the Buddhist Indian emperor Asoka and today used as a reference to mainland Southeast Asia, especially Theravada Buddhist areas.

20 http://www.royalfloraexpo.com/about_expo/intro.html (accessed December 2012).

21 Though in the higher country there will occasionally be frost on the ground in the morning in winter, such an event makes the front page of the newspaper. None of my informants had ever seen or heard of actual snow falling in the North, not even on the tallest peak. The word for "snow," *hima,* is Sanskrit, not Tai in origin.

22 A Thai unit dividing land; 2.5 *rai* is equal to one acre.

23 Lung was a staunch Thaksin supporter. His anger over Thaksin's ouster conflicting with his pride in Thaksin's proposed feats may have been the underlying reason why he so adamantly refused to go but still lauded the site.

24 One subtracts 543 from BE dates to arrive at CE. Buddhist Era 2549 is therefore 2006 CE.

25 The reader might be confused about what "Love the King . . . Sufficiency" means. Does the sign intend to say that the park's excess is the only "sufficient" reward for a king? How does one reconcile calls for sufficiency with the huge amount of labor and water needed to maintain the park (and to justify the destruction of the forest)? I asked a number of my informants about the slogan, and none of them answered my question directly. Those who considered themselves royalists (e.g., Maew and Tong) countered with, "It means Thai people love the king" (often stated to me in English, even when I had conducted the entire previous conversation in Thai—here was a chance to show the foreigner that he was truly foreign here); those of my informants who were (quietly and privately) opposed to the monarchy claimed that the slogan was meaningless.

26 The "red/yellow" divide split Thailand, growing around 2007 and peaking during the political violence of 2010. During the period of my research at Ratchaphruek in 2006, this split was in its infancy. At the time of Ratchaphruek, the yellow shirts were unchallenged as symbols of monarchical love and were worn by the supporters of Thaksin as well as by his opponents. During the course of my fieldwork, the first few red shirts appeared in Chiang Mai, often on sale at the very same places where yellow or blue shirts (for the queen) were being sold. In the months just after Thaksin's ouster, although there was a good deal of anger in Chiang Mai, this anger had not yet coalesced into the street protest movement. After the election of 2011, when Thaksin's sister Yingluck won the PM seat, the Yellow Shirt movement dissipated into multiple factions and its message became coherent, while the Red Shirts remain at the time of writing (2013) politically powerful.

27 The Chatukam amulets had the image of a deity (of disputed origin) on one side and on the other an auspicious symbol that varied from brand to brand. These deities originated in a temple in Nakhon Si Thammarat in Thailand's south, and the amulets were widely believed to be capable of bestowing miraculous amounts of wealth upon their bearers.

28   The number is significant both in that the current king is the ninth Chakri king of Thailand and in that the number nine—*kao*—is a close homonym for the word "to step forward," thus making it auspicious. Only those close informants of mine who had privately expressed antimonarchical attitudes suggested that the result of 999 on the king's birthday was evidence that the lottery system was rigged; others to whom I mentioned it regarded the numbers as a genuine sign of the king's *barami*.

29   The word is Japanese, not Thai.

CHAPTER 5: Rebuilding Lanna

1   The reaction against high-rise architecture also reflected a more emboldened intelligentsia. Educated leftists who had flocked to the communist insurgency (had *khao pa*, "entered the forest") in the 1970s were by the late 1980s drifting back under the Thai government's amnesty plan, following the dissolution of the Thai Communist Party. Many became academics and adopted localist or anticonsumerist causes.

2   With Thaksin's ouster in 2006 and the rise of military rule, many of these groups also split. Each was anti-Thaksin during his administration; but some, like Thanet, could no more stomach military rule than they could Thaksin, while others, like the Love Chiang Mai Group, were ardently "Yellow."

3   Technically including Christian churches and Muslim mosques.

4   Including the city wall, which, significantly, is not in the previous category.

5   *Phu wa*, an official appointed by the Ministry of the Interior.

6   Here, I define "civil society" as the loose network of nongovernmental organizations (NGOs). Chiang Mai hosts a large number of these, ranging from groups affiliated with Chiang Mai University, various community-based groups, and hill-tribe focused groups to NGOs associated with Burmese refugee networks.

7   One should also note the compatibility of this statement with Fishel's analysis of *barami* versus transparency in Thai political discourse (2001).

8   Pavin Chachavalapongpun (2010) notes a similar language ("selling off the nation") as key in the discourse of those opposing Thaksin Shinawatra.

9   Thailand has no state religion, a fact that Aek, as a government official, should know. Yet the monarch must be a Buddhist, and most Thai understand "religion," *satsana,* one of the pillars (*lak*) of the Thai nation to be Buddhism.

10   Chatthip argues that Thai peasant culture is naturally antistate and anticapitalist and rooted in Buddhist belief. He advocates that NGO practice adopt these notions—a call that gained no small amount of support during the height of the anti-Thaksin years (prior to 2006) . However, he reifies both the idea of "Thai" and the centrality of Buddhism to this fundamentally "Thai" thought.

11   See references to the famous Northern monk Khuba Siwichai elsewhere.

12   A claim that aroused the ire of other academics, planners, and monks.

13   Pseudonym.

14 In fact, this is not an entirely accurate characterization. International standards of human rights often conflict with social norms that stress mutual obligation over individual independence. For instance, one could imagine a scenario where an entire family is made to account for one of its members' crime.

15 Here again we see the association of an abandoned building with misfortune and ghosts.

16 Pseudonym.

GLOSSARY

amnat. Power, authority, right, etc., exercised without a moral direction; amoral power.

atthan. Cursedness, inauspiciousness.

barami. Power, charisma, authority stemming from moral righteousness.

bun. Merit in a Buddhist sense.

chao. A lord, used for both earthly kings and powerful spirits. Pronounced with a short falling tone and an unaspirated *ch,* distinguishing it from *chao* (person), which is pronounced with an aspirated *ch* and long flat tone.

chao khao. Highlanders, hill tribes. Mostly refers to members of the Hmong, Karen, Lisu, Akha, Mien, etc., ethnic minorities.

Chao Luang Kham Daeng. Chief spirit of the Chiang Mai area, with his central shrine in Chiang Dao.

chao nai. Literally, "nobility," but here referring to one kind of possessing spirit, *phi chao nai.*

chao noi. Literally, "small lord," but here referring to a possessing spirit who is a child.

charoen. To progress, to prosper, to grow. Implies wise progress, lasting change. In its noun form (e.g., "progress"), *khwam charoen;* in its adjectival form (e.g., "progressed"), *charoen laeo.*

chat. Nation, ethnicity. See Thongchai 1994.

chon. Bandits, thieves. Not to be confused with *chon* (person), which has an aspirated *ch.*

farang. A white foreigner, Caucasian, westerner.

fon phi. Dancing while possessed by spirits.

hian. To haunt in an angry, violent manner. A spirit that haunts in this way.

ho kham. Literally, "golden hall," a palace. Herein refers to the central hall of Ratchaphruek.

ho phi. The central structure in a spirit shrine.

Inthakin. The city pillar of Chiang Mai, housed at Chedi Luang temple.

kam mueang. Literally, "city words." Northern Thai language.

kan phatthana. See *phatthana.*

kha. A serf, a servant.

khantok. An "invented tradition" consisting of a Northern Thai dinner with a floor show, often mixing Northern Thai, Shan, and hill-tribe dances.

khuet (Northern Thai). A taboo.

khon mueang. A Northern Thai person. Usually assumed to be ethnically Yuan or Yong and Buddhist.

khuang (Northern Thai). An open plaza in Northern Thai architecture.

khwam charoen. See *charoen*.

Lanna. A kingdom, occasionally independent and occasionally vassal, centered on Chiang Mai (or, briefly, Chiang Rai or Chiang Saen), beginning in the thirteenth century. In modern usage, Northern Thailand, sometimes excluding Nan Province.

lok. To haunt, to fool, to trick.

mandala (Sanskrit). Literally, "a circle"; herein refers to a relatively borderless polity centered on the body of the monarch and an urban sacred center.

mueang. A city, a polity. Comparable in some usages to Sanskrit *mandala*.

Ngiao (Northern Thai). A Shan, a member of an ethnic minority spanning the Thai and Burmese border speaking a Tai language.

phatthana. To develop. While still usually positive, it lacks the religious connotations of *charoen*. In noun form ("development"), *kan phatthana*.

phi. Ghost, spirit. In Northern Thai use, less negative than in Central Thai use.

phi a-hak (Northern Thai). Guardian spirit of a city or place.

phi pu ya. Ancestral spirit.

phi tai hong. A ghost created by an inauspicious death (especially resulting from an accident or sudden disease).

phra-det. Kingly power, force, might. To be compared with *amnat*.

phra-khun. Another form of kingly power, but persuasive, coaxing, rather than coercive. To be compared with *barami*.

pret. A hungry ghost, suffering from karmic punishment.

sak. Sacrality, magical power.

suep chata mueang. Ritual performed to bolster the fortunes of the city.

siwilai. "Civilization," cultivation.

Tai. Ethnic and linguistic group encompassing Thai (Siamese), Northern Thai, Shan, Lao, and others.

tamnan. Chronicles, legends.

Thai-Yai. Official, Central Thai term for Shan, an ethnic group spanning the Thai-Burmese border and speaking a related language.

thaksa. System of sacred space surrounding a city.

thansamai. Modernity, up-to-dateness.

thep. An angelic spirit.

thewada. An angelic spirit, comparable to the Sanskrit *deva*.

wai. A gesture of greeting, thanks, devotion, and/or respect performed by placing the hands together in front of oneself, elbows down at the sides, and lowering the head slightly. Those lower in rank will perform an earlier and deeper *wai*, and those higher in rank (although not monks or kings) will reciprocate afterwards.

watthanatham. Culture.

wiang. A walled city.

yak. A giant, a demon. Fierce *yak* often guard the entrances to temples, especially in Central Thailand.

yan. A neighborhood, an area of the city.

yok khru (Northern Thai). An event honoring a certain teacher, holy person, or spirit. Comparable to Central Thai *wai khru.*

Yuan. Predominant ethnic group in Chiang Mai. Less inclusive than *khon mueang.* Contrastive with Khoen, Yong, Thai-Yai, etc. Often written "Thai-Yuan."

REFERENCES

Amporn Jirattikorn. 2003. Suriyothai: Hybridizing Thai national identity through film. *Inter-Asia Cultural Studies* 4, no. 2: 296–308.

———. 2008. Pirated transnational broadcasting: The consumption of Thai soap operas among Shan communities in Burma. *Sojourn* 23, no. 1: 30–62.

Anan Ganjanapan. 1984. The idiom of Phi Ka: Peasant conception of class differentiation in Northern Thailand. *Mankind* 14, no. 4, special issue 3: 325–329.

Anderson, Benedict R. O'G. 1972. The idea of power in Javanese culture. In *Culture and politics in Indonesia*, ed. Claire Holt, Benedict R. O'G. Anderson, and James Seigel, pp. 1–70. Ithaca, NY: Cornell University Press.

———. 1977. Withdrawal symptoms: Social and cultural aspects of the October 6 coup. *Critical Asian Studies* 9, no. 3: 13–30.

Aroonrat Wichiankhieo. 1982. *Lanna Thai Sueksa*. Chiang Mai: Chiang Mai Teacher's College.

Aroonrat Wichiankhieo and Gehan Wijeyewardene. 1986. *The laws of King Mangrai (Mangrayathammasart): The Wat Chang Kham, Nan manuscript from the Richard Davis Collection*. Canberra: Australia National University.

Askew, Marc. 1996. The rise of Moradok and the decline of the yarn: Heritage and cultural construction in urban Bangkok. In *Sojourn* 11, no. 2: 183–210.

Bangkok Post. 2002. Terrorists attack school bus: Suspicions centre on small ethnic groups. June 5.

———. 2012. Dhammakaya "knows" Jobs' afterlife, August 20. http://www.bangkokpost.com/breakingnews/308543/dhammakaya-boasts-steve-jobs-afterlife (accessed April 21, 2013).

Barmé, Scot. 1993. *Luang Wichit Wathakan and the creation of a Thai identity*. Singapore: Institute of Southeast Asian Studies.

Bowie, Katherine. 1997. *Rituals of national loyalty*. New York: Columbia University Press.

Buddhadatta, Mahathera. 1962. *Jinakālamālī*. London: Pali Text Society. Bunnell, Tim. 2013. City networks as alternative geographies of Southeast Asia. *TRaNS: Trans-regional and -national studies of Southeast Asia* 1, no. 1. Seoul: Sogang University.

Buntha Siphimchai, Khomnet Chetthaphatthanawanit, and Silao Ketphrom. 1996. *Khuet: Kho Ham Nai Lanna*. Chiang Mai: Chiang Mai University.

————. 2004. *Mai Mi Wat Nai Thaksa Mueang Chiang Mai: Bot Phisut Khwam Ching Doi Nak Wichakan Thong Thin*. Chiang Mai: Social Research Center. In Thai.

————. 2005. *Sustainable cities in Chiang Mai: A case of a city in a valley (Mueang Yangyuen nai Chiang Mai: Naeokhit lae prasopkan khong mueang nai hup khao)*. Chiang Mai: Chiang Mai University.

Dube, Saurabh. 2010. *Enchantments of modernity: Empire, nation, globalization*. New York: Routledge.

Duncan, James S. 1990. *The city as text: The politics of landscape interpretation in the Kandyan kingdom*. Cambridge: Cambridge University Press.

Evans-Pritchard, E. 1976. *Witchcraft, oracles and magic among the Azande*. Oxford: Oxford University Press.

Ferguson, Jane. 2010. Another country is the past: Western cowboys, Lanna nostalgia, and bluegrass aesthetics as performed by professional musicians in Northern Thailand. *American Ethnologist* 37, no. 2: 227–240.

Fishel, Thamora Virginia. 2001. Reciprocity and democracy: Power, gender, and the provincial middle class in Thai political culture. PhD diss., Cornell University.

Foster, Michael Dylan. 2008. *Pandemonium and parade: Japanese monsters and the culture of Yokai*. Berkeley: University of California Press.

Freud, Sigmund. 2003 [1919]. *The uncanny*. Trans. David McLintock and Hugh Haughton. New York: Penguin Books.

Funahashi, Daena Aki. 2013. Wrapped in plastic: Transformation and alienation in the new Finnish economy. *Cultural Anthropology* 28, no. 1: 1–21.

Geertz, Clifford. 1980. *Negara: The theatre state in nineteenth-century Bali*. Princeton, NJ: Princeton University Press.

Gordon, Avery. 2008. *Ghostly matters: Haunting and the sociological imagination*. Minneapolis: University of Minnesota Press.

Haeman Chatemee. 2006. *The memory (Rak Chang)*. Bangkok: RS Film. 105 min.

Handley, Paul M. 2006. *The king never smiles: A biography of Thailand's Bhumibol Adulyadej*. New Haven, CT: Yale University Press.

Hanks, Lucien M. 1962. Merit and power in the Thai social order. *American Anthropologist* 64, no. 6: 1247–1261.

Hansen, Anne. 2008 Gaps in the world: Violence, harm and suffering in Khmer ethical narratives. In *At the edge of the forest: Essays on Cambodia, history, and narrative in honor of David Chandler*, ed. David Chandler, Anne Ruth Hansen, and Judy Ledgerwood, pp. 47–70. Ithaca, NY: Southeast Asia Program, Cornell University.

Harms, Erik. 2010. *Saigon's edge: On the margins of Ho Chi Minh City*. Minneapolis: University of Minnesota Press.

Headley, Robert K., Kylin Chhor, Lum Kheng Lim, Lim Hak Kheang, and Chen Chun. 1977. *Cambodian-English dictionary, volume I*. Washington, DC: Catholic University of America Press.

Heidegger, Martin. 1977 [1954]. *The question concerning technology, and other essays*. New York: Harper & Row.

Herzfeld, Michael. 1986. Closure as cure: Tropes in the exploration of bodily and social disorder. *Current Anthropology* 27: 107–120.

———. 2002. The absent presence: Discourses of crypto-colonialism. *South Atlantic Quarterly* 101, no. 4: 899–926.

———. 2005. *Cultural intimacy: Social poetics in the nation-state.* 2nd ed. New York and London: Routledge.

———. 2006. Spatial cleansing. *Journal of Material Culture* 11, nos. 1–2: 127–149.

———. 2010. Engagement, gentrification and the neoliberal hijacking of history. *Current Anthropology* 51, no. S2, Engaged anthropology: Diversity and dilemmas, S259–S267.

Hirschman, Charles. 1987. The meaning and measurement of ethnicity in Malaysia: An analysis of census classifications. *Journal of Asian Studies* 46, no. 3: 555–582.

Hobsbawm, Eric J., and Terence O. Ranger. 1983. *The invention of tradition.* Cambridge: Cambridge University Press.

Holt, John Clifford. 2009. *Spirits of the place: Buddhism and Lao religious culture.* Honolulu: University of Hawai'i Press.

Hong Lysa. 1998. Of consorts and harlots in Thai popular history. *Journal of Asian Studies* 57, no. 2: 333–353.

Irvine, Walter. 1984. Decline of village spirit cults and growth of urban spirit mediumship: The persistence of spirit beliefs, the position of women and modernization. *Mankind* 14, no. 4: 315–324.

Jackson, Peter. 1998. The magic monk in boom time Thailand: The cult of Luang Phor (Reverend Father) Khoon. *Asia Pacific Magazine* 11: 4–7.

———. 2004. The Thai regime of images. *Sojourn* 19, no. 2: 181–218.

———. 2010. Virtual divinity: A twenty-first-century discourse of Thai royal influence. In *Saying the unsayable: Monarchy and democracy in Thailand,* ed. Søren Ivarsson and Lotte Isager, pp. 29–60. Singapore: Nordic Institute of Asian Studies.

Johnson, Andrew Alan. 2007. Authenticity, tourism, and self-discovery in Thailand: Self-creation and the discerning gaze of trekkers and old hands. *Sojourn* 22, no. 2: 153–178.

———. 2010. Rebuilding Lanna: Constructing and consuming the past in urban Northern Thailand. PhD diss., Cornell University.

———. 2011. Re-centering the city: Spirits, local wisdom, and urban design at the Three Kings Monument of Chiang Mai. *Journal of Southeast Asian Studies* 42, no. 3: 511–531.

———. 2012. Naming chaos: Accident, precariousness, and the spirits of wildness in urban Thai spirit cults. *American Ethnologist* 39, no. 4: 766–778.

Jonsson, Hjorleifur. 2005. *Mien relations: Mountain people and state control in Thailand.* Ithaca, NY: Cornell University Press.

———. 2010. Above and beyond: *Zomia* and the ethnographic challenge of/for regional history. *History and Anthropology* 21, no. 2: 191–212.

Kapferer, Bruce. 1988. *Legends of people, myths of state: Violence, intolerance and political culture in Sri Lanka and Australia.* Washington, DC: Smithsonian Institution.

———. 2003. *Beyond rationalism: Rethinking magic, witchcraft and sorcery.* New York: Berghahn Books.

Karuna Raksawin. 2002. *The study of Chiang Mai public open space for city activities (Kan sueksa thi long wang sattharana nai mueang Chiang Mai phuea kan prakop kitchakam nanthanakan radap mueang).* Chiang Mai: Chiang Mai University.

Kasian Tejapira. 2002. The postmodern of Thainess. In *Cultural crisis and social memory: Modernity and identity in Thailand and Laos,* ed. Shigeharu Tanabe and Charles F. Keyes, pp. 202–230. Honolulu: University of Hawai'i Press.

Keyes, Charles. 1973. The power of merit. In *Visakha Puja B.E. 2516,* pp. 95–102. Bangkok: The Buddhist Association of Thailand.

———. 1975. Buddhism in a secular city: A view from Chiang Mai. In *Visakha Puja B.E. 2518:* 62–72. Bangkok: The Buddhist Association of Thailand.

———. 2002. National heroine or local spirit: The struggle over memory in the case of Thao Suranari of Nakhorn Ratchasima. In *Cultural crisis and social memory: Modernity and identity in Thailand and Laos,* ed. Shigeharu Tanabe and Charles F. Keyes, pp. 202–230. Honolulu: University of Hawai'i Press.

———. 2006. The destruction of a shrine to Brahma in Bangkok and the fall of Thaksin Shinawatra: The occult and the Thai coup in Thailand of September 2006. Asia Research Institute Working Paper No. 86. http://www.ari.nus.edu.sg/docs/wps/wps06_080.pdf.

———. 2013. The village economy: Capitalist AND sufficiency-based. A northeastern Thai case. In *Exploring sufficiency economy: Ethics, practices, challenges,* ed. Seri Phongphit, Istvan Rado, and Nate Long. Bangkok: Prajhadipok Institut.

King, Ross. 2010. *Reading Bangkok.* Singapore: NUS Press.

Kirsch, A. Thomas. 1977. Complexity in the Thai religious system. *Journal of Asian Studies* 36, no. 2: 241–66.

Klima, Alan. 2002. *The funeral casino: Meditation, massacre, and exchange with the dead in Thailand.* Princeton, NJ: Princeton University Press.

———. 2006. Spirits of "dark finance" in Thailand: A local hazard for the International Moral Fund. *Cultural Dynamics* 18, no. 1: 33–60.

Kraisri Nimmanhaemin. 1965. Put vegetables in baskets and people into towns. In *Ethnographic notes on Northern Thailand,* ed. Lucien M. Hanks and Jane Richardson Hanks, pp. 6–9. Ithaca, NY: Southeast Asia Program, Cornell University.

———.1967. The Lawa guardian spirits of Chiengmai. *Journal of the Siam Society* 55, no. 2: 185–226.

Lambek, Michael. 2002. *The weight of the past: Living with history in Mahajanga, Madagascar.* New York: Palgrave MacMillan.

Langford, Jean M. 2009. Gifts intercepted: Biopolitics and spirit debt. *Cultural Anthropology* 24, no. 4: 681–711.

Leach, Edmund Ronald. 1973. *Political systems of highland Burma: A study of Kachin social structure.* Boston: Beacon Press.

Lefebvre, Henri. 1996. *Writings on cities.* Trans. Eleonore Kofman and Elizabeth Lebas. New York: Wiley.

Le May, Reginald. 1986 [1926]. *An Asian arcady: The land and peoples of northern Siam.* Cambridge: W. Heffner.

Loos, Tamara Lynn. 2006. *Subject Siam: Family, law, and colonial modernity in Thailand.* Ithaca, NY: Cornell University Press.

Low, Setha. 2003. *Behind the gates: Life, security, and the pursuit of happiness in fortress America.* New York: Routledge.

Mala Khamjan. 2008. *Ghosts of Lanna (Phi nai Lanna).* Chiang Mai: Happy Book Publishing.

Manee Phayaomyong. 1994. *Twelve months of Lannathai customs (Prapheni sipsong duean Lanna Thai).* Lanna Studies documents number 3. Chiang Mai: S. Sapkanpim.

Manit Wanliphohdom, Sisak Wanliphohdom, Phiset Jiajanphong, and Sujit Wongthet. 2002. *Lord Phrom in the Yonok Chronicle (Phrachao Phrom wiraburut nai Tamnan khong Yonok-Lanna).* Bangkok: Matichon.

McDaniel, Justin Thomas. 2011. *The lovelorn ghost and the magical monk: Practicing Buddhism in modern Thailand.* New York: Columbia University Press.

McMorran, M. V. 1984. Northern Thai ancestral cults: Authority and aggression. *Mankind* 14, no. 4: 308–314.

Mills, Mary Beth. 1995. Attack of the widow ghosts: Gender, death, and modernity in northeast Thailand. In *Bewitching women, pious men: Gender and body politics in Southeast Asia,* ed. Aihwa Ong and Michael Peletz, pp. 244–273. Berkeley: University of California Press.

———. 1999. *Thai women in the global labor force: Consuming desires, contested selves.* New Brunswick, NJ: Rutgers University Press.

Morris, Rosalind C. 2000. *In the place of origins: Modernity and its mediums in Northern Thailand.* Chapel Hill, NC: Duke University Press.

———. 2002. Failures of domestication: Speculations on globality, economy, and the sex of excess in Thailand. *Differences* 13: 45–76.

Muecke, Marjorie A. 1984. Make money not babies: Changing status markers of Northern Thai women. *Asian Survey* 24, no. 4: 459–470.

Mukhom Wongthes. 2003. *Intellectual might and national myth: A forensic investigation of the Ram Khamhaeng controversy in Thai society.* Bangkok: Matichon.

Nelson, Diane. 1999. *A finger in the wound: Body politics in quincentennial Guatemala.* Berkeley: University of California Press.

Nidthi Eoseewong. 1991. Sao khrua fa. *Silapa Watthanatham* 12, no. 6: 180–185.

Nophakhun Tantikun. 2003. *The Story of Lord Phab (Wirokam Phaya Phap: Nan techa haeng khwaeng nong chom san sai).* Chiang Mai: Mingkhwan.

O'Connor, Richard. 1990. Siamese Tai in Tai context: The impact of a ruling center. *Crossroads* 5, no. 1:1–21.

Pa-oon Chantarasiri. 2004. *The letter (Chot Mai Rak).* Bangkok: Sahamongol Film. 109 min.

Parle, Julie. 2003. Witchcraft or madness? The Amandiki of Zululand, 1894–1914. *Journal of Southern African Studies* 29, no. 1: 105–132.

Pasuk Phongpaichit and Christopher John Baker. 1995. *Thailand, economy and politics.* Kuala Lumpur: Oxford University Press.

———. 2009. *Khun Chang Khun Phaen.* http://pioneer.netserv.chula.ac.th/~ppasuk /kckp/kckpmain.htm (accessed June 20, 2009).

———. 2010. *Thaksin.* 2nd ed. Seattle: University of Washington Press

Pattana Kitiarsa. 2003. You may not believe, but never offend the spirits. In *Global goes local: Popular culture in Asia,* ed. Timothy Craig and Richard King, pp. 160–176. Vancouver: UBC Press.

———. 2005. Beyond syncretism: Hybridization of popular religion in contemporary Thailand. *Journal of Southeast Asian Studies* 36, no. 3: 461–487.

———. 2006. In defense of the Thai-style democracy. http://www.ari.nus.edu.sg/showfile.asp?eventfileid=188 (accessed December 2012).

———. 2010. An ambiguous intimacy: Farang as Siamese occidentalis. In *The ambiguous allure of the West: Traces of the colonial in Thailand,* ed. Rachel Harrison and Peter Jackson, pp. 57–74. Ithaca, NY: Cornell Southeast Asian Program Publications.

Pavin Chachavalapongpun. 2005. *A plastic nation: The curse of Thainess in Thai-Burmese relations.* Lanham, MD: University Press of America.

———. 2010. Temple of doom: Hysteria about the Preah Vihear Temple in the Thai nationalist discourse. In *Legitimacy crisis in Thailand,* ed. Marc Askew, pp. 83–117. Chiang Mai: Silkworm Books.

Peleggi, Maurizio. 1996. "National heritage and global tourism in Thailand." *Annals of Tourism Research* 23, no. 2: 432–448.

———. 2002a. *Lords of things: The fashioning of the Siamese monarchy's modern image.* Honolulu: University of Hawai'i Press.

———. 2002b. *Politics of ruins and the business of nostalgia.* Bangkok: White Lotus Press.

Pemberton, John. 1994. *On the subject of "Java."* Ithaca, NY: Cornell University Press.

Penth, Hans. 1986. History of the Chiang Mai city wall (*Prawat kamphaeng wiang Chiang Mai doi sangkep*). In *The Chiang Mai city wall (Kamphaeng mueang Chiang Mai),* pp. 10–17. Chiang Mai: Thipphanet.

———. 1994. *A brief history of Lan Na: Civilizations of north Thailand.* Chiang Mai: Silkworm Books.

Phra Maha Sanga (Chaiyuang) Thirasonwaro. 2004. Chiang Mai nai manothat rueang wat lae thaksa. In *Mai Mi Wat Nai Thaksa Mueang Chiang Mai: Bot Phisut Khwam Ching Doi Nak Wichakan Thong Thin,* pp. 27–41. Chiang Mai: Social Research Center.

Ping Amranand and William Warren. 2000. *Lanna style: Art and design of Northern Thailand.* Bangkok: Asia Books.

Punna. 2009. About the Punna. http://www.punnagroups.com/development/about-punna (accessed January 2009).

Rhum, Michael R. 1987. The cosmology of power in Lanna. *Journal of the Siam Society* 75: 91–107.

———. 1994. *The ancestral lords: Gender, descent, and spirits in a northern Thai village.* DeKalb: Northern Illinois University Press.

Rimmer, James, and Howard Dick. 2009. *The city in Southeast Asia: Patterns, process, and policy.* Singapore: NUS Press.

Robert, Christophe. 2005. "Social evils" and the problem of youth in post-war Saigon. PhD diss., Cornell University.

Royal Flora. 2007. http://www.royalfloraexpo.com (accessed May 2007; now off-line).

Saichol Sattayanurak. 2002. The establishment of mainstream thought on "Thai Nation" and "Thainess" by Luang Wichit Wathakan. *Tai Culture* 7, no. 2: 7–34.

Said, Edward. 1978. *Orientalism.* New York: Vintage Books.

Saipin Kaewngarmprasert. 1996. Politics in the Thao Suranari Monument (Kanmueang nai anusawari Thao Suranari). MA thesis, Thammasat University.

Saitip Sukatipan. 1995. Thailand: The evolution of legitimacy. In *Political legitimacy in Southeast Asia,* ed. Muthiah Alagappa, pp. 193–223. Stanford, CA: Stanford University Press.

Sanguan Chohtsukrat. 1969. *Northern Thai customs (Prapheni Thai Phak Nuea).* Ayutthaya: Odian Satoh.

―――. 1972. *Collected Lanna Thai chronicles (Prachum tamnan Lanna Thai).* Ayutthaya: Ohdian Satoh.

Sanya Phonprasit. 1988. *Into a new land (Su Phaendin Mai).* Bangkok: Duang Kamon.

Sarasawadee Ongsakul. 1982. Kan patirup kansueksa nai Lanna: Kan sang ekaphap haeng chat (P.S. 2446-2475). *Sueksasat* 10, no. 2: 31–38.

―――. 1992. Wat Chet Yot nai thana Ayu Mueang Chiang Mai (Chet Yot Temple in the Ayu Mueang position). *Sinlapakon* 35, no. 3: 20–33.

Sarasawadee Ongsakul, Dolina W. Millar, and Sandy Barron. 2005. *History of Lan Na.* Chiang Mai: Silkworm Books.

Schien, Louisa. 1997. Gender and internal orientalism in China. *Modern China* 23, no. 1: 69–98.

Scott, James. 2010. *The art of not being governed: An anarchist history of upland Southeast Asia.* New Haven, CT: Yale University Press.

Seri Atsali. 1966. *15 Phao Nai Thai: Chak Tamrap Kao.* Phranakhon: Phitthayakhan.

Shalardchai Ramitanon. 1984. *Phi Chao Nai.* Chiang Mai: Chiang Mai University.

Sidel, John. 1995. "The Philippines: The languages of legitimation." In *Political legitimacy in Southeast Asia,* ed. Muthiah Alagappa, pp. 136–169. Stanford, CA: Stanford University Press.

―――. 2004. Bossism and democracy in the Philippines, Thailand, and Indonesia: Towards an alternative framework for the study of "local strongmen." In *Politicising democracy: The new local politics of democratization,* ed. John Hariss, Kristin Stokke, and Olle Tornquist, pp. 51–74. Basingstoke: Palgrave Macmillan.

Siegel, James T. 2006. *Naming the witch.* Stanford, CA: Stanford University Press.

Simmel, Georg. 1950 [1903]. The metropolis and mental life. In *The Sociology of Georg Simmel,* ed. Kurt H. Wolff, pp. 324–339. Glencoe, IL: Free Press.

Sit But-in. 1980. *The worldview of Thai Lanna people (Lokkathat chao Thai Lanna).* Chiang Mai: Book Center.

Sluhovsky, Moshe. 1996. A divine apparition or demonic possession? In *The Sixteenth Century Journal* 27, no. 4: 1039–1055.

Somchote Ongsakhul. 1987. The fight over the cable car climbing Doi Suthep: One century of conflict between "Bangkok" and "Lanna" (*Kan to su rawang chao thueng krachao loi fa khuen doi suthep: Nueng sathawat haeng khwam khat yaeng rawang "Krung Thep" kap "Lanna"*). *Aesia Boritat* 8, no 2.

Sommai Premchit and Pierre Doré. 1991. *The Lan Na twelve-month traditions: An ethno-historic and comparative approach.* Chiang Mai: Chiang Mai University.

Srisak Wanliphokhom. 1994. Khun Chueang: Khwam samnuek ruang thang watthanatham khong khon nai lum nam khong ton bon. *Mueang Boran* 20, no. 1.

Stallybrass, Peter, and Allon White. 1986. *The politics and poetics of transgression.* Ithaca, NY: Cornell University Press.

Stengs, Irene. 2009. *Worshipping the great moderniser: King Chulalongkorn, patron saint of the Thai middle class.* Seattle: University of Washington Press.

Sulak Sivaraksa. 1992. *Seeds of peace: A Buddhist vision for renewing society.* Berkeley, CA: Parallax Press.

Sunait Chutintharanon. 2000. Historical writings, historical novels and period movies and drama: An observation concerning Burma in Thai perceptions and understanding. *Journal of the Siam Society,* 88.1 and 2: 53–57.

Suraphol Damrikul. 1986. Naeo khwam khit nai kan anurak mueang prawattisat Chiang Mai. In *Kamphaeng Mueang Chiang Mai,* pp. 176–181. Chiang Mai: Thippanet.

Surin Maisrikrod. 1999. Joining the values debate: The peculiar case of Thailand. *Sojourn* 14, no. 2: 402–413.

Suriya Samutkhupthi, Pattana Kitiarsa, Sinlapakit Tikhantikul, and Janthana Suraphinit. 1999. *Spirit-medium cult discourses and crises of modernity in Thailand (Song chao khao phi).* Bangkok: SAC Princess Maha Chakri Sirindhorn Anthropology Centre.

Suthep Sunthonphetsat. 1986. Rabop khwam chuea kap phatthana kan kayaphap khong mueang Chiang Mai. In *Kamphaeng Mueang Chiang Mai,* pp. 176–181. Chiang Mai: Thippanet.

Swearer, Donald K. 1987. The northern Thai city as sacred center. In *The city as a sacred center: Essays on six Asian contexts,* ed. Bardwell L. Smith and Holly Baker Reynolds, pp. 103–112. Leiden: E. J. Brill.

Swearer, Donald K., and Sommai Premchit. 1998. *The legend of Queen Cama: Bodhiransi's Camadevivamsa, a translation and commentary.* SUNY series in Buddhist studies. Albany: State University of New York Press.

Swearer, Donald K., Sommai Premchit, and Phaithun Dohkbuakaeo. 2004. *Sacred mountains of Northern Thailand and their legends.* Chiang Mai: Silkworm Books.

Tambiah, Stanley Jeyaraja. 1975. *Buddhism and the spirit cults in north-east Thailand.* Cambridge: Cambridge University Press.

———. 1976. *World conqueror and world renouncer: A study of Buddhism and polity in Thailand against a historical background.* Cambridge: Cambridge University Press.

Tamnan Mueang Suwanna Khom Kham. 1969. *Prachum Phongsawadan* 72, no. 45.

Tanabe, Shigeharu. 1991. Spirits, power, and the discourse of female gender: Phi Meng cult of Northern Thailand. In *Thai constructions of knowledge,* ed. Manas Chitakasem and Andrew Turton, pp. 183–212. London: School of Oriental and African Studies.

Taylor, Philip. 2004. *Goddess on the rise: Pilgrimage and popular religion in Vietnam.* Honolulu: University of Hawai'i Press.

Terwiel, B. J. 2012 [1994]. *Monks and magic: An analysis of religious ceremonies in central Thailand.* Copenhagen: NIAS Press.

Thak Chaloemtiarana. 2003. Move over Madonna: Luang Wichit Wathakan's *Huang Rak Haew Luk.* In *Southeast Asia across Three Generations,* ed. James Siegel and Audrey Kahin, pp. 145–164. Ithaca, NY: Cornell Southeast Asia Program Publications.

———. 2007. *Thailand: The politics of despotic paternalism.* 2nd printing. Ithaca, NY: Cornell Southeast Asia Program Press.

Thammakhian Kanari. 1985. Pratu pen AIDS thi nakhon Chiang Mai (Gates are/have AIDS in Chiang Mai). *Matichon* 23, October 23 (2528 BE).

Thanet Charoenmueang. 1993. *Ma Chak Lanna.* Bangkok: Manager Press.

———. 2004. "Wat nai Thaksa Mueang" nai Yutthasat Kan Fuen Fu Watisat. In *Mai Mi Wat Nai Thaksa Mueang Chiang Mai: Bot Phisut Khwam Ching Doi Nak Wichakan Thong Thin,* pp. 76–81. Chiang Mai: Social Research Center.

Thanit Jitnukul. 2009. *Pai in love.* Bangkok: Megabox.

Thawi Sawapanyangkun. 1976. *Tamnan Mueang Chiang Tung.* Chiang Mai: Chiang Mai University.

Thiw Witchaykhatka. 1986. Fuen adit pratu mueang Chiang Mai thi pratu tha phae phuea anurak thang borankhadi. In *Kamphaeng Mueang Chiang Mai,* pp. 37–68. Chiang Mai: Thippanet.

Thong Chaichat. 1974. *Tamnan Chao Chet Phraong Chiang Mai.* Chiang Mai: Sanguan.

Thongchai Winichakul. 1994. *Siam mapped: A history of the geo-body of a nation.* Honolulu: University of Hawai'i Press.

———. 2000a. The quest for "Siwilai": A geographical discourse of civilizational thinking in the late 19th and early 20th c. Siam. *The Journal of Asian Studies* 59, no. 3: 528–549.

———. 2000b. The others within: Travel and ethno-spatial differentiation of Siamese subjects 1885–1910. In *Civility and savagery: Social identity in Tai states,* ed. Andrew Turton, pp. 38–62. Richmond: Curzon Press.

———. 2010. Coming to terms with the West: Intellectual strategies of bifurcation and post-westernism in Siam. In *The ambiguous allure of the West: Traces of the colonial in Thailand,* ed. Rachel Harrison and Peter Jackson, pp. 135–152. Ithaca, NY: Cornell Southeast Asia Program Publications.

Thon Tonman. 1974. *Tamnan Phuen Mueang Chiang Mai.* Chiang Mai: Khanakamakanchatphim Ekasan Than Prawattisat Samnak Nayok Rathamontri.

Turton, Andrew. 1972. Matrilineal descent groups and spirit cults of the Thai-Yuan in Northern Thailand." *Journal of the Siam Society* 60, no. 2: 217–256.

Van Esterik, Penny. 2000. *Materializing Thailand.* Oxford: Berg.

Vatikiotis, Michael R. J. 1984. Ethnic pluralism in the northern Thai city of Chiangmai. PhD diss., Oxford University.

Vickery, Michael. 1991. The Ram Khamhaeng inscription, a Piltdown skull of Southeast Asian history? In *The Ram Khamhaeng Controversy, Collected Papers,* ed. James R. Chamberlain, pp. 3–52. Bangkok: Siam Society.

Vidler, Anthony. 1999. *The architectural uncanny: Essays in the modern unhomely.* Cambridge, MA: MIT Press.

Walker, Andrew. 2010. Royal sufficiency and elite misrepresentation of rural livelihoods. In *Saying the unsayable: Monarchy and democracy in Thailand,* ed. Søren Ivarsson and Lotte Isager, pp. 241–266. Singapore: NIAS Press.

Wassana Nanuam. 2009. *Lap Luang Phrang.* Bangkok: Post Books.

Weber, Max. 2003 [1905]. *The Protestant ethic and the spirit of capitalism.* New York: Dover.

Weiner, Margaret J. 1995. *Visible and invisible realms: Power, magic, and colonial conquest in Bali.* Chicago: University of Chicago Press.

Wijeyewardene, Gehan. 1986. *Place and emotion in northern Thai ritual behaviour.* Bangkok: Pandora.

———. 1990. Thailand and the Tai: Versions of ethnic identity. In *Ethnic groups across national boundaries in mainland Southeast Asia,* ed. Gehan Wijeyewardene, pp. 48–73. Singapore: ISEAS.

Williams, Raymond. 1975. *The country and the city.* Oxford: Oxford University Press.

Wirth, Louis. 1964 [1938]. Urbanism as a way of life. *American Journal of Sociology* 44:1–24.

Withi Phanitchaphan. 2005. *Withi Lanna.* Chiang Mai: Silkworm Books.

Wolf, Margery. 1990. The woman who did not become a shaman. *American Ethnologist* 17, no. 3: 419–430.

Wolters, O. W. 1999 [1982]. *History, Culture and Religion in Southeast Asian Perspectives.* Ithaca, NY: Cornell Southeast Asia Program Press.

Woodhouse, Leslie Ann. 2009. A "foreign" princess in the Siamese court: Princess Dara Rasami, the politics of gender and ethnic difference in nineteenth-century Siam. PhD diss., University of California, Berkeley.

Wyatt, David. 1991. Contextual arguments for the authenticity of the Ram Khamhaeng inscription. In *The Ram Khamhaeng Controversy, Collected Papers,* ed. James R. Chamberlain, pp. 439–452. Bangkok: Siam Society.

———. 1994 [1989]. Assault by ghosts: Politics and religion in Nan in the eighteenth century. In *Studies in Thai history,* pp. 173–182. Chiang Mai: Silkworm Books.

Wyatt, David K., and Aroonrat Wichiankhieo. 1998. *The Chiang Mai chronicle.* Chiang Mai: Silkworm Books.

Yesterday. 2009. http://www.yesterday.co.th (accessed May 2009).

Zakharia, Fareed. 1994. Culture is destiny: A conversation with Lee Kwan Yew. *Foreign Affairs* 72, no. 2: 109–126.

INDEX

abandoned buildings, 6, 9, 12, 15,
16–18, 23–25, 44, 148, 167n.15
allochrony, 54, 69, 105, 108, 110, 136,
162n.6
amulets. *See* Buddhism, and amulets
Anderson, Benedict, 11, 72, 87
animism, 1, 34, 42, 49–50, 53, 59–60;
and Buddhism, 1, 42, 45, 70, 76,
89, 130, 137, 149. *See also* mediums;
spirits
architecture, 5, 6, 98–101, 109–112,
130, 137–138, 142, 147, 153,
166n.1. *See also* gated community;
high-rise
artists, 20, 65, 96–103, 106, 110–113,
122
aspiration, 7–16, 27, 39, 84
authenticity, 57, 103, 105, 133

Bangkok, 3, 6–7, 10–11, 15–16,
20, 33, 39, 42, 61, 64, 69–70, 91,
96–99, 112–113, 133, 152, 160n.10,
164n.3; attitudes towards Lanna,
38, 54, 96, 99, 100–109, 112–114,
119, 127, 157n.3, 162n.6, 164n.6;
historical influence in Lanna, 36–38,
60, 65, 68–70, 82, 95, 160n.10
barami, 1–2, 6, 9, 40, 67, 87, 92–95,
105, 125–126, 134, 155, 166n.7; of
the city, 33, 40–41, 88, 92, 116, 125,
134, 142, 155; of monarchs, 32–33,
40, 65–67, 85, 118, 122–126,
137, 155–156, 160n.10, 162n.30,
166n.28; of spirits, 40, 75–77, 88,
90, 105–106, 116, 154

Brahminism, 49, 161n.23
Buddhism, 1, 11, 14, 34, 38–45,
49–51, 56–60, 76, 88, 91, 117–118,
131, 154, 158n.8, 158n.12, 159n.3,
163n.10; and amulets, 90, 120,
123, 136–137, 151, 159n.17,
165n.27; the Buddha, 46, 47, 48;
and capitalism, 137, 166n.10; and
development, 132, 154–156; history
in Thailand, 5, 38, 50–51, 56, 58,
60, 86, 104, 161n.15, 165n.19;
and monarchy, 117–122, 126,
151, 166n.9; and monks, 13, 22,
25, 32, 38, 42, 45, 51–53, 59–63,
89–92, 123, 130, 140, 143, 145,
158n.12, 163n.10; and nationalism,
121,136,141,166n.9, 166n.10;
and syncretism, 45, 50, 52, 70, 76,
89, 91, 161n.23, 162n.2, 163n.10;
Thammayut order, 51–52, 54–55,
161n.23
Burma, 22, 25, 34–35, 50, 86, 100,
106–107, 126, 158nn.8–10,
158nn.13–14, 161n.15, 166n.6;
Burmese people, 7, 22–26, 34–36,
40, 49, 56, 157n.1, 158n.9,
158nn.13–14, 161n.15; in Lanna
history, 34–37, 40, 56, 86, 103,
160n.8; religion, 118, 162n.4; in
Thai nationalism, 25–26, 34, 103,
154, 160n.8, 161n.25. *See also* spirits

Caucasians. See *farang*
center-oriented space, 2–3, 32–33,
40–44, 49–51, 59–61, 64–70,

ABOUT THE AUTHOR

Andrew Alan Johnson is assistant professor of social sciences (anthropology) at Yale-NUS College in Singapore. He received his PhD in anthropology from Cornell University in 2010 and has held positions at Sogang University, the National University of Singapore's Asia Research Institute, and Columbia University. He has published several articles on the subject of Thailand and popular religion. His current research on urban popular religion is based in Bangkok.

OTHER VOLUMES IN THE SERIES

Khmer Women on the Move: Exploring Work and Life in Urban Cambodia
Annuska Derks

The Anxieties of Mobility: Migration and Tourism in the Indonesian Borderlands
Johan A. Lindquist

The Binding Tie: Chinese Intergenerational Relations in Modern Singapore
Kristina Göransson

In Buddha's Company: Thai Soldiers in the Vietnam War
Richard A. Ruth

Lục Xì: Prostitution and Venereal Disease in Colonial Hanoi
Vũ Trọng Phụng
Translated by Shaun Kingsley Malarney

Refiguring Women, Colonialism, and Modernity in Burma
Chie Ikeya

Natural Potency and Political Power: Forests and State Authority in Contemporary Laos
Sarinda Singh

The Perfect Business? Anti-Trafficking and the Sex Trade along the Mekong
Sverre Molland

Seeing Beauty, Sensing Race in Transnational Indonesia
L. Ayu Saraswati

Potent Landscapes: Place and Mobility in Eastern Indonesia
Catherine Allerton

Forest of Struggle: Moralities of Remembrance in Upland Cambodia
Eve Monique Zucker

Production Notes for Johnson | *Ghosts of the New City*

Cover design by Mardee Melton

Text design and composition by Jansom
with display type in Garamond 3 Hawn
and text type in Garamond 3 Hawn

Printing and binding by Sheridan Books, Inc.

Printed on 55 lb. House White Hi-Bulk D37,
360 ppi.